Altogether Lovely

THE PERFECT MAN

Blessings!
12/17/08

CHÉRIE BLAIR

FOREWORD BY MIKE BICKLE

uniquedove
creations

Kansas City, Missouri
www.uniquedove.com

Altogether Lovely—THE PERFECT MAN

By Chérie Blair with Jesus Christ, Author and Finisher (HEB 12:2).

Portions of text are revised from Mike Bickle's
teachings on the Song of Solomon. Used by permission.
Foreword by Mike Bickle. Afterword by Audra Close.

Designed by Chérie Blair. Cover photography by Melissa Isaacs.
Edited by Audra Close, Gary Cooper, Elizabeth Gensch,
and Jennifer Sansom. Capitalization added for emphasis.

Printed in the United States of America

ISBN 978-0-9820786-0-0

This is a gift to my

Beloved!

I have found the

One my heart loves.

I will hold him and never let Him go!

He laid down His life to *save* mine.

He fulfills my every dream.

He *provides* my every need.

He is absolutely everything I *desire.*

He is my Best Friend. He completes me.

Truly, my Bridegroom is Altogether Lovely!

He is the Perfect Man; His name is

Jesus Christ!

Chérie Lynn Blair

Thank You!

Acknowledgements

Jesus Christ: Words cannot express my eternal gratitude to You, my Maker and eternal Husband. You have imparted the divine kisses of Your Word to my heart and sealed me with Your jealous flame of love. Thank You, Father, Son, and Spirit. Apart from You I can do nothing!

FRIENDS OF THE BRIDEGROOM

John and Elaine Blair: The Lord has greatly blessed me with you as my parents. Thank you both for training me up in the way I should go (PROV 22:6). Your faithfulness to God and dedication to our family is reaping a plentiful harvest in the lives of your children.

My family: Thank you all for your encouragement and support. Your prayers have kept me on the path of life. I thank God for giving me a family who loves the Lord. I love you *all* so dearly.

Audra Close: You are my favorite *sister*! Your steadfast commitment to our friendship has been a plumb line in my life. Your prayers have accelerated my maturity in the Lord. I am so blessed by your generous heart. Thanks for all you have sacrificed and the countless ways you have contributed to making this dream a reality. You are a rare treasure!

Tommy Nelson: Thank you for sowing seeds of covenantal marriage in our culture through your relational study on the Song of Solomon.

Mike Bickle: Thank you for making the Song of Solomon a lifelong pursuit. Your extensive research, devotional prayer, and commitment to God's Word are preparing the Bride for partnership with our Beloved. Thank you for your encouragement to turn the Song into prayerful dialogue and to write books about it. This has motivated me to meditate on Jesus' Love Song and turn it into creative expression. Thank you also for your word about wrapping our faces in the mantle of God's name. Jesus has declared His glory to my heart through this composition. I will keep asking for the kisses of His Word!

Lou Engle: I am provoked by your pursuit of our Beloved. Thank you for calling us to a forty-day fast from June 30 to August 8, 2008. This divine season of ascending the mountain of the Lord has truly been a kiss from the Lord. He has given me a refreshing spring in the midst of the wilderness. May Jesus continually reveal His glory to you.

Gary Wiens, Dana Candler, Lisa Gottshall, Diane Hallam, and Rhonda Calhoun: Thank you for studying the Song of Solomon and sharing your discoveries with the IHOP–KC community. You have followed the path of the shepherds before you. Thank you for the fresh tracks you have laid for this generation to find our way forward.

SOS Group: Thank you for persevering in our study of the Song. Our discussion on Song 5:8-16 is what provoked me to write this book!

Gary and Debra Cooper: Thank you for opening your home for us to continue our Song of Solomon study. I am blessed by your hospitality.

Audra Close, Gary and Debra Cooper, Elizabeth Gensch, Matt and Christina Worwood, Shawn Kovac, Joel Sholar, and Jenn Sansom: Thank you for looking up verses and helping with the editing process.

Melissa Isaacs: Thank you for the spontaneous photo shoot.

IHOP–KC worship teams: Thank you for your faithfulness to exalt the name of Jesus Christ day and night 365 days a year. You have truly made the House of Prayer a *singing seminary.* Your songs, choruses, melodies, and prayers are invaluable. This heavenly music penetrates my heart as I mine the Scriptures to discover the nature of Jesus. I find myself continually captivated by the Biblical phrases that flow forth like streams of Living Water to my soul. I am ever grateful to you for this escort into the place of deeper encounter with our Beloved!

IHOP–KC Leadership, Faculty, Staff, and Intercessors: Thanks to those who teach the knowledge of God. Thanks to everyone behind the scenes who keeps this ship afloat as we build at sea. Thanks also to those who keep the furnace burning with ongoing worship and intercession. Your lives arise as fragrant incense before God's throne.

Gospel Communications: Thank you for creating BibleGateway.com. Your online search engine has made it possible to look up thousands of verses and quote Scripture in compliance with copyright guidelines.

Lightning Source: Thank you for your print-on-demand services and for making it possible to self-publish my first two books.

Everyone: I have so much to be grateful for. Thank you for imparting friendship and smiles into my life. You have done this unto the Lord. To all who read this book, thank you for supporting my endeavor to ascribe to the Lord the glory due His name. I pray our Beloved will encounter your heart with His beauty as you fix your eyes on the only One who is *Altogether Lovely—The Perfect Man,* Christ Jesus!

God's richest blessings!
Chérie Blair
Intercessory Missionary
International House of Prayer
Kansas City, Missouri

Foreword

By Mike Bickle

Dare to fall in love with Jesus Christ! This is our highest pursuit. The Holy Spirit is restoring the *first commandment* to first place in the Church worldwide (MATT 22:37-39). Jesus makes it clear that cultivating wholehearted love for God is the greatest lifestyle. The foundational truth that equips us to love God is to know and feel His affection for us. God loves us in the way that God loves God. Jesus feels the same intensity of love for us that the Father feels for Him (JOHN 15:9). Loving God always results in an overflow of love for ourselves and others.

Flowing out of her pursuit of divine intimacy, Chérie Blair presents a timely, powerful, and captivating cry of a lovesick heart. Hear the voice of the Bride inviting you to encounter the glory of our Father God in the image of Jesus Christ as she proclaims the splendor of her Beloved. A banqueting table has been lovingly prepared for you. Push delete on the busyness of your life to partake in the delicacies of this literary feast! Chérie's composition will provoke you to pursue the knowledge of God as you give yourself in wholehearted love to your Beloved. The most powerful revelation of Jesus in Scripture (SONG 5:10-16) will truly become a heart reality as you pause to verbalize the Word of God and worship Jesus, who is Altogether Lovely!

Mike Bickle
Director
International House of Prayer
Kansas City, Missouri

My *beloved* is white and ruddy,

chief among ten thousand.

His head is like the finest *gold*;

his locks are wavy, and black as a raven.

His eyes are like *doves* by the

rivers of waters, washed with milk, and fitly set.

His cheeks are like a bed of *spices*,

banks of scented herbs.

His *lips* are lilies, dripping liquid *myrrh*.

His hands are rods of gold set with beryl.

His body is carved *ivory* inlaid with sapphires.

His legs are pillars of marble set on bases of fine gold.

His countenance is like Lebanon,

Excellent as the cedars. His mouth

is most sweet, yes, he is

altogether lovely...

Song 5:10-16

Contents

My heart is *overflowing* with a good *theme*;

I recite my *composition* concerning the *King*;

my tongue is the pen of a ready *writer*.

You are *fairer* than the sons of men ...

⤙

Psalm 45:1-2

It is the *glory* of God

to conceal a matter;

to search out a matter

is the glory of *kings*.

❦

Proverbs 25:2 NIV

Introduction

In Search of Treasure

BETROTHED

The Perfect Man—does such a being exist? Have you ever dreamt of finding the *one* who would somehow make your life complete and satisfy your every desire? I finally found Him! All the other *lovers* of this world faded away when I discovered that Jesus Christ is my Bridegroom (SONG 3:4). I do look forward to entering the holy union of marriage on this side of eternity, but there remains a *union* with only One Beloved, which far surpasses any earthly experience. Only God Himself can fulfill the desires of your heart. If you have received Jesus Christ as your Lord and Savior, you are betrothed to the King of kings.

> *Your Maker is your husband, the LORD of hosts is His name.*
> ISAIAH 54:5

Our Maker, the Lord of hosts, is our Husband (Is 54:5). There is going to be a *wedding*! Our Beloved is returning soon. Jesus Christ will split the sky and return for His Bride. For this we make ourselves ready!

HIDDEN TREASURE

My purpose in writing this book is not to share profound insights. If it were, you should stop reading. Rather, it is to provoke others and myself to pursue the Lord that we may obtain the knowledge of the Father and His Son. I have written journals and used countless pens to fill hundreds of pages with words from sorrow to joy, prayers to answers, dreams to sacrifice, and unending praise and adoration of my Savior, King, and eternal Bridegroom. In attempting to compose a book on a few attributes of Jesus Christ, I am simply positioning myself to receive an impartation of divine revelation as I seek the One I love. Like you, I am searching. Who can know the Uncreated God, the Eternal One? This is only an initial response to the question posed by the daughters of Jerusalem in the Song, "What is your Beloved more than another?"

Beloved, have we obtained the knowledge of God as if it were a thing to be grasped? It is not enough to know *about* Him. We must *know* Him personally during our brief internship on the earth if we are to rule and reign with Him eternally. We develop a relationship with the Living God through prayer, worship, and Bible study. At the International House of Prayer Missions Base in Kansas City, Missouri, worship and prayer continue from dawn to dusk and through the watches of the night. Misty Edwards, an IHOP–KC worship leader, has written a song expressing our desire to know Jesus intimately.[1] She declares to the Lord, "I don't wanna talk about You like You're not in the room. I wanna look right at You. I wanna sing right to You. So give me dove's eyes. Just give me undistracted devotion to only You!" I pray this for you and myself that we may forever commune with our Beloved!

Let us search for hidden treasure and mine the Scriptures that we may know our Beloved. Let us follow the path of the flock and feed beside the shepherd's tents—those who have trod the ancient path before us (SONG 1:8)—so that somehow together we may increase in the knowledge of the Holy One. Let us behold the Lord in all His glory so that we may exalt the name that is above every other name as we proclaim with all creation, "Jesus Christ is Lord!"

Therefore God also has highly exalted Him and given Him the name which is above every name, that at the name of Jesus every knee should bow, of those in heaven, and of those on earth, and of those under the earth, and that every tongue should confess that Jesus Christ is Lord, to the glory of God the Father. —Philippians 2:9-11

BELOVED DARLING

Like many believers, I have struggled with my identity—wanting to be *important*. While touring the United Kingdom, I marveled at the front page of a London paper, which read, "Who is Cherie Blair?" This headline question posed by journalists seemed quite appropriate.

I first became aware of my British counterpart while trying to book a reservation for a youth hostel. Laughter filled the phone line the moment I stated my name. Needless to say, my identity as the prime minister's wife became the going joke. "How's your husband, Tony?" "What are you doing with an American passport?" "Can I have your autograph?" My dad joined me during a brief business trip to England, so I gave him a tour of its capital city. He told everyone, "I got a tour of London by Cherie Blair!" I used to joke about sending my bills to "10 Downing Street" to see if they might be paid—of course I knew better than to actually try. Not too long after publishing my first book, I searched for the new title online by author. I was not surprised to find it listed alongside an upcoming autobiography by Tony Blair's wife.

The question remains, "Who is *Chérie* Blair?" One thing is certain; my Husband is renowned. Since the Lord affirmed me as His Bride, I have gained confidence to partner with my eternal Husband knowing that who I am is not defined by any temporal earthly status.

My full name is Chérie Lynn Blair. I learned the significance of my first name in a junior high French class. The accent is placed over the first é according to the spelling of a term that communicates *darling* or *beloved*. I discovered when visiting France that this is also a term of endearment reserved for use between husbands and wives, which caused most single men to blush as they attempted to try an alternate pronunciation. Many people have complimented me for this beautiful name. I have always enjoyed it but secretly wished it were in the Bible.

It finally occurred to me that my name is woven throughout the entire Song of Solomon. I am the Lord's *Beloved Darling*.

> *I found the One my heart loves ...*
> SONG 3:4 NIV

I once studied the Song as a marriage handbook while dating a young man. I was sure we would spend the rest of our lives together. Once this relationship ended, I hid my face from the intimate words on those pages, subconsciously vowing never to read the book again until my wedding day. Whenever I heard or saw its passionate expressions, I was reminded only of heartache. One day, someone suggested reading it as a love letter from Jesus. As I turned my eyes once again to the poetic verses, the intimate phrases came alive. I discovered that Jesus is really *the One my Heart Loves*!

I have been *saved* as long as I can remember. My kindergarten teacher at a private Christian school led me through a prayer to invite Jesus into my heart. My brother and I sang about Jesus with our parents every night before bedtime. We participated in youth group, summer and winter camps, outreaches to orphans in Mexico, Bible studies, and all kinds of church activities. I was so outspoken about my faith at a public high school that some who considered themselves *Christians* would openly mock me for being too extreme. I began eating lunch alone while reading my Bible. Upon transferring to a Christian school my junior year I gained a better foundation in the Scriptures. Our Bible instructor required each class to keep ongoing journals. This practice has proved invaluable in my walk with God. Over the years I have matured in my love for the Lord. However, the discovery of Jesus as my Bridegroom in February of 2002 seemed like a true conversion experience. This revelation has profoundly transformed my life!

My middle name, Lynn, never held much importance. It did not sound pretty as far as I was concerned. Once I learned the significance of my first name, I decided to research the meaning of Lynn. I came across a card at a store that defined it as a *flowing brook*. My mom found another definition: *abundant blessing*. This is the very thing Jesus declares in the Song, "You are a garden fountain, a well of flowing water streaming down ..." (SONG 4:15 NIV). I have begun to realize that God is taking the wounds of my past and turning them into a *flowing brook of abundant blessing*.

I dearly love my family, but our last name, Blair, has often sounded dull and boring. In fact, it used to remind me of an obnoxious character I watched on a television show in the 80's. My grandpa researched our lineage and Christian heritage, which should have given me a sense of honor. This did not change the fact that I got teased unmercifully with phrases like, "Blare out loud." Not to mention there was a bully in my fourth grade class named Blair. My dad tried to educate me about our coat of arms and family name. He frequently told me about the *Blair Castle* in Scotland. One year, my cousin and I decided to take a trip together and explore the United Kingdom. A friend drove us to *our castle* where we learned the meaning of Blair: *valley*. Never mind that we could not find any memorabilia in its museum to prove our connection. While our venture seemed futile, I am reminded of the picturesque valley where the castle was located. In fact, the destination of any stream is a valley, for water continually flows to lower ground. I began to see God's plan to work humility in my heart as I read about this in Hannah Hurnard's allegory, *Hinds' Feet on High Places*.

God has fashioned each of us with a unique destiny and purpose. The Lord has revealed through my name that He is transforming me, His

> *He must*
> *increase,*
> *but*
> *I must*
> *decrease.*
> JOHN 3:30

Beloved Darling, that I might become a *flowing brook of abundant blessing poured out into the low places.* I must be emptied of myself and filled with Him in order to minister His love to others (JOHN 3:30). With confidence in my identity as *His Beloved Darling,* I am not so interested in proving my significance. Our true identity is found in Jesus. Pursuing the knowledge of God causes each of us to willingly decrease so that He may increase. Our primary purpose in life is to know Him and make Him known. The real question to consider is, "Who is Jesus Christ?"

FALLING IN LOVE

I have found the One my heart loves! I have fallen passionately in Love with my Creator and Savior, my eternal Bridegroom. I will hold Him and never let Him go (SONG 3:4). Even now I am falling in love with Jesus again. I pray for you to fall in love with Him as well. May He become the One your heart loves above all else. You have already stolen His heart (SONG 4:9). Jesus is our Beloved. We are His Bride. His desire is for you and me individually. He passionately loves each of us. My prayer is that the Holy Spirit may stir your heart and awaken you to deeper intimacy with Jesus. Whether beginning your journey or desiring to go deeper, I pray the words expressed on these pages arouse greater passion for your Beloved. May your gaze be ever fixed on the One who gave His life for you. You are His *joy*.

> Let us run with endurance the race that is set before
> us, looking unto Jesus, the author and finisher of our faith,
> who for the joy that was set before Him endured the cross,
> despising the shame, and has sat down at the right hand
> of the throne of God.   —Hebrews 12:1-2

May you run the race He has set before you, fixing your eyes on the finish line by looking to Jesus. May this *one thing* become your life passion—to gaze upon the beauty of the Lord and to inquire of Him!

> One thing I have desired of the LORD, that will I seek: that
> I may dwell in the house of the LORD all the days of my life,
> to behold the beauty of the LORD, and to inquire in His temple.
>   —Psalm 27:4

THE WORD OF MY TESTIMONY

As you pursue the Lord, I pray you become strong in His mighty power and daily put on His armor. You will need this to stand against the devil's schemes, which attempt to draw you away from His presence.

> Finally, my brethren, be strong in the Lord and in the power
> of His might. Put on the whole armor of God, that you may
> be able to stand against the wiles of the devil. For we do not
> wrestle against flesh and blood, but against principalities,
> against powers, against the rulers of the darkness of this
> age, against spiritual hosts of wickedness in the heavenly

places. Therefore take up the whole armor of God, that you may be able to withstand in the evil day, and having done all, to stand. —*Ephesians 6:10-13*

It is by the blood of the Lamb and the word of our testimony that we gain victory over the accuser. I pray that my testimony will encourage you to submit to God and resist the devil. As you draw near to Him, He will draw near to you. The enemy will flee (JAS 4:7-8). This is how we overcome: by His Blood and our Testimony!

Then I heard a loud voice saying in heaven, "Now salvation, and strength, and the kingdom of our God, and the power of His Christ have come, for the accuser of our brethren, who accused them before our God day and night, has been cast down. And they overcame him by the blood of the Lamb and by the word of their testimony, and they did not love their lives to the death …" —*Revelation 12:10-11*

Jesus is the Lamb of God who takes away our sins. His blood was shed so that we might live. When we confess Jesus as Lord, we are saved. We receive forgiveness for our sins through His death and resurrection. Eternal life is our inheritance. With Jesus Christ as our Lord and Savior, we are born again. Our sinful nature passes away and we become new creatures. We are no longer condemned because we believe in Him (JOHN 1:29; 3:3-7, 16; ROM 10:9; 2 COR. 5:17; ROM 8:1-2).

God is the Word. In the beginning, before anything was written, His Word existed. The Word of God became a person, Jesus Christ. This Perfect Man lived with us. The Word is also the sword of His Spirit. Having God's Word in our hearts helps to prevent us from sinning against God. Then, when Satan lies and tries to condemn us, we can quote the Word of God and stand on the truth and promises of Christ. When His Word is in us, we know the truth, and it is His truth that sets us free (JOHN 1:1-2, 14; 8:32; PS 119:11; EPH 6:17).

The Lord is our Testimony. We testify that He is our God and that He has set us free. Without Him we can do nothing, but through Him we can do all things. We bear witness of His faithfulness in our lives. No matter what our circumstances, we can look back on the events of our lives and see how the Lord has helped and blessed us. If the Lord is our Savior, we should not be deceived into thinking we have no testimony. Instead, we need to draw into His presence with gratitude. We have so much to thank Him for, including eyes to read and minds to perceive. Developing thankful hearts helps us see God's faithfulness when our faith is lacking. The Lord cannot and will not contradict His nature (JOHN 15:5; PHIL 4:13; HEB 13:5-6, 15; 2 TIM 2:13).

My favorite quote was once, "My life has been the poem I would have writ, but could not both live and utter it," by Henry David Thoreau. It has since changed. The Lord caused me to rephrase these words into my own vision statement: "My life is the poem that God has writ, so I will both live and utter it." My days are numbered by Christ. He has already ordered my steps. All of my days

My life is the poem that God has writ, so I will both live and utter it.

CHÉRIE BLAIR

were written in His book before I ever lived one of them (PS 139:16). My goal is to live in such a way that my life may arise as a beautiful love song to my Beloved.

Therefore, I choose to live according to His design by following the unique path He has set before me. I will not be short-changed by the enemy's game-plan. The devil wants to destroy everyone who gives glory to God. But the Lord desires to prosper His children. He gives abundant life (1 PET 5:8-9; JER 29:11; JOHN 10:10). And I will do more than live this poem that God has written. I will utter it in words and various forms of creative expression. In doing so, this testimony will defeat the one who accuses God's Beloved Bride while giving glory, honor, and victory to the Lord, Jesus Christ. Beloved friends, let us rise up. We will overcome the evil one in our generation and those to come by the *blood of the Lamb* and the *word of our testimony.*

FERVENT PRAYER

With our eyes fixed steadily upon Jesus, we pray for others to fall in love with Christ, asking for the knowledge of God to increase in their lives (JAS 5:16). William Ford tells how God found him when he was not looking for God.[2] When Ford was a backslidden Christian, his mother and others were praying. He once heard a preacher speak on prayer, saying, "The only difference between the grip of a praying mother and a pit-bull is lipstick! Devil, get your hands off my son. I plead the blood of Jesus!" One night Ford was at a dance club. Little did he know that the disk jockey had gotten saved. The guy started mixing in a sermon by S. M. Lockridge.[3] It went like this: "My King was born King. The Bible says He's a Seven Way King. He's the King of the Jews—that's a racial King. He's the King of Israel—that's a national King. He's the King of righteousness. He's the King of the ages. He's the King of Heaven. He's the King of glory. He's the King of kings and He is the Lord of lords. Now that's my King. Well, I wonder ... Do you know Him?" Ford thought to himself, "Dog, yeah, I know him." At this point he could

> *The prayer of a righteous man is powerful and effective.*
>
> JAMES 5:16 NIV

not even get on beat. He knew he could no longer run because the hand of God was on his life. Since then, this sermon has become an integral part of Ford's personal prayer life.

PRAY FOR THE KNOWLEDGE OF GOD

I pray for myself, for my family, for you, for your family, and others, that the Father of glory would give us the knowledge of His Son. I ask that He would impart to each of us a hunger, passion, and insatiable desire to intimately know this Perfect Man, Christ Jesus. We must have knowledge of the Holy One!

For this reason I bow my knees to the Father of our Lord Jesus Christ, from whom the whole family in heaven and earth is named, that He would grant you, according to the riches of His glory, to be strengthened with might through His Spirit in the inner man, that Christ may dwell in your hearts through faith; that you, being rooted and grounded in love, may be able to comprehend with all the saints what is the width and length and depth and height—to know the love of Christ which passes knowledge; that you may be filled with all the fullness of God.   *—Ephesians 3:14-19*

Therefore I also, after I heard of your faith in the Lord Jesus and your love for all the saints, do not cease to give thanks for you, making mention of you in my prayers: that the God of our Lord Jesus Christ, the Father of glory, may give to you the spirit of wisdom and revelation in the knowledge of Him, the eyes of your understanding being enlightened; that you may know what is the hope of His calling, what are the riches

*of the glory of His inheritance in the saints, and what is the
exceeding greatness of His power toward us who believe …*
                                                 —Ephesians 1:15-19

*For this reason we also, since the day we heard it, do not
cease to pray for you, and to ask that you may be filled
with the knowledge of His will in all wisdom and spiritual
understanding; that you may walk worthy of the Lord,
fully pleasing Him, being fruitful in every good work and
increasing in the knowledge of God; strengthened with all
might, according to His glorious power, for all patience and
longsuffering with joy; giving thanks to the Father who
has qualified us to be partakers of the inheritance of the
saints in the light.*   *—Colossians 1:9-12*

*I will praise You, O LORD, among the peoples, and I will
sing praises to You among the nations. For Your mercy is
great above the heavens, and Your truth reaches to the
clouds. Be exalted, O God, above the heavens, and Your
glory above all the earth.*   *—Psalm 108:1-5*

These Scriptures are foundational prayers. May Christ dwell in our hearts through faith that we may experience the fullness of God's Love. May the Lord give us His Spirit of wisdom and revelation that we may behold His glory. And may we forever increase in the knowledge of God as we praise His name among the nations. As we discover the mysteries of God, I pray we may each live worthy of our precious Lord's calling, fully pleasing Him, bearing fruit in every good work. As Christ's pure and spotless Bride, we will carry His glory to the ends of the earth.

For the earth will be filled with the knowledge of the glory of the LORD, as the waters cover the sea. —Habakkuk 2:14

PROVOKED TO PURSUIT

Please remember this book is not meant to be exhaustive. Rather, it is to motivate each of us to seek the Lord as we grow in relationship with our Beloved. When I first discovered Jesus as my eternal Bridegroom through the Song, I began to paint, dance, sing, and write with divine creativity. My identity shifted from what I *do* to who I *am* before the Lord. Jesus reminds me daily that I ravish His heart with one glance. A single movement of my heart overwhelms Him with love for me. Yet, I scarcely understand how to be a *flowing brook of abundant blessing* carrying His love *into the valley* of this world. I am just learning to pray that the Body of Christ would come forth in maturity. I have so far to go before entering into the fullness of love and union with My Beloved. I do not consider that I have attained anything but am pressing on to the goal of knowing Jesus (PHIL 3:12-15).

Our journey is just beginning. May we be provoked to pursuit of the Living God by this simple composition. One day we will stand before our Beloved as His pure and spotless Bride. Let us set our hearts on the pilgrimage into Bridal partnership with our Beloved King. May loving God truly be our lifelong quest. I pray my initial thoughts set forth in *Altogether Lovely—The Perfect Man* will serve as a springboard to launch us into further study of Jesus' glorious splendor. Our Beloved is Altogether Lovely!

My *dove*, my perfect one

is *unique*...

the *favorite*

of the one who bore her.

⌘

Song 6:9 NIV

The Song

A Divine Love Story

Before focusing in on seven verses that portray our Beloved's glory, let us first consider the entire Song of Solomon. This brief overview is abbreviated from Mike Bickle's extensive teaching on the Song. You may already be familiar with this interpretation as a love story between Jesus and His Bride, or perhaps this is your first time to view the text through the lens of our relationship with Jesus. Wherever you are along your journey, I invite you to read this Song of all songs again.

DIVINE LOVE SONG

The Song of Solomon is a poetic *love song* inspired by the Holy Spirit to express the truth of Scripture and illustrate the Gospel of Christ. It is often translated as an allegory between Jesus Christ and His Bride (individual believers or the corporate Church). There are three primary characters. King Solomon, depicted as the Bridegroom, represents Jesus Christ, the triumphant resurrected Lord of lords and King of kings. The Shulamite is a picture of the Bride of Christ who will eventually experience full spiritual maturity. The Daughters of Jerusalem convey the spiritual condition of dullness and immaturity characteristic of many believers. The ultimate goal of studying this love song is to cultivate lifestyles of wholehearted love and pursuit of our Beloved Bridegroom, Jesus Christ. When I first discovered the Lord as my eternal Bridegroom, I began to journal the Song in the form of prayers to Jesus and His responses to me. My heart soared with new passion for my Beloved. The Lord continually uses this Song to establish me in my identity as His Bride and to awaken my heart with greater love for Him. We can each identify with the Shulamite's journey as it parallels various seasons in our own life experiences.

Song of Solomon One

If we surrender our lives to Jesus Christ, our Savior, we are His Bride. Our journey into mature partnership with our Beloved begins with longing for the kisses of God's Word. We discover that Jesus' affection is more satisfying than all earthly pleasures. This revelation awakens fervency to love the Lord with our entire beings. He leads us to abide in the Vine through intimate communion. We face a spiritual crisis when we recognize the depravity of our sinful nature. Though we see the darkness of our hearts, we also realize our loveliness in God's eyes. Our *Counseling Shepherd* teaches us the way forward in our weakness. Jesus then expresses the heart of the *Affectionate Father* by embracing and affirming us at His table of redemption. Here we receive increasing revelation of the salvation Jesus provided for us through the Cross. We understand the abundance of His suffering for love. In response, our fragrant worship ascends to God as perfume. In this season we may think of the Lord in terms of what we receive from God instead of what He receives from us. Obedience to Jesus is not yet our highest goal in life. He strategically leads us to slow down, receive His love, and eventually carry His love to others.

Song of Solomon Two

Although we are immature in love, the Lord affirms our beauty. When we understand the redemptive riches in Christ, we discover our highest identity as His Bride. We are Christ's fragrance amidst a fallen world. Confidence in our Bridal identity is essential in order to experience

Jesus as the One who provides spiritual refreshment. We will never enjoy the Lord's presence beyond our comprehension of His love for us in our weakness (ROM 5:6-8; 1 JOHN 4:10). At the Cross, He provides nourishment leading to joy in His presence. We no longer live under shame. His banner of *Love* redefines our lives. He causes negative circumstances to work for our good (ROM 8:28). Spiritual pleasure awakens desire for deeper experiences of intimacy with Jesus. Through the ministry of the Holy Spirit, we receive the fullness of God's love. The Lord uses seasons of satisfaction to cultivate spiritual growth while cautioning others to be gentle with His fervent yet easily distracted Bride. When the voice of our Beloved challenges us to leave our comforts, we are confronted with another spiritual crisis: *fear.* Jesus invites us to join Him in partnership. When we are tempted to refuse His invitation, He encourages us to run *to* Him, not *away from* Him. Convicted by the Holy Spirit, we cry to God for deliverance from compromise. As the *Sovereign King,* Jesus effortlessly conquers all opposition.

SONG OF SOLOMON THREE

Jesus withdraws His presence to cultivate longing in our hearts. He has drawn us to Himself in worship and invited us into partnership. Now it is time for us to run with Him in ministry. We experience the loving chastisement of our Heavenly Father until we arise to follow Jesus. We soon realize that our hearts are only safe in the context of complete obedience. Our insight into the Lord's loving leadership motivates us to new depth in our commitment. We are no longer afraid to leave our comforts because we believe our hearts will be secure. With excitement, we teach others our discoveries. Our Father is committed to bringing each of us forth as a glorious mature Bride for His Son, Jesus Christ. There is a day to come when the Church will crown Jesus as King. All of history will culminate in the glorious Wedding Day between Jesus and His Bride (REV 19:1-16). Jesus is the *Safe Savior* who ensures our arrival upon that great Wedding Day through His intercession and provision. The Lord will finish the good work He started (PHIL 1:6). He is going to receive us with the gladness of a Bridegroom (IS 62:5).

SONG OF SOLOMON FOUR

Jesus Christ is our *Heavenly Bridegroom.* After withdrawing His presence during a season of divine chastisement, He breaks the silence by affirming our budding virtues. The Lord uses this strategy to equip us for spiritual warfare against Satan's accusations. Though we are weak believers, He speaks to us with cherishing words so that we may become His mature Bride. Our Beloved's declaration of His passionate affection empowers us to commit our lives to Him in obedience. We have confidence to embrace the Cross and become like Him. Jesus is a passionate Bridegroom committed to winning our hearts. He reveals His desire for us and romances us by declaring the truth of our identity as His eternal Bride. As we drink from the Living Water, abiding daily in Him, we become flourishing gardens with godly lives and fruitful ministries (JOHN 4:14; 7:37-38; 15:5). Fully confident in God's love, we can more readily invite His north winds of testing and south winds of blessing to transform our hearts. We give our entire lives to the Lord in order to become His fragrance and spread the testimony of Jesus to the nations. We want Him to receive His inheritance. This is a major turning point in our journey.

SONG OF SOLOMON FIVE

Jesus answers our request for both the north and south winds by fully possessing us as His inheritance. This is a pivotal chapter in the Song.

The focus shifts from our inheritance in Jesus to His inheritance in us. We want to love Jesus as He loves us that we may become the Father's gift to His Son (EPH 1:18). The Lord knows the best combination of adversity and blessing suitable to bring each of us into full maturity and partnership. He appears as the *Suffering Servant* with the bitter north winds. Christ embraced the cross and invites us to share in the fellowship of His sufferings (HEB 12:2; MATT 16:24; PHIL 3:10). Earlier Jesus withdrew His manifest presence to discipline us because of our disobedience. Now He withdraws His presence to test our faithfulness in difficult circumstances. This *dark night* is our ultimate test of maturity. Our inheritance—feeling God's nearness (intimacy) and serving with Him in ministry (partnership)—seems so distant. It appears as though all of His promises have vanished. In reality, we stand vulnerable before God. The test is clear. Will we become offended at the Lord for withdrawing His presence and allowing us to be severely mistreated, or will we respond with greater passion for Jesus? We have the opportunity to respond in love and humility by turning our pain into worship. Declaring the beauty of our *Majestic God* is the focus of *Altogether Lovely—The Perfect Man.* The Lord is our Faithful Friend. With our hearts overflowing in love for Jesus, we can boldly withstand the enemy's temptations to "curse God and die" (JOB 2:9). When others accuse the Lord of abandoning or wounding us, we can proclaim the truth of Jesus' perfect leadership over our lives. This testimony will launch us into greater intimacy with God and ministry to people.

SONG OF SOLOMON SIX

Lovesick responses during the *dark night* of our souls provoke other believers to ask, "Where is your Beloved? How can we know Jesus intimately like you do?" We teach these *daughters* how to grow in maturity and intimacy with the Lord by sharing what we have learned from our own experiences. Young believers glean from our lives as we encourage them to feed on the beauty of Jesus through the Word of God. In this way, we begin to partner with the Lord in gathering souls for the Great Harvest. Jesus returns His manifest presence and breaks this second season of silence. In His evaluation of our struggle, He says, "My Beloved, you have prevailed. In the great test you have come forth victoriously." The trials now seem worth all the pain. With one of the greatest statements in God's Word, Jesus declares that our eyes of loving devotion overcome Him. He celebrates the beauty imparted to us by the Holy Spirit through tribulation. This is the fruit produced by divine testing, obedient responses, and the revelation of the Lord's affections for us. We each capture the heart of our Bridegroom in a unique way. We are His Bride, His favorite one! Believers also esteem our spiritual maturity. Even the host of heaven rejoices with eternal gladness as we step into our position as Christ's Bride. Ultimately, we conquer all darkness in our hearts and triumph over the enemy through our authority in Christ Jesus. With such victory in our lives we are overcome with love, concern, and desire for the whole Church.

SONG OF SOLOMON SEVEN

God's grace adorns us. He nourishes us with healthy spiritual diets, which enables us to impart to others. We are equipped to nurture, edify, and reproduce life in the Kingdom of God. Our lives are completely submitted to the will of the Lord. The eyes of our understanding are enlightened with spiritual wisdom and revelation (EPH 1:17-18). Others are protected by our ability to discern spiritual enemies. We take our thoughts captive in obedience to Christ so that our minds are not vulnerable to Satan's attacks (2 COR 10:5). Our hearts are filled with holy resolve to obey God even under pressure. Jesus commissions us to nurture people, impart the Holy Spirit, and maintain lives of intimacy with Him. We captivate His heart by our devotion as we embrace the first commandment of loving God and the Great Commission of proclaiming His Gospel. The Father has promised to give Jesus the nations as His inheritance (Ps 2:8). Jesus wants His Bride to participate with Him in this Great Harvest of souls. We do so by drinking the cup of His will without hindrance. At the beginning of our journey, we were burned out from laboring without love. Now, as a result of God's restoration, we want to labor with Him in His vineyards. The Lord takes delight in the abundance of fruit produced from our lives of intimacy and partnership with Him. We are Jesus' inheritance. He deeply desires ongoing intimate communion with each of us. Our Bridal partnership is expressed in obedience to Jesus and continual intercession. Love for our Beloved, Jesus Christ, motivates us to war against the enemy's schemes.

SONG OF SOLOMON EIGHT

This journey into partnership with the Lord is eventually expressed through humility and boldness in public ministry as well as full union and communion with the Lord. We long to boldly display our affections for Jesus that all may see, yet we recognize the need to walk with humility and restraint. We prayerfully discern how to publicly express our intimacy with Jesus in ways that edify others (1 Cor 14:12). In trying circumstances, God's invisible work supports us. His loving intervention leads us through this strategic period. The Holy Spirit prepares us to emerge from our wilderness voyage with loving and leaning hearts. This is the ultimate goal of our journey. If we surrender our lives to Jesus and follow Him through every season, we come forth as His victorious Bride. God uses weakness to manifest His power and strength (2 COR 12:9). He is our divine source and eternal reward. Jesus is a *Consuming Fire.* In the great climax, our Beloved reminds us how He has awakened our hearts and then invites us to receive His bridal seal of divine *love.* We each commence our journey with His kiss and conclude it with His seal of love. The fire of God's passionate zeal empowers our hearts with His supernatural love. The Lord's eternal flame of love will withstand the rivers of persecution and floods of temptation. Jesus Christ's love for us has conquered the grave. No opposition can prevent our Beloved from bringing us into full maturity if we walk in obedience to Him. Our spiritual identity is found in God's evaluation of our beauty. This assurance gives us confidence to walk in partnership with the Lord. We are aware of our accountability to tend the vineyard of our own hearts and lead others into fruitfulness. With urgency we intercede for the Church to be brought forth into full maturity and for Jesus' return (REV 22:17, 20).

ROLE OF SUFFERING

However romantic this eight-chapter love song seems at first glance, further study illuminates the suffering interwoven among these poetic Scriptures. The pain of shame, exhaustion, lovesickness, chastisement, persecution, death to self, and other experiences all play a significant role in God's design. The crucible of suffering refines each of us like silver. Every impurity is removed in the fires of love and testing. The Father ultimately presents a worthy Bride to His Son Jesus.

Our journey begins with an awakening to love and recognition of our unworthiness. This initial taste of discontentment is found when we are stirred with desire for intimacy and cry out for the divine kisses of our Beloved, Jesus (SONG 1:2-4). We experience a spiritual crisis when we discover our sinful depravity and realize our hearts have become *burned out* from tending vineyards other than our own (SONG 1:5-11). In the midst of this, Jesus reveals Himself as our Tender Shepherd. He grants us a season of rest. Jesus expresses the Father's affectionate heart by establishing us in Bridal identity (SONG 1:12-2:7).

Our Sovereign King interrupts this refreshing time by challenging us to leave our comforts (SONG 2:8-17). In this first dark night, we initially refuse our Beloved's invitation to partner with Him in His zeal for the harvest. Our unwillingness is the result of immaturity rather than deliberate disobedience; nevertheless, He will not permit even the slightest area of compromise. Upon finding Him, we determine not to forsake Him again. Our hearts are set on pursuing the Lord even to the mountain of suffering (SONG 3:1-4; 4:6).

The second dark night we experience is an escort into the knowledge of God. Although our early struggles feel painful to our hearts, they are minor compared to the suffering we encounter through the Lord's chastisements and refining fires. The Father and His Son add the north winds of adversity to the south winds of blessing in Their jealousy to make us pure and blameless. We are equipped for the impending time of testing through renewed intimacy with the Lord and His expression of enjoyment over us (SONG 4:1-5:1).

Jesus invites us to share in the fellowship of His suffering by calling us to open to Him after He has endured the Cross (SONG 5:2). We may not immediately respond to His call because of its inconvenience, but after hesitating for a moment, we declare, "My heart began to pound for Him." We rise to discover myrrh dripping "on the handles of the lock" (SONG 5:4-5 NIV). Wounded with lovesickness for our Beloved, we search for Him again. While pursuing our Bridegroom, we are beaten and persecuted. Still, nothing is able to deter us. We plead with others to tell our Lover, "I am faint with love" (SONG 5:8 NIV).

Our final response to divine testing is one of hearts that are fully in love. When asked why we would be captivated by the very one who abandoned us, we make an astounding declaration of Jesus' beauty and perfect leadership (SONG 5:9-16). Having followed our Beloved through suffering, we are now confident of His excellence. There is no longer any hindrance preventing us from entering into partnership with Him. We will do anything for Love.

Understanding our journey through the Song provides a foundation that gives each of us confidence to trust the Lord's leadership in the midst of suffering. Though pain itself has no inherent value, it serves as an escort into intimacy with Jesus. Our response to pain determines our final destiny. Will we refuse chastisement and reject our Beloved, or will we arise to find Him even in the dark nights?

Fashioning vessels of honor that are equipped to carry God's glory to the nations requires breaking, crushing, and purifying in the Refiner's Fire to purge all the dross. It is a long and painful process, but He will bring forth His fragrant aroma from our lives if we surrender to the Flame. He is the Potter. We are the clay (IS 64:8). We must allow Him to crush us into fine powder, that He may reform us into His image. He sends the north winds of adversity and south winds of blessings to bring each of us forth as His pure and spotless Bride (SONG 4:16).

We must develop eternal perspective and remember that these present sufferings are not worth comparing to the glory that will be revealed in us (ROM 8:18). Let us say, "Yes," to the Lord regardless of our temporal circumstances. Whoever desires to become mature in bridal love must be willing to drink the cup of Christ's suffering. In Chapter 8, "His

Lips: Invitation to Suffering," we will consider our Beloved's invitation to join Him in the fellowship of the cross.

THE JOURNEY

In some measure, Jesus has led me along this road of partnering in His suffering. Following is a monologue composed from my experience.

Why so cold, O heart of mine? Why refuse such Love Divine? Come, O Lord, and tenderize this hardened heart that's bought the lies, "He loves you not; you're filthy and poor. You can't even earn it; just look at your score!" But You tell me how I have stolen Your heart, when all I have done is a dance and some art. I'm not even worthy; can't You see that I'm dirty? Don't stare at me; I'm dark. You'll see a bruise, a scar, a mark—where I once let love in but was wounded by men. Yet, I long to know this Love of One who calls me His dove. Why should I hide behind a veil? Must I remain locked in this cell? Come quickly, my Lover; do not delay. Kiss me with Your Word and take me away. Your Love to me is more delightful than wine. Oh, satisfy my heart with the fruits of Your Vine.

My Beloved, I slept but my heart was awake. I dreamt of the early days when You awakened my heart. All I could see then was my brokenness, but You considered me lovely. You answered my cry and kissed me with the deep things of Your Word. You removed the veil that kept me hidden. You drew me into the courts of Your heart. You led me by streams of Living Water into Your presence. Together we caught the little foxes of compromise that spoiled our vine. You showed Your love to the one You called "not my loved one." I tasted of Your love and found it better than the choicest wine. You danced with me, O Lover of my soul. I discovered the earth had nothing I desired besides You. Everything then seemed so new, so fresh. Yet, with time, it has grown so old, so stale. I pondered what became of our flame of love. I wondered if the passion of our romance had died. That's when You came! I heard You knock and call my name. How I longed to see Your face, but it was so late. The day had become night; all I wanted was respite. I had taken off my robe. It was too burdensome to put on again. Just then, You thrust Your hand through the opening. My heart began to pound. I realized my foolishness and quickly opened the door. I looked, but You were not there. I called. You did not answer. I remembered the first time You beckoned and I turned You away. How immature I was then. I could only think about the wounds I had suffered by men. I thought to myself, "How could I be; why would I be wounded again?" Even then, I knew You would heal and transform my heart. So, I rose up. I sought after You. Though I became distracted by other lovers, I found none faithful. All along, You blocked my path so I could not find my way to another. Then, scarcely had I passed the ones I had mistaken, those masquerading lovers, when I found You, the One my heart loves. That's when I held You and vowed never to let You go!

Now what have I done? This time You came calling me, "My darling, My dove, My perfect one." Oh, why did I hesitate? Why did I consider it inconvenient to rise up from my comfort to embrace the One I once promised to hold onto? What was I thinking? Would I rather sleep than be with You? Forgive me for not rising up at once to open for You. My Love, why did You leave? Didn't You know my heart was awake anticipating Your coming? I am sorry for making excuses. Don't You know that I am lovesick? Tell me, where have You gone? And what is this myrrh You left on the doorknob? Now it's dripping from my hands. My Lord, why are You covered in burial spices? What did You mean by saying that Your head was drenched with dew? Where have You been? Where did You go? Must You suffer? Must I suffer, too? Never mind, just tell me where You are!

Has anyone seen my Beloved? Whatever may happen I will pursue the Love of my life. Whatever the cost, I will share in His suffering; no price is too high. I must find my Love. So beat me if you will, you watchers of the night. Take my veil away, you keepers of the wall. I will not give up. No, I will not lose heart. I will keep on searching 'til once again I find this One my heart loves. If anyone finds Him, tell Him I am faint with love!

Oh, Jesus, what is it about You? I really must know. What drew me to You? Oh, is it so? That I have been so captivated by You and have found in You a Love so true? My Beloved, what is it about You that I adore? Just one glance; my heart is overcome. Just one Word and now I am undone. When will You see me here gazing, longing, praying as I wait for You? For one more glance! For one more Word!

Lord, You've wounded me with love. You've stricken me with lovesickness. Though You slay me, yet I will trust You, for You wound me as a Friend. Jesus, You are faithful. Your leadership is perfect. This is what I love. You are dazzling and excellent. No one can compare. You know how to bring me forth as Your Bride. Though You lead me into the wilderness and blow the north winds of adversity, I remember Your south winds of blessing. I will meditate on Your promises. This suffering is not unto death. It is for Your glory. You will restore my vineyards. You will fashion me into Your pure, spotless, radiant Bride. So cleanse me. Refine me. Test me and try me. Do what You must to purify me. Still I will say, "I am Yours." Forever I will say, "You are mine." I will come up from this wilderness leaning on You. Once again, I will call You my Husband. All I have is Yours. I lay it at Your feet. I will partner with You through every dark night. I will arise and come with You even into Your suffering. I will take up my cross. I will drink of Your cup.

DEVOTIONAL PRAYER

This overview is an appetizer. A friend told me our journey is about heart movements toward Jesus. Mike Bickle reminds us, "To receive the full benefit of the Song, we must turn it into ongoing prayerful dialogue with Jesus" (see "Road Maps: Tools for Your Journey"). My first book, *Journey through the Song of Solomon*, is intended to help you mature in intimacy and partnership with Jesus. Your heart will be transformed as you turn the Song into prayer! This devotional study tool divides the Scriptures into short segments with space to journal through each verse (see "About Chérie: Uniquedove Creations"). Also, provided at the end of *Altogether Lovely—The Perfect Man* are pages for you to record initial thoughts and prayers as you begin journaling through Song of Solomon 5:8-16. Write your composition concerning the Perfect Man as you discover the hidden mysteries of your Beloved, Jesus (see "Invitation: Encounter Your Bridegroom" and "Journal: May Your Fragrance Arise"). May the Lord encounter your heart as you turn His love song into devotional prayer!

If you find my beloved...

tell him 1 am lovesick!
Song 5:8

What is your *beloved*

more than another beloved,

o *fairest* among women?

What is your beloved

more than another beloved,

that you so *charge* us?

᪥

Song 5:9

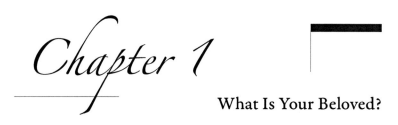

Chapter 1

What Is Your Beloved?

WHAT IS YOUR BELOVED?

The daughters of Jerusalem inquire of the Bride's lovesickness for her Beloved. Her reply poetically unveils the splendor of Jesus Christ.

PRAYER

Jesus, I am lovesick for You (SONG 5:8). I will go on searching until I find You (SONG 3:1). You are beautiful. There is no one like You. Let me see Your face. Show me Your glory (EXOD 33:18). I long to know You as I am known by You (1 COR 13:12). I desire to partake of Your divine nature (2 PET 1:4). I want to become one with You and the Father (JOHN 17: 11). Draw me away, that we may run together (SONG 1:4). Lead me in Your everlasting Way (PS 139:24). Reveal Your Majestic Splendor, that I may worship You in the beauty of Your Holiness (PS 29:2). Write Your Word upon my heart (PROV 7:3). Let the testimony of Jesus flow from my heart like rivers of Living Water (JOHN 7:38). My Beloved, You are holy. You are the only One worthy of all my praise (PS 99:5; 96:4). I love you. Amen.

THE MAJESTIC GOD

"What is your Beloved more than another beloved?" This question provokes a lovesick response from Christ's Bride. Out of the midst of severe testing arises one of the most extravagant expressions of love in

Scripture. The Bride's general statement of introduction is followed by descriptive phrases that comprise a dynamic proclamation of Jesus' glory. Although the meaning is somewhat hidden in the language of romantic poetry, further study reveals ten distinct attributes of God's nature. His lovesick Bride summarizes His comprehensive beauty as *Altogether Lovely*. This extravagant demonstration of wholehearted love directs others to gaze on the splendor of His beauty.

Ten Distinct Attributes

1. His head: Jesus' sovereign *leadership*

2. His locks: Jesus' *dedication* to God and the Church

3. His eyes: Jesus' focused *vision*

4. His cheeks: Jesus' diverse *emotions*

5. His lips: Jesus' *Word*

6. His hands: Jesus' divine *activity*

7. His body: Jesus' tender *compassion*

8. His legs: Jesus' *administration* of the Father's will

9. His countenance: Impartation of Jesus' *nature*

10. His mouth: *Intimacy* with Jesus

What is My Beloved?

Ask any newly engaged bride to describe her fiancé and you will get an earful of expressions that convey his superiority to every other man. Is this our response when we are asked about Jesus? When we have the internal reality of Jesus Christ as our Bridegroom, we will likewise respond with such joyful enthusiasm. I attended an exhibit where I was encouraging an artist with God's delight in his work. When a viewer interjected a false comment about God's nature, I tried to hold my tongue, but the stranger probed me about my thoughts. I instinctively described my Beloved with intense passion.

So what is my Beloved more than another? Who do I say Jesus Christ is? How does my God compare to all the gods of this world? To whom on earth can I liken Jesus (Is 40:18)? *Altogether Lovely* is my lovesick response. It is my testimony of Jesus Christ's splendor. He is fully God and fully Man. There is no other like Him. My Beloved has all authority in heaven and earth, yet He sympathizes with my weakness because of His humanity. He

To whom then will you liken God? Or what likeness will you compare to Him?

Isaiah 40:18

is humble, meek, and lowly. His compassions are new every morning. When I look into His eyes, He cleanses me with the water of His Word. He leads me by quiet waters, that I may drink from the Eternal Fountain of Living Water. His face displays His endless love. The Living Word became flesh and poured out His life unto death for me. His strength is absolutely perfect. He moves on my behalf. From the center of His being proceeds glorious light and truth. His foundation is immovable. He is my strength and the rock of my salvation. He is my firm support. God dwells within me. I cannot be shaken (Ps 46:5). He is glorious, majestic, and beautiful. Who can compare to Him? He is the most excellent of all men. The entrance of His Word brings light and understanding (Ps 119:130). His Words are truth and life reviving my soul (Ps 19:7). They are sweeter than the honeycomb (Ps 119:103). Truly He has the Words of eternal life (John 6:68). My Beloved is complete and perfect. My Maker, the God of the whole earth, is my Husband (Is 54:5). The earth has nothing for me. I desire Him more than anything temporal (Ps 73:25). His love is better than life itself. Only He can satisfy my soul (Ps 63:3, 5). This is the One who is worthy of all my affections (Rev 5:12). Dear friends, Jesus is my Beloved. He is my Best Friend. My Beloved is the Perfect Man!

Have you ever seen another like God? He created the heavens and the earth. He put the stars in the sky. His hands formed the land and the sea. He set boundaries for the sea and determined the measurements of the earth. Today, He continues to command the morning and causes darkness to cover the earth at night. He speaks to the clouds and they obey. He sends forth lightning, thunder, rain, and hail from their abode in heaven. He exalts kings and humbles them. When he hears the cry of the needy or afflicted, He listens. He answers those who call on His name. Of all the gods of this world, are there any except for the Lord God Almighty who acts on behalf of the ones He loves? Indeed, how could images formed with man's hands give aid to their human creators? But my Beloved is the uncreated God who formed and fashioned every creature that dwells on the face of the earth. He alone is worthy of praise. The Father sent His only Son who, although a Man, was God in flesh. In Him dwelt all the fullness of the Godhead in bodily form. He died for all, that He might redeem mankind from sin. He forgives me even for my sin of idolatry and pursuing *other beloveds* instead of Him. By His own blood He purchased me so that I might dwell together in unity with Him.

There is no one in heaven or on earth or under the earth who is like this One. He is glorious and majestic. He is awesome. My Lord is King over the whole earth (Ps 47:2). He is outstanding among ten thousand.

He is perfect in every way, and yet He became
sin. He was numbered among the transgressors
and removed iniquity so that I could live. He is
the fairest among men. His leadership is perfect.
All His ways are just and true. His eyes are ever
upon me. I cannot hide from His gaze. He has
one desire: that all would be saved—that none
should perish—but that all would enter into the
covenant of everlasting life and love with Him.

For the LORD
Most High
is awesome;
He is a great
King over
all the earth.

PSALM 47:2

He loves with an everlasting love that no man can comprehend. His
affections cannot be denied. His *love* is strong as death; its jealousy
unyielding as the grave. He is faithful and merciful. He is slow to anger
and rich in love. These are His ways. He speaks with kindness and
humility so that all may see and comprehend the height, depth, width,
and length of His great love. He became nothing and was led like a
lamb to the slaughter. He did not open His mouth to defend Himself,
though He had the power to break free and escape such torment. For
the joy that was set before Him, He endured the Cross. He scorned its
shame, that He might gain the prize of a pure, spotless Bride who will
rule and reign with Him for all eternity!

How can another beloved compare? Have you not known? Have you
not heard, O children of the King? With His own arms, He stretched
out the heavens like a curtain. In strength and dignity, He sits above
the circle of the earth. He brings princes to nothing and makes judges
useless. He rides upon the clouds and makes darkness His covering.
He thunders from heaven; the voice of the Most High resounds. He
sends out His arrows and scatters the enemy. He rescues those He loves
because He delights in them. He is Light in the midst of deep darkness.
Out of the brightness of His presence, clouds advance. He shines the

light of His countenance, that all may see the glory of His appearing. He speaks and mountains melt like wax in His presence. Who is God except the Lord? Who is a rock except my God? Have you not known? Have you not heard? Has it not been told to you since the foundation of the earth? Does not all of creation declare it? The Everlasting God, the Lord, the Creator of the ends of the earth—Jesus Christ is the One and only true God. This is my Beloved!

He is the only One worthy of my love. His Words are more desirable than my necessary meals. They satisfy more than the choicest food. They are sweeter than honey. They are more intoxicating than the best wine. He alone satisfies the longings in my heart. In all He does, He neither grows tired or weary. He arms me with strength. All His ways are perfect. His Word is proven. Therefore, I will praise Him.

This is my Beloved! This is my Friend! His ways are unsearchable. His wisdom is beyond comprehension. His Love is everlasting. There is no other beloved like my Beloved. He is the Perfect Man. Jesus Christ is Altogether Lovely!

OUR STORY

Dear friends, Jesus Christ is not just my Beloved. He is *our Beloved*. This is *our story*. Jesus is our Messiah. We are each His Bride. Our Bridegroom King will return to gather all believers for the Marriage Supper of the Lamb. We will dwell with Him for all eternity. Today, if you hear His voice, turn to this One whom I call my Beloved.

Although we cannot see the Lord, let us lovingly declare our Beloved's incomparable attributes as our Majestic God (SONG 5:9-6:5). When He withdraws His presence for a season, may our souls not become downcast. Let us not be offended. Instead, may extreme longing for the Son of God consume us. When it seems that every circumstance is in opposition to His nature, let us believe His goodness. Let us lay aside all self-focus that we may overcome our struggle. As we come into agreement with the perfect nature of our Beloved, these seven verses proclaiming His beauty will become our songs of love. The Bride's beautiful expression of worship in the Song of Solomon will pour forth from our lives. Out of the abundance of our hearts, we will speak (LUKE 6:45). Our tongues will become like pens of ready writers. Our hearts will overflow with this good theme declaring the glory of our Bridegroom. Let us eagerly recite our compositions concerning King Jesus (Ps 45:1). Our Beloved is *Altogether Lovely—The Perfect Man*!

My beloved is white and ruddy, chief among ten thousand. His head is like the finest gold; his locks are wavy, and black as a raven. His eyes are like doves by the rivers of waters, washed with milk, and fitly set. His cheeks are like a bed of spices, banks of scented herbs. His lips are lilies, dripping liquid myrrh. His hands are rods of gold set with beryl. His body is carved ivory Inlaid with sapphires. His legs are pillars of marble set on bases of fine gold. His countenance is like Lebanon, excellent as the cedars. His mouth is most sweet, yes, he is altogether lovely. This is my beloved, and this is my friend, O daughters of Jerusalem! —Song of Solomon 5:10-16

My *beloved*
is white and *ruddy* ...

∽

Song 5:10

Chapter 2
My Beloved—Fully God and Man

WHITE AND RUDDY:
The *divinity* and *humanity* of Jesus Christ

PRAYER

Father God, I ask for the divine kiss of Your Word upon my heart (SONG 1:2). Reveal the divinity and humanity of Your Son to my soul. Impart Your Spirit of wisdom and revelation. Enlighten my eyes with knowledge of the triune Godhead (EPH 1:17-18). Open my eyes to discover wondrous truth from Your Word (PS 119:18). I desire to gaze upon the beauty of the Lord all the days of my life (PS 27:4). Awaken my heart that I may behold the beauty of my Beloved, Jesus. Amen.

FULLY GOD AND FULLY MAN

Jesus is both light and flesh, divine yet human. Our Beloved is fully God and fully Man. He is the image of the invisible God (COL 1:15).

The Gospel according to John introduces the Word as God. "In the beginning *was* the Word." In the beginning "the Word was *with* God." His Spirit was hovering over the waters. And in the beginning "the Word was *God.*" In the very beginning—when the earth was

> *He is the image of the invisible God, the firstborn over all creation.*
>
> COLOSSIANS 1:15

formless, void, and covered in complete darkness—the Word created the heavens and the earth (GEN 1:1-2; JOHN 1:1-3). Everything was made through the Word. Nothing was made without Him.

> *For by Him all things were created that are in heaven and that are on earth, visible and invisible, whether thrones or dominions or principalities or powers. All things were created through Him and for Him. And He is before all things, and in Him all things consist.* —Colossians 1:16-17

In the beginning the Word spoke into darkness saying, "Let there be light." Immediately light shone forth (GEN 1:3). "And the Word became flesh" (JOHN 1:14). True Light, the image of the invisible God, entered the world in the form of a Man (JOHN 1:9). "In Him was life, and the life was the light of men" (JOHN 1:4). The Word came to earth proclaiming, "I am the light of the world" (JOHN 8:12). Our Beloved is a brilliant light shining far brighter than the sun. He is clothed in light as if it were a garment (PS 104:2). Lightning proceeds from His throne (REV 4:5). Out of His brightness, clouds move forward (PS 18:12). Even darkness is as light to Him (PS 139:12). John the Baptist was sent from God to testify of this Light that all might believe (JOHN 1:6-7). Those in darkness have seen a great light (MATT 4:16). Using Solomon's language, John was proclaiming, "The One coming after me is *white. He is dazzling and excellent. The Lamb of God is radiant light.* This Man is *distinguished among ten thousand.* There is none like Him." When the Word became flesh, He pierced the darkness (JOHN 1:5, 14). This glorious Light could not be overpowered. Jesus Christ is the Word of God made manifest (ROM 16:25-26). This Perfect Man who put the stars in their place has dwelt among us. God became a Man!

Jesus' ruddy complexion reminds us that the One who created light in the beginning took on flesh, that we might behold His Father's glory. How interesting that the appearance of the Father on His heavenly throne is also likened to white and red attributes.

Immediately I was in the Spirit; and behold, a throne set in heaven, and One sat on the throne. And He who sat there was like a jasper and a sardius stone in appearance; and there was a rainbow around the throne, in appearance like an emerald.
—Revelation 4:2-3

A jasper gem reflects various colors. This clear crystal represents God's glory (REV 21:11; 4:3). Both sardius and carnelian gems can be found as reddish in appearance representing Jesus human nature.

This correlation between Father and Son is no coincidence. The Son of God dwells in unapproachable light (1 TIM 6:16), yet He stepped down into darkness to reveal His Father's glory. The Word that was spoken by God came to earth. Beloved, all the fullness of God dwells in this Perfect Man, Christ Jesus.

Beware lest anyone cheat you through philosophy and empty deceit, according to the tradition of men, according to the basic principles of the world, and not according to Christ. For in Him dwells all the fullness of the Godhead bodily.
—Colossians 2:8-9

Similarly, the Song of Solomon calls our attention to red and white attributes describing Jesus and His Bride (SONG 2:1). The Lily of the Valley is a plant with clusters of white flowers. The Rose of Sharon is a small tree with large reddish flowers. This imagery gives us a picture of the Bride purified by Christ's blood. Jesus may as well be characterized by the pure white lily and red-colored rose. He is the spotless Lamb who was slain. Our Beloved came to the earth as a Perfect Man and then humbled himself unto death. The uncreated God once robed in light exchanged His glory for garments of skin. He made Himself nothing and took the form of a servant. The Eternal One who made man in His image was Himself born of a woman. As a Child, our Lord grew in wisdom and stature. He was submissive to His parents.

> *Then he went down to Nazareth with them and was obedient to them. But his mother treasured all these things in her heart. And Jesus grew in wisdom and stature, and in favor with God and men.* —Luke 2:51-52 NIV

He was a Son, yet He learned obedience by the things which He suffered.

HEBREWS 5:8

Can we comprehend what it means that our Creator laid aside His omnipotence to become a Baby dependent on a mother to nurse Him? As if this humility were not enough, our Beloved also learned obedience through His suffering (HEB 5:8). When He had lived thirty-three years on earth, Jesus' obedience to the Father's will led Him to endure the torture of death on a cross.

> *Christ Jesus, who, being in the form of God, did not consider it robbery to be equal with God, but made Himself of no reputation, taking the form of a bondservant, and coming in the likeness of men. And being found in appearance as a man, He humbled Himself and became obedient to the point of death, even the death of the cross.* —Philippians 2:5-8

Who has believed our report? And to whom has the arm of the LORD been revealed? For He shall grow up before Him as a tender plant, and as a root out of dry ground. He has no form or comeliness; and when we see Him, there is no beauty that we should desire Him. He is despised and rejected by men, a Man of sorrows and acquainted with grief. And we hid, as it were, our faces from Him; He was despised, and we did not esteem Him. —Isaiah 53:1-3

Do we believe this report? Jesus Christ, a Jewish Man, is our Messiah. He is the One of whom the Prophets spoke, and yet He was more than a prophet. He was and is God incarnate. Jesus is white and ruddy. He is fully God and fully Man, entirely divine yet completely human. Yes, I believe the Living Word. There is no other like Him!

GLORY TO GOD

Jesus lived on the earth. He died on a cross. He rose from the grave. He is alive today. And He is coming back again!

> *"He's not a baby in a manger anymore.*
> *He's not a broken man on a cross.*
> *He didn't stay in the grave.*
> *And He's not staying in heaven forever.*
> *'Cause He's alive."*
>
> Copyright © 2007 Misty Edwards. Used by permission.

Jesus Christ is Lord! He has been given the name above every other name (PHIL 2:9). Our Beloved was exalted to the highest place and now sits enthroned at the right hand of God (EPH 1:20). He is our great High Priest forever making intercession on our behalf (HEB 2:17).

Chapter 2: My Beloved—Fully God and Man

There is a Man—the Perfect Man, Christ Jesus—seated at the right hand of God. Some of my favorite songs exalt the beauty of this Man.

My heart is overflowing
I speak concerning my beloved
King whose Name is Light
This One is white and ruddy
This One stands out among ten thousand
His head glows like gold, so bright

Brighter than the sun You shine,
Flames of fire are in Your eyes
Jesus, You are
Fairer than the sons of men

Your Father's Words, they dwell inside,
No other man is more alive
Jesus, You are
Fairer than the sons of men

No one has ever seen God
But Jesus, Your person radiates
The glory of His frame
You are the Faithful Witness
You are the One who speaks the Name of
The Father of all lights

I can hear the angels singing,
"Glory, glory to God in the highest!"
There's never been a man who's more alive
More alive than You Jesus

My heart is overflowing with a good theme. I speak concerning my Beloved King. God became the Perfect Man. Jesus took on flesh. He forever radiates the glory of His Father. How beautiful. The God Man, Jesus Christ, is alive. Glory to God! Can you hear the angels singing?

Then I looked, and I heard the voice of many angels around the throne, the living creatures, and the elders; and the number of them was ten thousand times ten thousand, and thousands of thousands, saying with a loud voice: "Worthy is the Lamb who was slain to receive power and riches and wisdom, and strength and honor and glory and blessing!" And every creature which is in heaven and on the earth and under the earth and such as are in the sea, and all that are in them, I heard saying: "Blessing and honor and glory and power be to Him who sits on the throne, and to the Lamb, forever and ever!" Then the four living creatures said, "Amen!" And the twenty-four elders fell down and worshiped Him who lives forever and ever.   *—Revelation 5:11-14*

Let us join in with this heavenly chorus. Let us lift our voices and sing, "Glory to God in the highest!" He is worthy of all our praise.

And suddenly there was with the angel a multitude of the heavenly host praising God and saying: "Glory to God in the highest, and on earth peace, goodwill toward men!"   *—Luke 2:13-14*

My *beloved* is ...
chief among ten *thousand*.

∽

Song 5:10

Chapter 3

Chief among Ten Thousand

CHIEF AMONG TEN THOUSAND:
Jesus' incomparable *superiority* to all

PRAYER

Jesus, draw me after you so that I may experience the superior pleasure of communion with my Beloved. Lord, your love is better than wine (SONG 1:2-3). The earth has nothing I desire besides You (Ps 73:25). Encounter my heart so that I may truly believe You are fairer than the sons of men (Ps 45:2). Amen.

KING OF GLORY

Our Beloved is Chief among ten thousand. He is more excellent than *all* men ever to live on the earth. Jesus Christ is incomparably superior to all people, pleasures, and experiences in our fallen world. He is the *only* Perfect Man. He is distinguished among the multitudes.

Therefore God also has highly exalted Him and given Him the name which is above every name, that at the name of Jesus every knee should bow, of those in heaven, and of those on earth, and of those under the earth, and that every tongue should confess that Jesus Christ is Lord, to the glory of God the Father. —Philippians 2:9-11

The Father has given His Son a name that is above every other name. Beloved, let us lift up our eyes and behold our King of Glory.

Lift up your heads, O you gates! And be lifted up, you everlasting doors! And the King of glory shall come in. Who is this King of glory? The LORD strong and mighty, the LORD mighty in battle. Lift up your heads, O you gates! Lift up, you everlasting doors! And the King of glory shall come in. Who is this King of glory? The LORD of hosts, He is the King of glory.

—Psalm 24:7-10

Who is this *King of Glory*? He is *Jesus Christ*, the *Son of the Living God*. In Him the fullness of the Godhead dwells (COL 2:9; ROM 1:20). He is the *Father*, the *Son*, and the *Holy Spirit*. Moses appealed to the Lord, "Please, show me Your glory" (EX 33:18). The Lord allowed His goodness to pass before Moses as He proclaimed His name, "The Lord, the Lord God, merciful and gracious ..."

The LORD, the LORD God, merciful and gracious, longsuffering, and abounding in goodness and truth, keeping mercy for thousands, forgiving iniquity and transgression and sin, by no means clearing the guilty, visiting the iniquity of the fathers upon the children and the children's children to the third and the fourth generation. *—Exodus 34:6-7*

Like Moses we long to behold the Lord's beauty and to see Him face to face. If we desire like David to gaze upon His beauty and inquire in His temple what will we discover? The Lord revealed His glory to Moses by proclaiming His name. He is the *God of Abraham, Isaac, and Jacob* (EXOD 3:6), the *Everlasting God* (GEN 21:33), and the *Holy*

One of Israel, our *Savior* (Is 43:3). Consider the numerous ways our Beloved has made His name known to us throughout Scripture.

You may have heard the Lord referred to by one of His Hebrew names. He is called *Jehovah Elohim, the Lord God* (GEN 2:4); *Adonai, Lord* (GEN 15:2); *El Shaddai, Almighty God* (GEN 17:1); *Jehovah Jirah, The Lord Will Provide* (GEN 22:14); *Jehovah Rophe, The Lord Who Heals* (EXOD 15:26); *Jehovah Nissi, The Lord Is My Banner* (EXOD 17:15); *Jehovah M'Kaddesh, the Lord Who Sanctifies* (LEV 20:8); *Jehovah Tsidkenu, The Lord Our Righteousness* (JER 23:6); *Jehovah Rohi, The Lord Our Shepherd* (PS 23:1); *Jehovah Shalom, The Lord Is Peace* (JUDG 6:24); *Jehovah Shamma, The Lord Is There* (EZEK 48:35); *Jehova Sabaoth, The Lord of Hosts* (Is 1:24); *El Nahsah, The God Who Forgives* (PS 99:8); and *El Roi, The God Who Sees* (GEN 16:13). There is a great deal of information worthy of study on the Lord's various names. Simply search for "Names of God" online and you will find thousands of websites on this subject.

The Lord first revealed His name to Moses as *YHWH,* which is transliterated from Hebrew. With vowels added, *YAHWEH* translates the meaning of this covenant name according to God's declaration, "*I AM WHO I AM*" (EXOD 3:14). The Gospel of John records seven of Jesus' famous *I AM* statements. The Son of God declared, "*I AM* ..." "the *Bread of Life*" (JOHN 6:35), "the *Light of the World*" (JOHN 8:12), "the *Door of the Sheep*" (JOHN 10:7), "the *Good Shepherd*" (JOHN 10:11), "the *Resurrection and the Life*" (JOHN 11:25), "the *Way,* the *Truth,* and the *Life*" (JOHN 14:6), and "the *True Vine*" (JOHN 15:1). Our Beloved is the great *I AM* (JOHN 8:58; 18:6; EXOD 3:14).

"Jesus" comes from the Hebrew name *Joshua (Je-Hoshua, Y'shua),* which means *Jehovah is Salvation.* The Hebrew word for *Christ* is

Messiah (Meshiach), which means *The Anointed One*. Jesus Christ is the *Anointed One*, our *Savior*. He is our *Messiah*.

Our Beloved is the *Root of Jesse*, the *Offspring of David*, and the *Bright Morning Star* (IS 11:1-10; REV 22:16). Jesus' name is the *Branch* (IS 4:2). He is called *"Wonderful, Counselor, Mighty God, Everlasting Father, Prince of Peace"* (IS 9:6). He is the *Ancient of Days* (DAN 7:9). He appeared in the Old Testament as the *Angel of the Lord* (GEN 16:7; 18:2; 21:17; 22:11; 24:7; 31:11; 32:24; EXOD 3:6, 13:21). He is the *Glory of God* (JOHN 17:1, 5; IS 42:8; 48:11). He is *Alpha and Omega*, the *Eternal One*. He has no beginning, and He has no end. He is the One who *Was*, who *Is*, and who *Is to Come* (REV 4:8). He is the *Head of the Church* (COL 1:8). He is the *Faithful Witness*, the *Firstborn from the Dead*, and the *Ruler over Kings of the Earth* (REV 1:5). He is the *First and Last* (REV 1:17; 2:8; IS 41:4; 44:6). He is the *Most Excellent Way* called *Love* (1 COR 12:31-13:13). There is no God besides the Lord. Truly there is no one like our Beloved!

Thus says the LORD, the King of Israel, and his Redeemer,
the LORD of hosts: "I am the First and I am the Last;
besides Me there is no God."   *—Isaiah 44:6*

It is interesting to note that the Son and the Father are called by the same names. They are both *Creator* (JOHN 1:3-10; GEN 1:1; IS 40:28; 44:24), *Savior* (JOHN 4:42; ACTS 4:12; IS 43:11; 45:21-22), *Judge* (JOHN 5:27; MATT 25:31; JOEL 3:12), *Light* (JOHN 8:12; IS 60:19), *Shepherd* (JOHN 10:11, 16; PS 23:1; IS 40:11), *Redeemer* (LUKE 1:68; REV 5:9; HOS 13:14; IS 41:14), *Bridegroom* (REV 21:2; MATT 25:1; IS 62:5; HOS 2:16), *Husband* (2 COR 11:2; JER 31:32), *Almighty* (REV 1:7-8; GEN 17:1), *I AM* (JOHN 8:58; EXOD 3:14), *Holy One* (ACTS 3:14; IS 43:15), *First* and *Last* (REV 22:13; IS 44:6), *Master* (MATT 23:8; MAL 1:6), *Rock* (1 COR 10:4; PS 18:31), *Lord of lords* (REV 19:16; 1 TIM 6:14; DEUT 10:17), and *King of Israel* (JOHN 1:49; IS 44:6). All of the Father's nature is manifest through His Son.

Jesus is the *Word of God* (JOHN 1:1; REV 19:13) and the *Wisdom of God* (1 COR 2:7; PROV 8). He is exalted by His name, *Yah.* Our Beloved is *Father to the Fatherless* and *Defender of Widows* (PS 68:4-5). He is the *Sun of Righteousness* (MAL 4:2) and the *Just Judge* (PS 7:11). The Lord is a *God of Covenant* (GEN 6:18). The Lord is our *Shield,* our *Strength,* and our *Refuge.* He is our *Very Present Help* in times of trouble. He is both *Master* and *Friend.* He is the *Second Adam,* the *Great High Priest,* the *Chief Apostle,* the *Great Physician,* and the *Lamb of God* who was slain before the foundation of the world. He is the *Stone the Builders Rejected,* yet He became the *Chief Cornerstone.* He is the *Author and Finisher* of our faith. He is our *Advocate* and our *Deliverer.* He is the *Blessed only Potentate,* the *King of kings,* and the *Lord of lords* (1 TIM 6:15).

This is our *King of Glory!* Jesus is the *Lord Almighty.* He is *Chief among Ten Thousand.* There is no God like Jehovah. Truly our God is an *awesome* God!

EXALT HIS NAME

The Lord, He is God! Out of His countless names, we still lack a word sufficient to describe this Perfect Man. Not one utterance does Him justice. We could assign the loftiest expressions to our Beloved but they all fall short. What shall we do? Let us ascribe to the Lord the glory due His name! Let us worship God in the beauty of His holiness (PS 29:2). Before the morning dawns, let us arise to declare His glory. All day

Ascribe to the LORD the glory due his name ...

PSALM 29:2 NIV

long, let us magnify the Lord. In the watches of the night, let us meditate on the splendor of our Beloved (Ps 63:6; 119:147-148). Let us never cease to exalt the name of Jesus Christ and to sing His highest praise. Dear friends, let us extol our God at all times. He is worthy of praise!

Sing to the LORD a new song; sing to the LORD, all the earth. Sing to the LORD, praise his name; proclaim his salvation day after day. Declare his glory among the nations, his marvelous deeds among all peoples. For great is the LORD and most worthy of praise; he is to be feared above all gods. For all the gods of the nations are idols, but the LORD made the heavens. Splendor and majesty are before him; strength and glory are in his sanctuary. Ascribe to the LORD, O families of nations, ascribe to the LORD glory and strength. Ascribe to the LORD the glory due his name; bring an offering and come into his courts. Worship the LORD in the splendor of his holiness; tremble before him, all the earth. Say among the nations, "The LORD reigns." The world is firmly established, it cannot be moved; he will judge the peoples with equity. Let the heavens rejoice, let the earth be glad; let the sea resound, and all that is in it; let the fields be jubilant, and everything in them. Then all the trees of the forest will sing for joy; they will sing before the LORD, for he comes, he comes to judge the earth. He will judge the world in righteousness and the peoples in his truth.

–Psalm 96 NIV

Consider the psalmist's exhortation. Let us sing to the Lord a new song. Let us proclaim His salvation every day. With all creation, let us sing of our Beloved's salvation, glory, and marvelous deeds. He stretches out the heavens like a curtain and measures the waters in the hollow of His hand (Is 40: 12, 22). Who is like our God? All the gods of this earth are merely idols. They did not make the heavens. Neither will they come to judge the earth. No one can compare. Only He is worthy to be praised and feared above all gods.

Our Beloved created us for His pleasure. We live to glorify Him. May our lives forever arise as songs of love to Him. May everything we do be all for His glory (1 COR 10:31). Let us live to declare His splendor, majesty, strength, and honor. This is our Beloved. He is Chief among ten thousand. Let us give Him all the glory and honor due His name. Let us enter His presence with sacrifices of thanksgiving and shouts of joy. Yes, let us sing! Let us worship Him in the splendor of His holiness and tremble with the fear of the Lord. The heavens rejoice, the earth is glad, and the sea resounds (Ps 96:11). All creation

> *The LORD reigns, let the earth be glad; let the distant shores rejoice.*
>
> PSALM 97:1

testifies of the majesty of the Lord. What else can we do except join in such praise? May our voices blend with the great multitude in heaven saying, "Alleluia! For the Lord God Omnipotent reigns!" (REV 19:6). Let all of heaven and earth rejoice. There is no one like our God!

O LORD, our Lord, how excellent is Your name in all the earth, who have set Your glory above the heavens!   —Psalm 8:1

Is it any wonder the Psalms are full of His praises? Even as I attempt to describe this Perfect Man, my heart overflows with a good theme. His rivers of Living Water spring up from my soul. My tongue is like a pen in the hands of an eager writer. Therefore, I will recite my composition of love concerning my King.

My heart is overflowing with a good theme; I recite my composition concerning the King; my tongue is the pen of a ready writer. You are fairer than the sons of men; grace is poured upon Your lips; therefore God has blessed You forever … Your throne, O God, is forever and ever; a scepter of righteousness is the scepter of Your kingdom. –Psalm 45:1-2, 6

Friends, I cannot contain this Fountain of Life dwelling inside. His Holy Spirit has made known the Man, Christ Jesus. I must declare the goodness of the Lord. I will lift my voice and sing, "Jesus, You are fairer than the sons of men!"

Our Beloved is the King of Glory. His name is exalted above every name. He says, "Look to Me, and be saved, all you ends of the earth! For I am God, and there is no other! I have sworn by Myself ... to Me every knee will bow. Every tongue shall take an oath" (Is 45:22-23).

Therefore God exalted him to the highest place and gave him the name that is above every name.
PHILIPPIANS 2:9 NIV

God declared this of Himself in the Old Testament, and in the New Testament the same is declared about His Son. Though Jesus is equal to God, He took the form of a servant, humbling Himself even unto death. For this reason the Father exalted His Son and gave Him the highest name (PHIL 2:6-9). Our Beloved is *Chief among ten thousand*, the King of Glory. At His name everyone will bow. All will confess that Jesus Christ is Lord (PHIL 2:10-11). This Perfect Man is the Lord Almighty. No God existed before Him. There will be none after Him. He is the only Savior of the world. He alone is God. There is no other (Is 43:10-11; DEUT 4:35; 6:4; 32:39).

"One will say, 'I am the LORD's'; another will call himself by the name of Jacob; another will write with his hand, 'The LORD's,' and name himself by the name of Israel. Thus says the LORD, the King of Israel, and his Redeemer, the LORD of hosts: 'I am the First and I am the Last; besides Me there is no God. And who can proclaim as I do? … Have I not told you from that time, and declared it? You are My witnesses. Is there a God besides Me? Indeed there is no other Rock; I know not one.'"

–Isaiah 44:5-8

He is the One and only true God (JER 10:10). He will not give His glory to another (Is 48:11). Every created being in heaven, on the earth, and under the earth will worship Christ Jesus. So what are we waiting for? Let us acknowledge Him as Savior now. Let us ascribe to the Lord the glory due His name today. Beloved of God, let us lift up our heads that our King of Glory may enter into His inheritance. Let us invite His presence into our hearts, our homes, our offices, our schools, and every activity of our lives. Let us exalt our King of Glory! Who is like our God? He is King of kings. He is Lord of lords. He is holy. He is worthy. This song causes my spirit to soar:

You are Lord of lords, You are King of kings
You are mighty God, Lord of everything

Chapter 3: Chief among Ten Thousand

You're Emmanuel, You're the great I am
You're the Prince of Peace, Who is the Lamb

You're the Living God, You're my Saving Grace
You will reign forever, You're the Ancient of Days
You are Alpha, Omega, Beginning and End
You're my Savior, Messiah, Redeemer and Friend

I will sing to and worship the King who is worthy
I will love and adore Him, I will bow down before Him

Copyright © 1994 Imboden Music; Martha Jo Publishing

Let us sing this to our Beloved. Let us love, adore, and worship Him. Jesus is our Lord (Ps 45:11). May His song arise from within our souls. Let us lift our voices and praise our Creator who gives us life!

Deep calls unto deep at the noise of Your waterfalls; all Your waves and billows have gone over me. The LORD will command His lovingkindness in the daytime, and in the night His song shall be with me—a prayer to the God of my life.

—Psalm 42:7-8

Deep calls out to deep. The Spirit of God calls out to His Spirit who dwells inside of us. We were created to worship. We were made to declare His glory. Let us give Him thanks. Let us shout joyfully and rejoice (Ps 98:4). Whether we stand, lift our hands, leap for joy, break forth in dancing, throw splashes of vibrant colors on canvases, sing, shout, or make joyful noises—whatever we do let us bless the name of our Beloved!

> *Shout joyfully to the LORD ... Break forth in song, rejoice, and sing praises.*
>
> PSALM 98:4

Stand up and praise the LORD your God, who is from everlasting to everlasting. Blessed be your glorious name, and may it be exalted above all blessing and praise. You alone are the LORD. You made the heavens, even the highest heavens, and all their starry host, the earth and all that is on it, the seas and all that is in them. You give life to everything, and the multitudes of heaven worship you … —Nehemiah 9:5-6 NIV

Listen to the still small voice that whispers through the leaves of the trees, beckoning us to lift our voices like joyful songbirds. Our Beloved is worthy of all our affections. Let us waste our lives loving this Perfect Man. Jesus Christ is Altogether Lovely!

My beloved spoke, and said to me: "Rise up, my love, my fair one, and come away. For lo, the winter is past, the rain is over and gone. The flowers appear on the earth; the time of singing has come, and the voice of the turtledove is heard in our land. The fig tree puts forth her green figs, and the vines with the tender grapes give a good smell. Rise up, my love, my fair one, and come away! O my dove, in the clefts of the rock, in the secret places of the cliff, let me see your face, let me hear your voice; for your voice is sweet, and your face is lovely."
—Song of Solomon 2:10-14

His *head* is

like the finest *gold* ...

᥎

Song 5:11

Chapter 4

His Head—Perfect Leadership

ATTRIBUTE #1

His head: Jesus' sovereign *leadership* over all

PRAYER

Jesus, Your leadership is absolutely perfect. You cause all of the events in my life to work together for good (Rom 8:28). Help me to trust You even when I do not understand. Give me grace to persevere and rejoice in the midst of trials (Jas 1:2-4). When the circumstances of life discourage my heart, Lord, lift my head that I may yet praise You (Ps 3:3; 42:11). I will not love my life even unto death (Rev 12:11). I will follow wherever You lead. Good Shepherd, lead me on (Ps 23:1). Amen.

PERFECT LEADERSHIP

Jesus Christ has divine sovereignty over all things. He is the image of the invisible God. He created all things. He is head of the Church.

He is the image of the invisible God, the firstborn over all creation. For by Him all things were created that are in heaven and that are on earth, visible and invisible, whether thrones or dominions or principalities or powers. All things were created through Him and for Him. And He is before all things, and in Him all things consist. And He is the head of the body, the

church, who is the beginning, the firstborn from the dead,
that in all things He may have the preeminence. For it pleased
the Father that in Him all the fullness should dwell . . .
–Colossians 1:15-19

It pleased the Father to cause the fullness of God to dwell in His Son, that He might give Jesus authority over all things. After the Father of glory raised our Lord Jesus Christ from the dead, He gave Him the highest seat in heaven.

The God of our Lord Jesus Christ, the Father of glory . . . raised
Him from the dead and seated Him at His right hand in the
heavenly places, far above all principality and power and
might and dominion, and every name that is named, not only
in this age but also in that which is to come. And He put all
things under His feet, and gave Him to be head over all things
to the church. *–Ephesians 1:17, 20-22*

All dominion was given to this Perfect Man. He was granted supreme headship over the Church. He rules with divine excellence. He is the blessed and only Sovereign (1 TIM 6:15 NRSV). His wisdom is supreme. He is omniscient (all-knowing). His head is finest gold. Our Beloved's leadership is absolutely perfect.

It has taken me some time to come to the place where I can declare this wholeheartedly. I have had my share of shattered dreams. My heart has been broken. I have felt as though God had forgotten me. After graduating with a degree in graphic design, I quickly settled into my career at a greeting card company with hopes to soon be married—so I thought. Within eighteen months, my future came crashing down. The relationship ended and my position was eliminated. I returned to

California and moved in with my parents with plans to start over. In less than two months, I found a well-paying design position just five minutes away from home. Within a year, the Lord made it possible for me to pay off my portion of outstanding college loans. I was finally on my way to a successful life—so I thought.

Then, all at once, I injured my back in a freeway car accident and was diagnosed with carpal tunnel syndrome. To make matters worse, I was burned out creatively after a very brief career in corporate America. A co-worker asked the dreaded question, "What are you going to do now?" I felt crippled. My identity had become completely wrapped up in who I was as a *designer*. What would I do if I could not create? What was the point of my college education if I was already out of commission three years into the race? Fear suddenly gripped me as I watched all of my dreams shatter to pieces a second time. I spent a year in physical therapy, quit my job, and began substitute teaching. My parents sold our house and moved to Oklahoma to be near our relatives. I felt lost and alone. During this time, I found myself spiraling downward into depression and being tempted with thoughts of suicide.

When life seemed like a dead-end road, my Beloved proved Himself faithful. Though darkness tried to consume me, it could not. I had true Light, the Living God, dwelling inside. My desperate cry rose before Him. My Shepherd guided me through this valley where death's shadow was lurking. The Lord restored my soul. He guided me on the path to emotional, spiritual, and physical healing (Ps 23). For His name's sake, Jesus liberated me from demonic strongholds in my life. He healed my body,

He brought me out into a spacious place; he rescued me because he delighted in me.

PSALM 18:19 NIV

heart, and soul. He brought me out into a spacious place and delivered me because of His great delight in me (Ps 18:19). Time and time again God has proven His goodness. Day after day I find myself trusting Him still more!

Why should I say my way is hidden from God (Is 40:27)? Can the clay say to the Potter, "You don't know what you're doing (Is 29:16)?" In the past I may have felt disregarded by God or questioned His activity in my life. The Lord has since taught me how to respond rightly in difficult circumstances. Now when things do not seem to go according to my plan, I no longer despair. Though I may be disheartened at first, I more readily surrender to His will. Even when Jesus was in agony, He submitted to His Father's will (LUKE 22:42-44). I believe the Lord will ultimately cause everything to work out for my benefit.

And we know that all things work together for good to those who love God, to those who are the called according to His purpose. —Romans 8:28

Those who love God can have confidence in His perfect leadership. Because He is a God of justice, there is a day of reckoning in His heart for the atrocities that have taken place in the lives of His children. Vengeance belongs to Him. He will repay the enemy for every injustice, however great or small (Is 2:12; HEB 10:30).

But let us forget the past and reach toward what is ahead (PHIL 3:13). Everything Satan meant for evil, God will use for His glory. He turns our mourning into dancing and our sadness into joy (Ps 30:11). The Lord is the magnificent conductor of the symphony of our lives. He has already ordained every day before one of them began. Our Beloved divinely orchestrates the intricate details of each event (Ps 139:16).

He knows the end from the beginning. The goal is not that we have comfort in temporary circumstances. Our Beloved has a greater plan. He is refining us so that we may walk worthy of His calling (COL 1:10). Jesus is preparing each of us to become His pure and spotless Bride. Beloved, we are living for another age. These momentary troubles are actually getting us ready for eternity!

> For our light affliction, which is but for a moment, is working for us a far more exceeding and eternal weight of glory.
>
> —2 Corinthians 4:17

James tells us to count it all joy when we face various trials. When our faith is tested, we are being perfected so that we may be complete, lacking nothing (JAS 1:2-4). Frank Sinatra sang of those who are young at heart, "You can laugh when your dreams fall apart at the seams." Solomon likewise described the Proverbs 31 woman saying, "She can laugh at the days to come" (PROV 31:25 NIV). There will always be trials. Why should we be surprised?

> Beloved, do not be surprised at the fiery ordeal that is taking place among you to test you, as though something strange were happening to you. But rejoice insofar as you are sharing Christ's sufferings, so that you may also be glad and shout for joy when his glory is revealed.   —1 Peter 4:12-13 NRSV

We can glory in tribulation knowing that it produces perseverance, character, and hope (ROM 5:3-5). Let us rejoice that we share in Christ's sufferings now so that we may also rejoice when He returns.

Whatever the situation, I am learning to declare, "Lord, Your head is finest gold. Surely the boundary lines have fallen to me in pleasant places (Ps 16:6). Jesus, Your leadership is perfect." I have even begun to welcome the Lord's north winds of adversity, not just His south winds of blessing. I am beginning to realize how essential this prayer is to my spiritual growth.

> *Awake, O north wind, and come, O south! Blow upon my garden, that its spices may flow out. Let my beloved come to his garden and eat its pleasant fruits.* –Song of Solomon 4:16

Only our Beloved knows the right amount of testing and refreshing needed to bring us forth in maturity. He arranges every season. Winter allows us to flourish in springtime. Our branches must be pruned so that we may bear more fruit. This is the way His fragrance emanates from our lives. It is the only way our lives can bear fruit that will last (JOHN 15:16). We are His garden. Jesus takes delight in the fruit we produce (SONG 5:1). A children's book called *Oh, the Places You'll Go* portrays the ups and downs of life and our ultimate victory.[4]

> *You'll be on your way up! You'll be seeing great sights!*
> *You'll join the high fliers who soar to high heights …*
> *Except when you don't. Because, sometimes, you won't.*
> *I'm sorry to say so but, sadly, it's true*
> *that Bang-ups and Hang-ups can happen to you.*
> *You can get all hung up in a prickle-ly perch.*
> *And your gang will fly on. You'll be left in a Lurch.*
> *You'll come down from the Lurch with an unpleasant bump.*
> *And the chances are, then, that you'll be in a Slump.*
> *And when you're in a Slump, you're not in for much fun.*
> *Un-slumping yourself is not easily done.*
>
> *–Dr. Seuss*

I enjoy the playful way that Dr. Suess depicts our common struggle. King David gives us the prescribed method for *un-slumping* oneself. He speaks directly to His downcast soul (Ps 42:5). He says to himself, "Hope in God." It is as if David were saying, "Soul, why are you surprised at this fiery ordeal? Don't you know these trials

Why are you cast down, O my soul? Hope in God ...
Psalm 42:5

are working an eternal weight of glory? Stop worrying. Lord, I trust you completely. Your leadership in my life is absolutely perfect. Even though I don't quite understand, I will worship You." There is truly no better way to get out of a *slump* than by praising the Lord. So why are we downcast? What is there to be anxious about? We cannot add a single hour to our lives by worrying (MATT 6:27). Instead of fretting, we are instructed to give thanks as we pray.

> Be anxious for nothing, but in everything by prayer and supplication, with thanksgiving, let your requests be made known to God; and the peace of God, which surpasses all understanding, will guard your hearts and minds through Christ Jesus. —Philippians 4:6-7

God's peace guards us from despair every time we offer Him thanks. If we respond to hardship with gratitude, our lives arise as love songs before His heavenly throne. The only way for us to have victory in this life is to continually acknowledge, "His head is finest gold." We must declare it. Giving thanks to God lifts our souls out of despair. Jesus gives us a garment of praise to replace our spirit of heaviness (Is 61:3). There are really only two times to praise the Lord. Let us worship Him when we feel like it and when we do not. Let us give Him the rightful place of leadership as head of our lives, our households, our jobs, our finances, our relationships, our desires, our dreams, our everything. It is only in His will that we find true freedom. Let us surrender *all* our ambitions, *all* our hopes, and *all* our plans to our Beloved.

Of course we may plan our way, but the Good Shepherd directs our steps (PROV 16:9). Imagine setting out for a trip without a road map. It might be fun to explore for a while, but it would be difficult to find a particular location. Do we really think we know the way to go? Our Beloved not only knows our destination but also discerns the best route to get us there. We need only submit our will to His. We cannot trust in our own understanding. We must acknowledge Jesus' divine authority. He is our only way forward. Our Beloved will direct our path. We can trust His leadership.

> *Trust in the LORD with all your heart, and lean not on your own understanding; in all your ways acknowledge Him, and He shall direct your paths.* —Proverbs 3:5-6

We are completely dependent on the Lord. If we put our trust in His leadership, we will come up from the wilderness of this life leaning on our Beloved (SONG 8:5). Let us pray the same way He taught His disciples: "Your kingdom come. Your will be done on earth as it is in heaven" (MATT 6:10). The Lord's ways are perfect (PS 18:30). They are so much higher than ours (IS 55:9). Beloved, no matter what happens during this brief life on the earth, we must come to the point where we can declare, "Jesus, You are wise. Your head is finest gold. Your leadership is perfect. Though I cannot see the way before me, I will hope in

As the heavens are higher than the earth, so are My ways higher than your ways ...

ISAIAH 55:9

You. Even though I may not understand, I believe that You are for me and not against me. Lord, let Your will be done, not mine. I surrender everything to You. I am confident that You will bring me forth as Your radiant Bride. My Beloved, though You slay me I will trust you completely!" Let us lift our eyes up to the mountains and say, "My help comes from the Lord" (Ps 121:1-2). He cares. He loves us. We can trust Him implicitly. Our Beloved's head is finest gold. His leadership is undeniably perfect. Jesus Christ is Altogether Lovely!

His *locks* are wavy,

and black as a *raven*.

⤣

Song 5:11

Chapter 5

His Locks—Faithful Witness

ATTRIBUTE #2

His locks: Jesus' *dedication* to God and the Church

PRAYER

Jesus, I cannot fathom the extent of Your Loving devotion to me. Who are You as the Faithful Witness? Give me Your Spirit of wisdom and revelation as You declare the nature of Your Father to my heart (EPH 1:17-19). Lord, show me Your glory. Give me the knowledge of God, the knowledge of the Holy One. Thank you for Your zeal in pursuing me. Thank You for Your dedication in revealing to me the heart of Your Father. Amen.

FAITHFUL WITNESS

Jesus Christ is the Faithful Witness (REV 1:5). A Nazarite's long uncut hair was worn to signify his dedication to the Lord (NUM 6:2, 7-8 KJV). It was a symbol of strength. Although Jesus did not take the vow of a Nazarite, His hair represents His consecration and youthful vitality. These black and wavy locks express our Beloved's eternal devotion. Jesus is committed to making the Father known to His Bride.

No one has seen God at any time. The only begotten Son, who is in the bosom of the Father, He has declared Him.

—John 1:18

If there is a question about the nature of God, we need only consider His Son. Although no one has seen the Father, His Son Jesus made Him known. The Father confirmed Jesus' divine Sonship with a sign and voice from heaven declaring, "This is my Beloved Son in whom I am well pleased" (MATT 3:17; 17:5). Christ is the One about whom Isaiah prophesied, "For unto us a Child is born, unto us a Son is given ... His name will be called Wonderful, Counselor, Mighty God, Everlasting Father, Prince of Peace" (IS 9:6). Why would this Son be called Everlasting Father? Simple. Jesus Christ is God. He testified, "I and My Father are One" (JOHN 10:30). When Jesus' disciples asked Him to show them the Father, He replied, "He who has seen Me has seen the Father" (JOHN 14:9). Jesus came to the earth not only to atone for sin but also to show the world His Father's glory.

We reflected on the nature of Jesus Christ as both fully God and fully Man in Chapter 2, "My Beloved: Fully God and Man." This is how our Beloved manifests His Father's name (JOHN 17:6). Jesus is the image of the invisible God. All of God's fullness dwells in this Perfect Man (COL 1:15, 19). The Son is the radiance of God's glory. He is the exact representation of His being (HEB 1:3 NIV). His name is the Word of God (REV 19:13). He was in the beginning with God creating all things. Jesus was daily the Father's delight as a Master Craftsman (PROV 8:30). Our Beloved was God Himself. Everything was made through Him (JOHN 1:1-3). Whatever can be known about God has been made plain through His creation. All of His invisible qualities have been clearly seen from the beginning of time (ROM 1:19-20). Through the ages God spoke through the prophets, but now He speaks through His Son.

> *He is the image of the invisible God ...*
>
> COLOSSIANS 1:15

God, who at various times and in various ways spoke in time past to the fathers by the prophets, has in these last days spoken to us by His Son, whom He has appointed heir of all things, through whom also He made the worlds; who being the brightness of His glory and the express image of His person … —Hebrews 1:1-3

For thirty-three years on the earth, Jesus Christ faithfully revealed the Father's glory. He is the Faithful and True Witness (REV 3:14; 19:11). He made known all that His Father said (JOHN 15:15). When the Word became flesh, we saw the glory of God in Jesus' face (JOHN 1:14; 2 COR 4:6). Our Beloved is the great I AM. He always has been. He always will be. Before time began, Father and Son together put the stars in the sky and gave to them each a name (IS 40:26). They rejoiced as they created the universe and laid the earth's foundation. Then out of the dust mankind was fashioned in the very image of our Creator. But Adam and Eve did not heed the Lord's instruction not to eat of the tree of

> *For God … made his light shine … the glory of God in the face of Christ.*
>
> 2 CORINTHIANS 4:6 NIV

the knowledge of good and evil. In their arrogance they sinned against God. Because of their actions, this means that we too have sinned and fallen short of His glory (ROM 3:23). We once shared in a glorious union with the Godhead in the Garden of Eden, but that relationship was severed. Man was banned from this Paradise.

Our defiance did not in any way diminish the desire of our Maker to continue in eternal communion with those He created. The Father loved us so much that He sent His Son to become a Man. Therefore, Jesus humbled Himself by coming to the earth as a Child. He gave up

His title and position as God. For a season, He did not share in the Father's glory. He traded in His garments of unapproachable light for the simple clothing of dust. Skin covered His eternal glory. As a Son, our Beloved became obedient to His Father that He might ransom us. Because of our disobedience, we were appointed to die. There was only one way for us to escape this eternal damnation. A perfect sacrifice must be made. This offering could not be just anyone, because all men had now sinned. Neither could God kill Himself. The Father gave His Son to be both God and Man that we might be reconciled to Him.

The Holy Spirit conceived Jesus in the womb of a woman in order to bring Him forth on the earth as a human. Still, Christ retained His divine nature and was sinless. In all of heaven and earth, Jesus was the only one found worthy to pay the penalty for our sin. Only His blood could cover our door posts to prevent death's shadow from entering and taking our lives for all eternity. God loves us so much that He came to the earth to intervene on our behalf. Jesus was obedient even to the point of becoming a curse by hanging on a cross. As a Perfect Man He never sinned, yet He actually became sin. He took on all of our transgressions and infirmities on His own body. It is by His wounds that we are healed and set free from captivity to sin and death.

As the Father loved Me, I also have loved you ...
JOHN 15:9

Beloved, this is Jesus' vow of consecration to the Father and to us. He committed to make the Father known. As the Father loves the Son, so Jesus loves us (JOHN 15:9). He declared to us the Father's name, that the love with which the Father loves Him may be in us (JOHN 17:26). Though our Beloved laid down His robe of splendor, He carried His Father's glory that we might behold it in His face. And being One with the Father, Jesus fulfilled His promise to join Himself to us that we may share in their glory. This Perfect Man is the Faithful Witness. He came to testify of the Ancient of Days. Jesus was dedicated to fulfilling His Father's will. He did only the things He saw His Father doing (JOHN 5:19). Though equal to God, Jesus did not use this power to His advantage, but made Himself nothing and took the form of a servant. Our Beloved came not to be served but to serve (MARK 10:45).

Your attitude should be the same as that of Christ Jesus:
Who, being in very nature God, did not consider equality
with God something to be grasped, but made himself
nothing, taking the very nature of a servant, being made
in human likeness. And being found in appearance as
a man, he humbled himself and became obedient to
death—even death on a cross!   *–Philippians 2:5-8 NIV*

When tempted by Satan in the wilderness, Jesus did not succumb to the pressure to abort the plan set forth from eternity (MATT 4:1-11). In Gethsemane, He surrendered His will to the Father's, saying, "Father, not my will but Yours be done." Even when His locks were wet with the drops of the night and His sweat became like drops of blood, He remained steadfast (LUKE 22:42-44). The Pharisees accused Him: "You saved others; can't you save yourself?" Once again, He submitted to His Father. He was obedient even unto death. Our Beloved did not allow His *black and wavy locks* to be cut. In His love covenant lay Jesus' true strength. Though He appeared weak and broken on the cross, His crucifixion and resurrection forever conquered sin and death. For the joy set before Him, our Beloved became the ultimate sacrifice for our sins. Jesus does not desire that anyone should be condemned to eternal separation from His love. He longs that all might be reconciled to God

(2 PET 3:9). This is why He prays for all believers to be one with Him and to partake of the same glory He shares with the Father.

I do not pray for these alone, but also for those who will believe in Me through their word; that they all may be one, as You, Father, are in Me, and I in You; that they also may be one in Us, that the world may believe that You sent Me. And the glory which You gave Me I have given them, that they may be one just as We are one: I in them, and You in Me; that they may be made perfect in one, and that the world may know that You have sent Me, and have loved them as You have loved Me. Father, I desire that they also whom You gave Me may be with Me where I am, that they may behold My glory which You have given Me; for You loved Me before the foundation of the world. O righteous Father! The world has not known You, but I have known You; and these have known that You sent Me. And I have declared to them Your name, and will declare it, that the love with which You loved Me may be in them, and I in them. —John 17:20-26

In this Perfect Man, the fullness of God dwells. He came to testify of the Father's love. Jesus came to unite us with the Triune Godhead. He did not use the power and authority He had to deliver Himself from becoming the sin of the world. God *so* loves the world that He sent His only begotten Son, and that Son was faithful to express the heart of His Father. He is the Faithful Witness who has made known to us the Father's glory. And yet His brief earthly ministry is not the end of the story. Beloved, Jesus is alive. His Spirit lives within us. His name is Immanuel, "God with us" (MATT 1:23). He is omnipresent.

He is everywhere. He is always with us. He said He would never leave us nor forsake us (HEB 13:5). And He did not leave. Jesus sent our Counselor, the Holy Spirit (JOHN 14:26; 15:26; 16:7). The indwelling Spirit forever testifies of the Father's glory. He imparts the Father's love to our hearts. The Holy Spirit searches all things and makes known to us the deep things of God (1 COR 2:10). If we believe, rivers of Living Water flow from this well inside our hearts (JOHN 7:38). This is how the Faithful Witness continues to impart the knowledge of the Holy One to His Church. Beloved, this Perfect Man is alive today. He who keeps us will not sleep (PS 121:4). He never grows weary. With youthful zeal and vitality, He pursues us.

Have you not known? Have you not heard? The everlasting God, the LORD, the Creator of the ends of the earth, neither faints nor is weary. —Isaiah 40:28

I find it difficult to describe the Faithful Witness when I fail to grasp the extent of His dedication. What is the degree of His devotion to us? Never will He leave or forsake us? Do we comprehend our Beloved's Faithfulness? Have we ever known a greater love? He did not love His life unto death but laid it down for His friends (JOHN 15:13). Christ loved the Church and gave Himself for us (EPH 5:25). His love is strong as death and His jealousy cruel as the grave.

For love is as strong as death, jealousy as cruel as the grave; Its flames are flames of fire, a most vehement flame. Many waters cannot quench love, nor can the floods drown it. If a man would give for love all the wealth of his house, it would be utterly despised. —Song of Solomon 8:6-7

The emerald rainbow surrounding God's heavenly throne forever reminds us of His faithfulness (Rev 4:3). He has given us a covenant of love and mercy. He fulfills His vows to a thousand generations.

Therefore know that the LORD your God, He is God,
the faithful God who keeps covenant and mercy for
a thousand generations with those who love Him and
keep His commandments.   *–Deuteronomy 7:9*

Beloved, have we considered this? God is in covenant with man! How can this be? Whenever we see a rainbow in the sky, let us remember His promise. Jesus revealed His Father's glory that we too may testify of His faithfulness. Let us recount the many ways our Beloved has shown His faithfulness to us.

His *eyes* are like doves

by the rivers of waters,

washed with milk,

and *fitly set*.

❦

Song 5:12

Chapter 6

His Eyes—Focused Vision

ATTRIBUTE #3

His eyes: Jesus' focused *vision*

PRAYER

Jesus, I fix my gaze upon You. Lord, I long to behold Your beauty (Ps 27:4). Let me see the apple of Your eye (Deut 32:9-10). Open the eyes of my understanding (Eph 1:18). Wash me with the water of Your Word (Eph 5:26). Your eyes are ever focused on me. I cannot begin to count your endless thoughts toward me (Ps 139:17-18). I will fix my gaze upon You (Heb 12:2). Lord, show me Your glory (Exod 33:18). Amen.

PERFECT VISION

The eyes of the Lord are everywhere. There is nothing hidden from His perfect vision. He is called El Roi, *The God Who Sees* (GEN 16:13). Jesus Christ, the omniscient God, sees all things with perfect wisdom, understanding, and discernment. His knowledge is infinite. Nothing is out of His direct line of sight. Our Beloved perceives every thought and every intention of our hearts. He knows each one of us completely. The Lord is intimately acquainted with all our ways.

O LORD, You have searched me and known me. You know my sitting down and my rising up; You understand my thought afar off. You comprehend my path and my lying down, and are acquainted with all my ways. For there is not a word on my tongue, but behold, O LORD, You know it altogether. You have hedged me behind and before, and laid Your hand upon me. Such knowledge is too wonderful for me; it is high, I cannot attain it. —Psalm 139:1-6

Before I even begin to express the beauty of His eyes, the Lord already knows every word I will write. How can I begin to comprehend such knowledge? He is intimately acquainted with all of our thoughts and desires. He knows our past, our present, and our future. He never sleeps. His eye is ever upon His people (Ps 34:15). The eyes of the Lord search throughout the earth for hearts that are loyal to Him (2 CHRON 16:9). He sits above the circle of the earth looking upon all its inhabitants (Is 40:22). His eyes are like doves with singleness of vision.

> *The eyes of the LORD are on the righteous ...*
> PSALM 34:15

THE APPLE OF HIS EYE

To understand our Beloved's focused vision, we must first consider it in the light of His chosen people. If we look into the very center of His eye what will we discover? There in the central aperture lies Israel, the apple of God's eye (DEUT 32:9-10).

For thus says the LORD of hosts: "He sent Me after glory, to the nations which plunder you; for he who touches you touches the apple of His eye ... Sing and rejoice, O daughter of Zion! For behold, I am coming and I will dwell in your midst," says the LORD ... "And the LORD will take possession of Judah as His inheritance in the Holy Land, and will again choose Jerusalem. Be silent, all flesh, before the LORD, for He is aroused from His holy habitation!" —Zechariah 2:8-13

The Old Testament is a historical account of the Lord's devotion to His covenant people. His jealousy was repeatedly aroused for this rebellious nation. He is exceedingly zealous for Zion (ZECH 1:14). Our Beloved's love for Israel is unquenchable. His passion extends beyond the grave (SONG 8:6-7). Jealousy is this Husband's fury (PROV 6:34). Zeal for the house of the Lord consumes Him (JOHN 2:17). We will consider the Bridegroom's relentless pursuit through the lenses of Song of Solomon and Hosea in Chapter 8, "His Lips:

> *I am zealous*
> *for Jerusalem*
> *And for Zion*
> *with great zeal.*
> ZECHARIAH 1:14

Invitation to Suffering." The Lord is full of compassion. Everything He does is through His eyes of mercy. Though Israel went astray, He said, "I am returning again to Jerusalem with mercy" (ZECH 1:16). Rivers of water stream from His eyes. He weeps for Jerusalem.

Now as He drew near, He saw the city and wept over it, saying, "If you had known, even you, especially in this your day, the things that make for your peace! But now they are hidden from your eyes." —Luke 19:41-42

O Jerusalem, Jerusalem, the one who kills the prophets and stones those who are sent to her! How often I wanted to gather your children together, as a hen gathers her chicks under her wings, but you were not willing! See! Your house is left to you desolate; for I say to you, you shall see Me no more till you say, "Blessed is He who comes in the name of the LORD!" —Matthew 23:37-39

The Man Christians know as Jesus Christ is the Jewish Messiah. When Israel's long awaited *King* came as a Baby, His own people did not recognize Him (JOHN 1:11). And so salvation has been extended to the Gentiles in order to provoke His covenant people to jealousy. In recent times, many Jewish people have received Him as their Messiah and call Him by His Hebrew name, *Yeshua HaMeshiach.*

I grew up a Gentile believer understanding the Gospel only according to its impact on my life. How arrogant I was to disregard my Jewish brethren with whom the Lord's original covenant was made. Beloved Gentile brothers and sisters, salvation has come to us through the Jews. God has made Jew and Gentile one by the blood of our Jesus. He has broken the dividing wall of hostility and reconciled us both to God in one body through the cross (EPH 2:13-16). Israel has experienced partial blindness until the fullness of the Gentiles has come in (ROM 11:25). We have been grafted as wild branches into a natural olive tree. If God can join us to Himself, how much more can He affix the native branches once again (ROM 11:17, 24)? All Israel will be saved (ROM 11:26).

God is not finished with His promise concerning Israel. He is the God of Abraham, Isaac, and Jacob. He is unrelenting. Indeed, His eyes are fitly set upon His chosen people. He has set watchmen on the walls of Jerusalem who will give the Lord no rest until He establishes this holy city as a praise in the earth.

> I have set watchmen on your walls, O Jerusalem; they shall never hold their peace day or night. You who make mention of the LORD, do not keep silent, and give Him no rest till He establishes and till He makes Jerusalem a praise in the earth.
> –Isaiah 62:6-7

The Blood of the Lamb will once again cover the door posts of this nation. He will save the remnant of Israel by His very own blood. This invitation to pray for Jerusalem's peace is extended to us today.

Pray for the peace of Jerusalem: "May they prosper who love you. Peace be within your walls, prosperity within your palaces." —Psalm 122:6-7

STEADY GAZE

Beloved, we have been grafted into this covenant relationship. Jesus keeps both Jews and Gentiles as the apple of His eye (Ps 17:8). Our Beloved's eyes of undistracted devotion are forever focused upon us. We cannot escape His steady gaze.

Where can I go from Your Spirit? Or where can I flee from Your presence? If I ascend into heaven, You are there; if I make my bed in hell, behold, You are there. If I take the wings of the morning, and dwell in the uttermost parts of the sea, even there Your hand shall lead me, and Your right hand shall hold me … My frame was not hidden from You, when I was made in secret, and skillfully wrought in the lowest parts of the earth. Your eyes saw my substance, being yet unformed. And in Your book they all were written, the days fashioned for me, when as yet there were none of them. —Psalm 139:7-10, 15-16

I cannot begin to comprehend Jesus' infinite knowledge. Who are we that the omniscient One would think of us (Ps 144:3)? Yet He sees every details of our lives. More than we desire to see His beauty, He longs to fascinate us. Can we fathom the extent of His affections for us?

Behold, He peers through the lattice waiting for us to turn our gaze toward His (SONG 2:9). With just one glance of our eyes, His heart is ravished (SONG 4:9). If all it takes is one look to undo the heart of this King, just imagine what happens when we return His gaze with undistracted devotion. When we fix our eyes steadily upon our Beloved, He says, "Turn your eyes away. They overwhelm me" (SONG 6:5).

You have ravished my heart ... with one look of your eyes ...

SONG 4:9

Undistracted devotion? Do we know what that is? A steady gaze? Who has this? I am well acquainted with my weakness. My eyes are prone to distraction. I can understand why David prayed, "Turn my eyes from looking at worthless things" (PS 119:37). I can see why Job made a covenant with his eyes (JOB 31:1). We are easily preoccupied by temporal things even though everything in this world pales in comparison to the glory of our Beloved.

Writing a book about Jesus is revealing how quickly I am sidetracked. It seems as though I were climbing Mt. Everest, which could be an insurmountable challenge even for the most physically fit athletes. Such a feat would require extreme focus and determination. As I set my heart to press into the knowledge of Jesus, I find myself on target for a while until the next distraction diverts my focus. The multitude of conversations and activities vying for my attention are endless. I even set aside this time of consecration by cutting out nonessential activities and determining not to speak. My goal is simply to fix my gaze upon Jesus and "wrap my face in His name" (see "Invitation: Encounter Your Bridegroom"). I thought that removing everything from my peripheral vision would surely give me a steady gaze, but with external distractions removed, all kinds of thoughts and emotions come in like a flood.

What exactly does it take to make Jesus center? Dancers are familiar with terms like *spotting* and *centering*. With the whole world spinning wildly out of focus, a dancer must fix his/her eyes on the same spot at every turn. It is also necessary to keep one's body in perfect alignment while activating core muscles in order to maintain proper balance. This is strangely similar to life in our busy society. No wonder Paul exhorted the Colossians to set their minds on things above. As believers, we are to have Christ as the *spot* we look for at every turn. We must find our *center* in God. This is the only way we will be able to maintain proper balance in this life. Paul likewise told the Philippians to meditate on things that are true, pure, lovely, and praiseworthy (PHIL 4:8).

If then you were raised with Christ, seek those things which are above, where Christ is, sitting at the right hand of God. Set your mind on things above, not on things on the earth. For you died, and your life is hidden with Christ in God.

—Colossians 3:1-3

We are to focus on heavenly, not earthly things. Some like to say, "If you're too heavenly minded, you're no earthly good." I believe exactly the opposite is true. It is far too easy to be earthly minded. We must strain to be heavenly minded. This is the only way we will be of any earthly good. Everything in this world is passing away (1 COR 7:31). Those things which we see are only temporary, but what we do not see is eternal (2 COR 4:18). Let us therefore fix our eyes on Jesus.

Let us fix our eyes on Jesus, the author and perfecter of our faith, who for the joy set before him endured the cross, scorning its shame, and sat down at the right hand of the throne of God.
—Hebrews 12:2 NIV

*I will instruct
you ... I will
guide you
with My eye.*

PSALM 32:8

Our Beloved's gaze is steady. Jesus is not easily distracted. Our Lord was never diverted from His earthly mission. This focused vision is the joy that drove Him to the cross. His eyes were constantly directed heavenward. The Son did only what He saw the Father doing (JOHN 5:19). If we purpose to set our vision toward Him, we will be able to regain our center every time we get off balance. He will continually draw our eyes back to His. He says, "Just seek my face. I will guide you. Beloved, gaze at Me. I will instruct you." If we seek the Lord's face, His very eyes will guide us (Ps 32:8). Just as Jesus did only what He saw His Father doing, so will we begin to do only what we see our Beloved doing.

ENLIGHTENED EYES

We cannot see clearly. Things of this world have tainted our vision. Eventually we will see Jesus face to face and know Him intimately like He knows us. Still, at this time we are looking through dirty lenses.

*For now we see in a mirror, dimly, but then face to face. Now
I know in part, but then I shall know just as I also am known.*
                                        −1 Corinthians 13:12

Unlike ours, the eyes of our Beloved are entirely pure. They have not been defiled. He sees perfectly. When we look into His eyes we see according to heavenly wisdom.

*But the wisdom that is from above is first pure, then
peaceable, gentle, willing to yield, full of mercy and good
fruits, without partiality and without hypocrisy.   −James 3:17*

Jesus' eyes are filled with light and truth. When we gaze at Him, we see with a right perspective. For this reason we must look into the perfect law of liberty (JAS 1:25). In His light we see light (Ps 36:9). His commandments are pure (Ps 19:8). His

> *The commandment of the LORD is pure, enlightening the eyes ...*
>
> PSALM 19:8

truth enlightens the eyes of our understanding (EPH 1:18). As we look into the eyes of our Beloved, we discern His perfect ways. He opens our eyes like He opened the eyes of Balaam by causing a donkey to speak (NUM 22:31-32). He opens our eyes like He opened the eyes of the disciples with whom He spoke on the road to Emmaus (LUKE 24:30-32). If our eyes are fixed on Jesus, we see the glory of God like Stephen did when he was being stoned to death.

> But he, being full of the Holy Spirit, gazed into heaven and saw the glory of God, and Jesus standing at the right hand of God, and said, "Look! I see the heavens opened and the Son of Man standing at the right hand of God!" –Acts 7:55-56

Could it be that gazing upon Jesus might prepare us for persecution or possibly martyrdom? Like John, will we see a door standing open in heaven and visions of God's throne room (REV 4)? Will we see the heavens open like Jesus did at His baptism?

> When He had been baptized, Jesus came up immediately from the water; and behold, the heavens were opened to Him, and He saw the Spirit of God descending like a dove and alighting upon Him. And suddenly a voice came from heaven, saying, "This is My beloved Son, in whom I am well pleased." –Matthew 3:16-17

Jesus said His disciples would see the heavens open and the angels of God ascending and descending (JOHN 1:50-51). He promises to show us

Open my eyes, that I may see wondrous things from Your law.

PSALM 119:18

great things that we do not know (JER 33:3). As we fix our gaze, He opens our eyes to receive greater revelation from His Word (Ps 119:18). John describes the Word of God as one having eyes like flames of fire (REV 19:12-13). How could His eyes appear in the Song as rivers of water and in Revelation as flames of fire? It may seem contradictory to describe the Lord's eyes as both water and fire, but the sea of glass was also mingled with fire (REV 15:2). This is actually a picture of our Beloved's unquenchable love.

> *Its flames are flames of fire, a most vehement flame. Many waters cannot quench love, nor can the floods drown it …*
> *–Song of Solomon 8:6-7*

Jesus is zealous to cleanse His Bride. The Lord counsels the Church in Laodicea to buy refined gold and eye salve (REV 3:18). Though we were born spiritually blind, God has anointed our eyes and instructed us to wash so that our eyes might be opened (JOHN 9:1-7). He washes us with the water of His Word (EPH 5:26). He is like a Refiner's Fire purifying us in the fire of His love (MAL 3:2).

> *Christ also loved the church and gave Himself for her, that He might sanctify and cleanse her with the washing of water by the word, that He might present her to Himself a glorious church, not having spot or wrinkle or any such thing, but that she should be holy and without blemish. –Ephesians 5:25-27*

David asks the million-dollar question, "How can a young man keep his way pure?" There is one answer. He responds to his own question, saying, "By guarding it according to Your Word." When we live according to God's Word and seek the Lord with our whole hearts, we prosper spiritually (Ps 119:1-3). The entrance of His Word imparts light where there is darkness. It gives understanding when we lack wisdom (Ps 119:130). It is a lamp to our feet and a light to our path (Ps 119:105). All of Psalm 119 is an expression of David's delight in the *law* of the Lord. The Word of God literally guards our lives.

May the words from the mouth of our Beloved be our delight and our counselors (Ps 119:24). Let us treasure His Word in our hearts so that we might not sin against Him (Ps 119:11). This is how He cleanses us. It is by His Word. We must live according to the Lord's commandments and seek Him wholeheartedly. We must hide His Word in our hearts that we may not sin against Him (Ps 119:9-11). This intimacy of daily communion is what rids us of all impurities. The Lord washes us with the water of His Word, but this washing only comes through abiding in the Word of God (see Chapter 13, "His Mouth: True Satisfaction").

Our Beloved's eyes are like doves, ever fixed upon us with a steady gaze. With perfect discernment, the Lord guides each of us. Let us look into His glorious eyes by the rivers of water. He will wash us with the pure milk of His Word (1 Pet 2:2). Jesus will sanctify us that we might become His radiant Bride. May this Perfect Man's eyes of faithful devotion forever fascinate us!

His *cheeks* are like

a bed of *spices*,

banks of scented herbs ...

∾

Song 5:13

Chapter 7

His Cheeks—Joy in Affliction

ATTRIBUTE #4

His cheeks: Jesus' diverse *emotions*

PRAYER

Jesus, You are the Lord God, compassionate, slow to anger, and abounding in love (EXOD 34:6). Reveal Your diverse emotions. If jealousy is a Husband's fury, display your zeal (PROV 6:34). Encounter my heart through Your relentless pursuit. Give me understanding of your passion—Your love as strong as death and unyielding as the grave. I believe Your Word—Your desire is for me. Please demonstrate your affections. I long to know every facet of Your nature. I want to feel the rhythm of Your heartbeat. Tell me what Your thoughts are toward me. Amen.

HIS DESIRE

Our Beloved's cheeks are a bed of emotions that continuously emanate a sweet-smelling fragrance. Certain feelings are difficult to conceal. Happiness, sadness, excitement, embarrassment—these are all easily discerned in the display of emotions our cheeks so readily give away. Such visual communication precedes our words. Whether we like it or not, our cheeks reveal hidden emotions. I had a conversation with my cousin about his political campaign. In our improvised dialogue, he illustrated his strategy of knocking on doors, starting with a brief

I am my beloved's, and his desire is toward me.

Song 7:10

introduction and followed by a reminder about the mailer I should have received. Of course, I proceeded to tell him that I throw away all *junk* mail. Immediately his cheeks became bright red. This demonstration was obviously not going as planned.

What do our Beloved's cheeks reveal? Our heavenly Father is filled with excitement to see His children. Our eternal Bridegroom is forever delighted to see His Bride. His never-ending desire is for us (SONG 7:10). He wants to be with us all the time (JOHN 17:24). Beloved, do we realize that even now Jesus is rejoicing over us with singing?

The LORD your God in your midst, the Mighty One, will save; He will rejoice over you with gladness, He will quiet you with His love, He will rejoice over you with singing.

–Zephaniah 3:17

The Hebrew definition of *rejoice* conveys a message of spinning with wild emotion. Could this be the *joy* for which our Beloved endured the Cross and scorned its shame?

DESPISED AND REJECTED

Oh, that we may behold the unfailing love and endless desire which our Beloved expressed for us amidst His affliction. What horrors our Messiah must have suffered with the intense scourging, beating, and whipping He endured at His crucifixion.

I gave My back to those who struck Me, and My cheeks to those who plucked out the beard; I did not hide My face from shame and spitting.

–Isaiah 50:6

We hurled insults at Jesus. We despised and rejected our Beloved. But for the sake of love, God's only Son did not turn away His cheek.

I attended a public school system in Southern California from third to tenth grade. Like most schools, mine were driven by popularity. Rejection was a common wound inflicted during my formative years. Upon moving from Oklahoma to our new west coast home, I was first ridiculed for my hick accent. Having attended private school prior to this, my naivety about perverse jokes was the next object of scorn. The teasing soon progressed to my twig-like form, the way I walked, my name—someone was always sure to point out anything that could be used to make fun of me. At times I would reciprocate in defense. One day the name-calling resulted in an all-out-cat-fight and a Saturday detention. I managed to find one so-called *best friend* in elementary. We spent hours playing mostly at her house, but she made it clear that she was boss. Whenever we swam, she would constantly dunk me. To prove her superiority, she frequently slapped me on the cheek. This was before I knew about turning the other cheek, but I did just that (MATT 5:39). I recall numerous times when I went home in tears swearing never to talk to her again. Even so, I would always return to her house the next day, desperate for acceptance.

Whoever slaps you on your right cheek, turn the other to him also.

MATTHEW 5:39

In junior high, we found our niche. Unfortunately, the influence of our circle was not the most constructive. Another girl transferred in from a different school and somewhat stole my grade-school friend. Not long after, the two began smoking and dating eighteen-year-old guys. Then, at a slumber party, one of our friends served us some of her brother's alcohol. I was naturally considered *a prude* for not partaking in their revelry, though one of the girls bravely confided her respect for my decision. Eventually, my best friend and her new cohort gave me an ultimatum. I had begun hanging out with some Christians who were also honors students. This was seen as a threat to the reputation of our clique. The two ringleaders approached to deliver their message, "It's either us or them. You decide." Apparently I could not associate with both groups. This was certainly a turning point. Although I did not need to think twice about discontinuing my friendship with this spiteful crew, it was the toughest decision I faced in my young life.

All through high school I maintained my stance, openly expressing my faith and refusing to join the party scene. People would feel convicted and apologize for cussing in my presence. Still, many would mock me for my purity and passion for Jesus. I felt the sting of rejection over and over. We all experience it in one way or another. Had I succumbed to peer pressure, I might have perceived different responses as acceptance. I realize now that any false approval would have been nothing more than rejection disguised.

Now my childhood and teenage wounds seem so trivial. I have not suffered the torment inflicted upon Jews in Nazi prison camps. I have not borne the anguish of the African slave trade. I have not endured the persecution of those in the underground Church in China. There is only One who has known such grief.

> *He is despised and rejected by men, a Man of sorrows and acquainted with grief … He has borne our griefs and carried our sorrows; yet we esteemed Him stricken, smitten by God, and afflicted. But He was wounded for our transgressions, He was bruised for our iniquities; the chastisement for our peace was upon Him … And the LORD*

has laid on Him the iniquity of us all. He was oppressed and
He was afflicted, yet He opened not His mouth …
                                                    —Isaiah 53:3-7

Isaiah 53 is rich with language describing Jesus' suffering. He was pierced, bruised, spat upon. The punishment that brought us peace was upon Him. Our Beloved endured sorrow exceeding everything we have known. Jesus' own Father forsook Him. It was God's will to crush His Son and cause Him to suffer (Is 53:10). Who has known such rejection? The Israelites cried out in their affliction, "Look and see if there is any sorrow like my sorrow" (LAM 1:12 NRSV). Not even these knew sorrow like that of our Lord.

Having already done so Jesus now invites us to *turn the other cheek* (MATT 5:39). Why? He knows that a sweet-smelling aroma will pour forth from these beds of spices. Spices must first be crushed in order to produce a fragrance. In His crushing, Jesus' appearance was disfigured beyond recognition (Is 52:14). In our crushing, why are we surprised when our lives do not seem to display the beauty of a rose garden?

Jesus' garments are scented with myrrh, a burial spice (PS 45:8). His sacrifice is a pleasing aroma. There is a glorious fragrance that arises from our Beloved's cheeks. This garden of spices and sweet-smelling herbs is a window to the Lord's diverse emotions for His Bride. He is gracious, slow to anger, and abounding in loving-kindness. He forgives sins to a thousand generations. Though men turn against Him and strike the very giver of life, His love abounds.

How can God, who we despised, have compassion on the ones who smote His cheeks? We spit in His face! How could He have mercy? It is His nature. He delights in mercy. Our Lord does not wish for

*Looking
unto Jesus
... who for
the joy that
was set
before Him
endured
the cross ...*

HEBREWS 12:2

any to perish. He wants all to repent (2 PET 3:9). His desire is toward each of us (SONG 7:10). God loves the world so much that He sacrificed His only Son for our sins (JOHN 3:16). The only begotten of the Father is full of grace. Out of intense passion for creatures fashioned in His image, the Word became flesh and dwelt with us (GEN 1:27; JOHN 1:14). What was on His mind when Jesus left His glory? It was for the joy of bringing us into His glory that God's Son gave up His life for us (HEB 12:2). What great kindness and mercy our Beloved extends to us!

Eternal holy communion of Father and Son brought forth heaven and earth. Mankind shared this intimate communion in the Garden of Eden before sin entered the world. Adam and Eve disobeyed their Creator. When they heard Him walking through the garden, they hid themselves (GEN 3:8). Just as sin entered the world through one man, so atonement for sin comes through one Man (ROM 5:12-21). We are eternally separated from our Maker and require a perfect Mediator to bring us into fellowship with the Godhead. Only one who is fully God and fully Man can offer Himself as a perfect sacrifice (HEB 8:26-27). Our great High Priest has done so once for all! Oh, how God loves us, that He would give us His only Son, that Jesus would lay aside His glory and humble Himself unto death. Oh, how He loves us, that Jesus would endure rejection, humiliation, suffering, crushing, and even become a curse on our behalf. Will we ever know the extent of the price this Perfect Man paid to redeem us?

For the sake of love, the very Word of God became a Man. The Creator dwelt with His creation (JOHN 1:14). But when He came to His own, we did not receive Him (JOHN 1:11). Once again we turned God away. The first time the Father responded by sending His Son. Now that we rejected His Son, would He not also turn us away? He did not. Jesus Christ made intercession for His Beloved. On the cross He made His appeal, "Father, forgive them, for they do not know what they do" (LUKE 23:34). It would have been sufficient for Jesus to ask His Father for nothing more than to pardon our transgressions. Instead Jesus asked for the unthinkable. He prayed that we might be one as He and the Father are One. As His Father loved Him before the creation of the world, so Jesus loves us (JOHN 17:21-23). The Son of God requested that the very ones who had rejected both Father and Son would be eternally united in the Godhead.

> *"Father, I desire that they also whom You gave Me may be with Me where I am, that they may behold My glory which You have given Me; for You loved Me before the foundation of the world."* —John 17:24

The Father granted Jesus' petition and accepted the blood of His Son as full payment of our death penalty. Now to those who receive Jesus and believe in His name He gives the right to become children of God (JOHN 1:12). How great is His love!

> *Behold what manner of love the Father has bestowed on us, that we should be called children of God!* —1 John 3:1

Who can comprehend the emotions of the Living God? Do we really believe that God is always thinking about us? His thoughts toward us outnumber the sand (PS 139:18). What are His thoughts? We ravish the very heart of God (SONG 4:9). The Scriptures are bursting with expressions of the Lord's affections for His people. As we abide in the Word of God, let us ask Him to reveal His thoughts toward us. He speaks through the wind, the birds, the rain, and the sound of all creation. Our Beloved's voice surrounds us. The heavens declare His glory. The skies proclaim His wonder. All of creation testifies of who He is. Jesus loves to reveal His delight in us.

The heavens declare the glory of God; and the firmament shows His handiwork. Day unto day utters speech, and night unto night reveals knowledge. There is no speech nor language where their voice is not heard. Their line has gone out through all the earth, and their words to the end of the world. —Psalm 19:1-4

Consider the works of God's hands. They are evident to every people group across the globe. Their song is heard through the whole earth. Everything that has breath praises the Lord (Ps 150:6). God's creation forever declares His glory. He is full of love and compassion. His mercies are new every morning (LAM 3:23). In the day His love directs us. At night His song is with us (Ps 42:8). Can we hear Him singing over us (ZEPH 3:17)? He turns our mourning into dancing (Ps 30:11). In His presence is fullness of joy and pleasures forever (Ps 16:11). Let us quiet ourselves to listen. What is He speaking?

His *lips* are *lilies,*

dripping liquid myrrh.

❧

Song 5:13

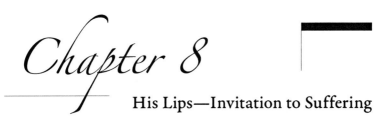

Chapter 8

His Lips—Invitation to Suffering

ATTRIBUTE #5
His lips: Jesus' *Word*

PRAYER

Jesus, I've never heard such gracious words as those that come from your lips (Ps 45:2). You do not condemn me. Instead You say, "Go and sin no more" (Rom 8:1; John 8:11). You speak with love, yet out of your mouth comes a sharp two-edged sword (Rev 1:16). It's your scepter of righteousness (Ps 45:6). Your Words of life convict my soul leading me to repentance. Thank You for alluring me into the wilderness and speaking tenderly to me (Hos 2:14). Your Words are Spirit and Life (John 6:63). Your testimony revives my soul, makes me wise, rejoices my heart, and enlightens my eyes (Ps 19:7-8). By Your Words I am warned (Ps 19:11). Living Word, I will not depart from the commands of Your lips (Job 23:12). Your loving-kindness and tender mercies preserve me (Ps 40:11). I hear You calling me to arise, "My dove, open to Me" (Song 2:10; 5:2). You woo me to take up my cross and follow You (Matt 16:24). Your kind Words motivate me to set my heart on a pilgrimage (Ps 84:5). I will pursue You to the mountain of myrrh and the hill of frankincense (Song 4:6). Thank You for beckoning me. Thank You for inviting me to partner with You on this journey! Amen.

THE WORD'S INVITATION

In the beginning, the Word spoke and creation was formed. Through His lips, our Beloved utters speech. All of heaven and earth move at the sound of His voice. And yet, Jesus' lips offer each of us His personal invitation to rise up and follow Him.

> *The voice of my beloved! Behold, he comes leaping upon the mountains, skipping upon the hills ... My beloved spoke, and said to me: "Rise up, my love, my fair one, and come away."*
> *–Song of Solomon 2:8, 10*

Where exactly is our Beloved inviting us to *come*? Imagine walking through a garden and discovering a beautiful lily. You hold it close to breathe in its fragrant aroma. As it brushes your lips, you instinctively kiss its delicate petals. In doing so, the taste of a familiar spice enters your mouth. Suddenly, a strange sensation fills your entire being. Just then you feel a drop glide onto your hand. Puzzled, you raise the peculiar oil to your nose. The sweet perfume of liquid myrrh now blends with an unpleasant odor. It is the scent of suffering.

Beloved, if we follow the Lord, we must go where He goes—to the mountain of spices. These are burial spices. He calls us to share in the fellowship of the Cross (PHIL 3:10). At first it may seem enjoyable to partake of sweet communion with our Bridegroom, but the scroll He offers will turn bitter in our stomachs (REV 10:9-10). Until the day breaks and the shadows flee—until He returns to establish His Kingdom on earth as it is in heaven—we must set our hearts to follow our individual pathways to share in His suffering (SONG 4:6).

Can we hear the voice of our Beloved? Our King's lips issue the call, "Listen! Consider and incline your ear. Forget everything you know that is comfortable. Arise, my love. Come away with me. I desire you." (Ps 45:10-11; Song 2:10). Today if we hear His voice, let us not harden our hearts (Ps 95:7-8). Let us follow our Beloved to the mountains!

Consider what a great invitation He has extended, that we might be with Him (John 17:24). This earth is not our home. Our citizenship is in heaven. As He left His Father's house, so we too must leave our father's house. He tells us not to love the world. We are to be in it but not of it. He invites us to arise and come away. We must forget all that is familiar and pursue Jesus into the unknown. Our Beloved is saying, "Forget what is comfortable. Follow Me. You are a stranger on the earth. Set your heart on a pilgrimage. Leave it all behind. Forget the past. Press on to what lies ahead—eternity. Forget your fears. Fix your eyes on the prize of your eternal inheritance. I am your joy and your great reward. Arise, my love. Follow me!" Can we hear His voice calling us higher?

Listen, O daughter, Consider and incline your ear ...
Psalm 45:10

The winter is past. The spring has come. It is time to leap upon the mountains with our Beloved. He is drawing us with loving-kindness (Jer 31:3). Let us press on toward the goal of knowing Christ Jesus. Let us set our gaze on the Author and Finisher of our faith. Let us enter into eternal fellowship with the triune Godhead: Father, Son, and Holy Spirit. Listen! Our King calls out, "Let Me see your face. Let Me hear your voice. Your voice is sweet and your face is lovely. My desire is for you. My jealousy is as fierce as the grave." Can we hear Him? He is calling out, "Rise up and come away. Do you want to be with Me where I am? Do not love the world. I was in the world and the world did not know me (John 1:10). Do you not know that friendship with the world is hatred toward Me (Jas 4:4)? Forget your earthly habitation. Think on things above and not on earthly things (COL 3:2). Do you want to share in My glory? What is it worth to you? Will you leave your own people and everything that is familiar? Will you count all things loss for the sake of knowing Me? Will you partner in the fellowship of My suffering? This is the cost of intimacy. Is it worth it? Arise, My beloved, and come away with Me!"

THE CUP OF SUFFERING

Consider the cost Christ first paid for intimacy with us. The Father so loves the world that He gave His very Son for the sake of love. Jesus is not asking us to do something He has not already done Himself. He left His Father's house. He gave up everything. Jesus laid down His life for us. Greater love has no one than this!

Before His crucifixion, Jesus went with His disciples to the Mount of Olives. There in the Garden of Gethsemane He invited His disciples to watch and pray. His soul being sorrowful unto death, Jesus withdrew and prayed, "Father, if it is Your will, take this cup away from Me; nevertheless not My will, but Yours, be done" (LUKE 22:42-46). Before He drank the cup of suffering, our Beloved was in anguish. He prayed earnestly and His sweat turned to drops of blood. When He returned to His disciples, He found them sleeping and again offered His invitation: "Rise and pray." This same spirit of slumber prevents many of us from entering into full partnership with Jesus.

Why do you sleep? Rise and pray, lest you enter into temptation.

LUKE 22:46

When our Beloved appears as the Man from Gethsemane, He finds us just as He found His disciples—sleeping. We hear His voice beckoning, "Open for me, my sister, my love, my dove, my perfect one; for my head is covered with dew, my locks with the drops of the night" (SONG 5:2-5). Our hearts yearn to be with Him, but when we rise to open, what do we find? On the handle of the lock, His hands leave the evidence of His affliction. Now our hands drip with this myrrh. We cannot touch what our Beloved has touched without becoming as He is. Indeed, we will drink from the very same cup.

> But Jesus said to them, "You do not know what you ask. Are you able to drink the cup that I drink, and be baptized with the baptism that I am baptized with?" They said to Him, "We are able." So Jesus said to them, "You will indeed drink the cup that I drink, and with the baptism I am baptized with you will be baptized."　　　　　　　　　　　　　　　　　—Mark 10:38-39

What is this cup Jesus mentioned to His disciples? It is the cup of His suffering. Jesus was led like a lamb to the slaughter and did not open His mouth (Is 53:7). Not a single utterance proceeded from His lips to defend the onslaught of accusation. With only one word Jesus could have silenced His persecutors, but the Word did not speak. Why? His silence spoke a thousand words. Jesus Christ bore the sin of many and made intercession for transgressors. He drank the cup of suffering.

PARTING WORDS

In the stillness of that night upon Calvary's cross, our Savior delivered seven final phrases referred to as the *Seven Last Words of Christ*.

1. "Father, forgive them, for they do not know what they do." –Luke 23:34

2. "Assuredly, I say to you, today you will be with Me in Paradise." –Luke 23:43

3. "Woman, behold your son! ... Behold your mother!" –John 19:26-27

4. "My God, My God, why have You forsaken Me?" –Mark 15:34

5. "I thirst!" –John 19:28

6. "It is finished!" –John 19:30

7. "Father, 'into Your hands I commit My spirit.'" –Luke 23:46

In those last moments of His thirty-three years on the earth, the One fully God interceded for our forgiveness. He gave us assurance of joining Him in eternity. Even so, this One who is also fully Man cried out in anguish. Jesus Christ, both God and Man, completed the work of His Father. After these final words, God's Son breathed His last. But His death is by no means the end of the story. On the third day our Beloved was raised to life!

COUNTING THE COST

We too are given life from the dead. Salvation crucifies our sinful nature and raises us to life in Christ. This is just the beginning of our journey. Jesus' lips are the doorway through which He offers us the invitation, "Arise." What is the cost? Those who follow the Lamb will suffer many things (PHIL 1:29). We must eat His body, drink His blood, and daily bear our cross (LUKE 9:23).

And he died for all, so that those who live might live no longer for themselves, but for him who died and was raised for them.
–2 Corinthians 5:15 NRSV

Beloved, Christ died for us that we may live for Him. What can separate us from His love? Can tribulation, persecution, famine, or any kind of danger stand in the way? No, in all these things we are victorious (ROM 8:35-37). Though enemies arise all around, we have this confidence: Jesus is our light and salvation. He will never leave us. What can man do to us? The Lord is our helper (PS 27:1-3; HEB 13:5-6). The righteous are never forsaken (PS 37:25 NIV). God commands His angels to watch over us (PS 91:11). In the midst of great waters, our Beloved is with us. Even in the fire, we are not burned (IS 43:2). Absolutely nothing can separate us from God's love. Why should anything avert us from following Him to the mountains?

The LORD is my helper; I will not fear. What can man do to me?

HEBREWS 13:6

I once heard a Middle Eastern pastor explain how the Lord has revealed Himself through dreams to multitudes of Muslims. It is extremely dangerous in his nation for Muslims to accept Christ. He said that one convert was questioned, "Do you know you could die?" The new believer replied, "Have you seen Him? You don't know what you're missing. I am ready to die for the sake of Christ!"

Have we counted the cost? Is it worth it? When our Beloved beckons us to leap upon the mountains, what is our response? Are we willing to drink from the cup that touched His lips? Do we hesitate? Do we find ourselves telling Him to go without us while we remain in our place of comfort? Does fear keep us from moving forward? Does realization of our weakness prevent us from joining Him? Are we willing to follow the Lamb wherever He goes? Are we willing to go even if it means we must pass through the valleys of death and weeping (PS 23:4; 84:6)? This is the divine invitation our Beloved extends. Are we willing to pay the price of following Him? Are we willing to enter into the fellowship of His suffering? Are we really ready to die for the sake of Jesus Christ?

But what things were gain to me, these I have counted loss for Christ. Yet indeed I also count all things loss for the excellence of the knowledge of Christ Jesus my Lord, for whom I have suffered the loss of all things, and count them as rubbish, that I may gain Christ and be found in Him, not having my own righteousness, which is from the law, but that which is through faith in Christ, the righteousness which is from God by faith; that I may know Him and the power of His resurrection, and the fellowship of His sufferings, being conformed to His death, if, by any means, I may attain to the resurrection from the dead. —Philippians 3:7-11

Beloved, He is worth it! Why would we offer a sacrifice that costs us nothing (2 SAM 24:24)? We have come too far to turn around. It is time to burn the bridges of our past. Let us arise from our beds of comfort. Let us incline our hearts to His invitation, leaving everything behind. Consider the glory that awaits. Let us worship our King, for He is our Lord. May we count all things loss for the sake of our Beloved!

GRACE UPON HIS LIPS

Jesus is the very One spoken of by the prophet Isaiah (IS 61:1-3). Our Beloved was anointed to preach good tidings to the poor and proclaim freedom to those in captivity. When this Scripture was fulfilled, those who bore witness marveled at His gracious words. The Lord had just returned to Galilee in the power of the Holy Spirit after being tempted by Satan in the wilderness. He was already gaining quite a reputation in the surrounding region. Everyone glorified Him as He taught in the synagogues. Jesus then came to His hometown, Nazareth. According to His usual practice, He went into the synagogue on the Sabbath day to read. He was handed the book of the prophet Isaiah. After reading the passage, our Beloved concluded that He was the fulfillment of its prophecy. He spoke not from a haughty spirit but humbly proclaimed He was anointed to heal our hearts and free us from oppression. Jesus always speaks with such grace upon His lips.

> And when He had opened the book, He found the place where it was written: "The Spirit of the LORD is upon Me, because He has anointed Me to preach the gospel to the poor; He has sent Me to heal the brokenhearted, to proclaim liberty to the captives and recovery of sight to the blind, to set at liberty those who are oppressed; to proclaim the acceptable year of the LORD." Then He closed the book, and gave it back to the attendant and sat down. And the eyes of all who were in the synagogue were fixed on Him. And He began to say to them, "Today this Scripture is fulfilled in your hearing." So all bore witness to Him, and marveled at the gracious words which proceeded out of His mouth …
>
> –Luke 4:17-22

Both the Song of Solomon and Hosea give evidence of our Beloved's gracious words. These books portray the Lord's affections as He speaks tenderly to His Bride (see "The Song: A Divine Love Story"). With grace our Beloved motivates us to follow Him even through hardship.

Let us briefly consider the divine chastisements experienced in the *dark night* of our souls as highlighted in Hosea. God commands Hosea to take an adulterous wife because Israel is guilty of adultery in departing from the Lord (Hos 1:2). The more He calls them, the further they abandon Him. He lovingly teaches His people to walk, heals them, leads them, removes their heavy burden, and feeds them, yet they refuse to repent (Hos 11:3-5).

God's chosen people continually pursued false lovers forgetting their true husband. With intimate longing, this Jealous Bridegroom acts as Judge to draw His unfaithful Bride back into covenant relationship. He declares, "I will wall her in and block her path so that she cannot find her way" (Hos 2:6). All of her celebrations come to a halt. When the Lord exposes her lewdness publicly, she realizes her true state of depravity (Hos 2:10-11). The King of Israel judges His people fiercely because of their blatant rebellion (Hos 5:1, 14-15). God's purpose in releasing His judgment is unto transformation. After alluring His Bride into the wilderness, He speaks tenderly. With compassion aroused, the Judge's lovesick heart is revealed as He declares, "I will not carry out my fierce anger" (Hos 11:9). God knows this demonstration of His love will ultimately cause His wayward Bride to return (Hos 3:1-5). After a season of cleansing, He then betroths her to Himself forever (Hos 2:17-20).

> *I am now going*
> *to allure her;*
> *I will lead her*
> *into the desert*
> *and speak*
> *tenderly to her.*
>
> Hosea 2:14 NIV

The Bride's actions in both the Song and Hosea lead to separation from her Beloved. While Hosea's wife turns away from her husband to pursue other loves, the Song of Solomon Bride turns the Lord away because of fear. Regardless of our situation, the Lord is faithful to bring each of us into union with Himself. The wounds He initiates produce deeper longing for His presence. In the Song, our Beloved invites us to share in the fellowship of His suffering by calling us to join Him after

He has endured the Cross (SONG 5:2). We may not immediately respond to His call because it seems inconvenient, but following our initial refusal, we rise to discover myrrh dripping on the handles of the lock (SONG 5:4-5). Wounded with lovesickness for our Beloved, we commence our search. While pursuing our Bridegroom, we are persecuted. This

If you find my beloved ... tell him I am lovesick!
SONG 5:8

does not deter us. We plead for others to tell our Beloved, "I am faint with love" (SONG 5:8). Through the lens of Hosea, we also see His display of love eliciting lovesick responses. God's judgment leads us to repentance and earnest pursuit (HOS 5:15). Through affliction, we discover the One who wounds is the One who heals (HOS 6:1). We begin to sing as in our youth and declare to our Beloved, "You are my God" (HOS 2:15, 23). In the end, we enjoy the fruitfulness of living in wholehearted love for the Lord (HOS 14:8).

The Father requires a spotless Bride for His Son, Jesus. He refuses to tolerate any form of idolatry. Through judgment, the Lord awakens desire in our hearts. When we are in despair, the loving discipline of His rod and staff actually brings us comfort (PS 23:4). He hedges us in on every side and then faithfully allures us into the wilderness where He speaks tenderly (HOS 2:14). Though we see only our darkness, He declares our loveliness (SONG 1:5). It is His goodness that causes us to repent (ROM 2:4). When we no longer find pleasure in what we once sought comfort, we seek satisfaction from our eternal Husband. With romance rekindled in our hearts, we willingly give up false comforts. In our weakness, our Beloved so kindly draws us (HOS 11:4). His gentle words provoke us to return to our First Love (HOS 2:7). Oh, how He loves us! His lips are truly anointed with grace (PS 45:2).

His *hands*
are rods of *gold*
set with beryl ...

∾

Song 5:14

Chapter 9

His Hands—Divine Activity

ATTRIBUTE #6
His hands: Jesus' divine *activity*

PRAYER

Jesus, my heart overflows with a good theme (Ps 45:1). I will remember your miracles. I will recount the ways You have acted on my behalf. I was in distress and called out. You rescued me because You delight in me. Thank You for delivering me from my powerful enemy (Ps 18:16-19). Thank you for revealing my sin. Thank you for exposing my hidden motives and showing me the little foxes that spoil my vineyard (Ps 19:12-13; Song 2:15). Your kindness leads me to repentance (Rom 2:4). I praise Your divine activity in my life. I love the way Your hand guides me and directs my path. It is all for Your glory and honor. Good Shepherd, lead me on! Amen.

DIVINE INTERVENTION

The hands of our Beloved are rods of gold set with jewels. He is armed with glorious strength. The divine activity of God is entirely perfect.

For since the beginning of the world men have not heard nor perceived by the ear, nor has the eye seen any God besides You, who acts for the one who waits for Him. —Isaiah 64:4

God acts on behalf of those who wait for Him. Have you ever felt the hand of God on your life? His miracles did not cease with the parting of the Red Sea. Beloved, He works on our behalf. We can see His divine activity all around. At certain times His intervention is more obvious. Let us remember His miracles (Ps 77:11). I can vividly recall several times I saw God's hand deliver me. Once, before making a weekly drive to another town for a missions class, I recall praying, "Jesus, I plead Your blood over this truck," for no apparent reason. About thirty minutes into my hour-long voyage along a stretch with limited civilization, I noticed a cloud of smoke in my rearview mirror. At first I thought I had just run over a patch of powder in the road. When the haze failed to dissipate, I realized something might be wrong. Just then a car passed me out of nowhere and pulled over at exactly the same time I drove onto the shoulder. The moment I stepped out of my Chevy *Blazer*, two men from the car in front of me yelled, "You're on fire!" I thought to myself, "I know!" For a brief second I did not even notice the fire under my truck. I was agreeing with what God had been doing in my heart to stoke the flames of passion for my Beloved. After I safely exited my vehicle, another man stopped his car behind us and came with an extinguisher to put out the fire. After the police, tow-truck, and members of my family came, I was able to resume my course in my mom's vehicle.

I will remember the deeds of the LORD; yes, I will remember your miracles of long ago.

Psalm 77:11 niv

My spirit was stirred. I could not contain my exhilaration. I began praising God aloud, yelling at the top of my lungs, proclaiming my amazement, and declaring His goodness. The fire in my soul continued to blaze violently for the next few days. My heart overflowed with a good theme (Ps 45:1). I was telling everyone, "Guess what happened!"

It was as if I had just won a million dollars. Excitedly, they would inquire, "What?" Imagine their perplexity when I proclaimed, "My truck caught on fire!" This got some puzzled expressions even after I explained the awesome miracle God had performed. The night of the incident, I arrived an hour and a half late to my three-hour class. After hearing my enthusiastic explanation for being tardy, my professor replied, "Chérie, there's never a dull moment with you." That is only because God is not dull. Reflecting on this event, I am compelled to bless the Lord. I believe He sent three *angels* to guard me (Ps 91:11). The flames could have caused an explosion had they reached my fuel tank, but my Beloved saved me. Before I even knew there was danger, He prompted me to pray for protection. I will remember this miracle!

Another time I was merging onto a five-lane freeway in California when a speeding car struck my vehicle. The impact turned my truck perpendicular to the road. With my door facing the eighty-miles-per-hour oncoming traffic, I braced myself and instinctively cried out, "God, help!" Without delay, He answered. A second collision thrust me into the carpool lane, where I came to an abrupt stop. I looked back through the passenger window to see a solid stream of parked cars. It seemed like an invisible barricade had been stretched across the interstate. Amazingly, I was able to drive to the shoulder without a scratch on my body. Then there was the time I hitched a ride on a bus in Greece. I am pretty sure its few passengers were members of the Italian or Greek mafia. I found myself in a rather precarious situation having no money or any idea

For he will command his angels concerning you to guard you ...

PSALM 91:11 NIV

of where I was going. One man offered me a place to stay with the group. I prayed fervently. My parents were relieved when I finally called home after two days without communication. I remember other times when I was caught in a downward spiral of negative emotions, overcome by depression, and tempted with suicidal thoughts. During one of these experiences the Lord reminded me that darkness could not consume me because the light of God's Spirit dwells inside of me. Where could I escape when even darkness is light to Him (Ps 139:7-12)? Needless to say, my Beloved intervened in these and many other perilous conditions.

Where can
I flee from
Your presence?

Psalm 139:7

We all have stories. I sat in a small group listening to others recount the works of the Lord. Their reports of near-death experiences were astounding. A friend of our family fell asleep at the wheel and totaled the truck he was driving. There is no way he should have survived. All the events surrounding his rescue and miraculous healing seem unbelievable. My best friend was nearly crushed to death between a moving truck and the garage door of a storage unit. Remarkably, she had no broken bones or internal wounds and was released from the hospital the same day. She eventually returned to view the site. The impression left in the door was that of a Man much larger than her frame. Jesus protected her body from being entirely compressed. Let us recall our Beloved's divine intervention. Truly we have a God who acts on our behalf. It is His pleasure to deliver us.

THE GREATEST MIRACLE

The gospels account for many miracles performed by the Lord during His earthly ministry. Jesus turned water to wine, multiplied food, walked on water, changed weather, healed diseases, cleansed lepers, restored sight to the blind, caused lame people to walk, forgave sins, delivered those possessed with demons, and raised the dead.

Not every wondrous work seemed timely. When Mary and Martha sent word that their brother was ill, the Son of God delayed for two days. Meanwhile Lazarus died and was buried. Why did Jesus not return to the town of Bethany immediately? His answer was given the moment He heard the news: "This sickness is not unto death, but for the glory of God, that the Son of God may be glorified through it" (JOHN 11:4). Both sisters believed Jesus could heal sickness, but death seemed so final. Martha said, "Lord, if You had been here, my brother would not have died" (JOHN 11:21). After Lazarus had been in the grave four days, Jesus ordered the stone to be removed. At first Martha objected. Jesus replied, "Did I not say to you that if you would believe you would see the glory of God?" (JOHN 11:40). Lazarus was resurrected to demonstrate Jesus' power.

> *Then Jesus said, "Did I not tell you that if you believed, you would see the glory of God?"*
> JOHN 11:40 NIV

Sometimes it is difficult to make sense of our circumstances. A friend shared with me the account of her husband's diving accident. He was paralyzed from the neck down and told he would never walk again. He is a godly man full of passion for Jesus. It would have been natural for the couple to ask, "Why us?" Instead they thanked the Lord for this opportunity to contend for healing. As I watched the extraordinary video of *Jamie's Recovery* on YouTube,[5] the sound of this powerful chorus resounded through the House of Prayer: "Whatever You do is just. Whatever you do is right. We trust You, Jesus!" I am encouraged by this amazing testimony of trusting the Lord amidst life's storms.

The time-lapsed video showed a grown man struggling to roll over on the ground, crawl, sit, stand, walk and eventually run as if each activity was accomplished for the very first time. This reminds me of the greatest miracle ever. When God came to the earth as a Baby, He was in essence paralyzed, having His divine power temporarily suspended. Can you imagine what this must have been like for Jesus? For a brief moment, the eternal God was limited to the realm of time. The Creator of heaven and earth was completely dependent on two human parents to nurture and care for Him. The omnipresent God was confined to a mortal body. The omnipotent God was taught to walk and talk. The omniscient God learned obedience. When this Child finally became a Man, His power was demonstrated through signs and wonders. At the height of His *recovery,* the crowds were ready to crown Him King.

He was received up into heaven, and sat down at the right hand of God.

MARK 16:19

Then He suffered a fatal blow. At the Cross, all hope seemed to vanish. His resurrection proved otherwise. Ultimately, Jesus ascended to heaven and sat at the right hand of God (MARK 16:19). Our Beloved was restored to the glory He shared with the Father before the world existed.

This miracle of Christ's humility and exaltation would have been sufficient to rival that of creation itself, but there is more. What our Savior accomplished is truly astonishing. The Perfect Man became a curse to redeem humanity. The great High Priest made a way for us to enter the holy of holies so those who believe might be one as He and the Father are One. This is truly the greatest miracle ever! No wonder the living creatures cry, "Holy," and the elders cast their crowns saying, "Worthy," as they praise the Father. Rightly do the myriads of angels join the celebration as all heaven worships the slain Lamb. Beloved, how could we ever cease to declare the marvelous works of the Lord? He is worthy to receive all honor and glory!

KINDNESS AND SEVERITY

Jesus' arms of gold were stretched out on the cross to redeem humanity. Is there any greater kindness than this? Regardless of the extent of Christ's suffering on our behalf, many people still question how a God of love could allow *bad* things to happen to *good* people. How often we forget that hell is what we truly deserve. It is not God who brought calamity upon mankind. Our sin separated us from Him and incurred His wrath. There is none righteous (ROM 3:10). We have all sinned. Jesus is perfect. He alone provides a way for us to be reconciled to God and no longer receive our due penalty of death. His mercy triumphs over judgment. Beloved, can we begin to comprehend the kindness and severity of the arm of the Lord? His love requires justice.

Behold, the LORD's hand is not shortened, that it cannot save … But your iniquities have separated you from your God … Your hands are defiled with blood … No one calls for justice … Therefore justice is far from us … For our transgressions are multiplied before You, and our sins testify against us … So truth fails, and he who departs from evil makes himself a prey. Then the LORD saw it, and it displeased Him that there was no justice. He saw that there was no man, and wondered that there was no intercessor; therefore His own arm brought salvation for Him; and His own righteousness, it sustained Him. For He put on righteousness as a breastplate, and a helmet of salvation on His head; He put on the garments of vengeance for clothing, and was clad with zeal as a cloak. According to their deeds, accordingly He will repay, fury to His adversaries, recompense to His enemies … So shall they fear the name of the LORD from the west, and His glory from the

rising of the sun; when the enemy comes in like a flood, the
Spirit of the LORD will lift up a standard against him …
"The Redeemer will come to Zion, and to those who turn
from transgression in Jacob," says the LORD.

—Isaiah 59:1-4, 9, 12, 15-20

The God of love wears garments of vengeance. He repays fury to His adversaries and recompense to His enemies. Who are His enemies? Anyone who befriends the world is an enemy of God (JAS 4:4). If we try to live according to God's Word while giving allegiance to the world's customs, we divide our hearts between two masters (LUKE 16:13). On the cross, Jesus' arms worked salvation for those who turn from their wicked ways and confess Jesus Christ as Lord. On the day of vengeance, His arms will work salvation by slaying every enemy of the Cross.

We are familiar with Jesus as the slain Lamb, but do we know the Jesus in red? I used to read Isaiah 63 as depicting Christ's victory on the cross until I discovered my Beloved as the Judge of the earth. His garments will be stained red with the blood of His enemies when He treads the winepress and tramples them in His fury.

Who is this who comes from Edom, with dyed garments from
Bozrah, this One who is glorious in His apparel, traveling in
the greatness of His strength?—"I who speak in righteousness,
mighty to save." Why is Your apparel red, and Your garments
like one who treads in the winepress? "I have trodden the
winepress alone, and from the peoples no one was with Me.
For I have trodden them in My anger, and trampled them
in My fury; their blood is sprinkled upon My garments, and
I have stained all My robes. For the day of vengeance is in My

heart, and the year of My redeemed has come. I looked, but there was no one to help, and I wondered that there was no one to uphold; therefore My own arm brought salvation for Me; and My own fury, it sustained Me. I have trodden down the peoples in My anger, made them drunk in My fury, and brought down their strength to the earth." —Isaiah 63:1-6

Beloved, are we ready to stand beside Jesus? Will we agree that His divine activity is entirely perfect when He kills His adversaries? On that day will we be His friend or His enemy? We must grasp both the kindness and severity of our Lord so we will not be offended because of Him (MATT 11:6).

I have long wrestled with God's judgment verses His love assuming that these represent opposite aspects of His character. Whenever my dad mentioned God's coming wrath, I would rebuke him for being too *judgmental* and exhort him to be more loving. He encouraged me to read about God's relentless fury in the Old Testament. My focus on Christian virtue in the New Testament led me to believe my father needed enlightenment. Now I am beginning to comprehend God's true nature. His severity and kindness are the same attribute. We have all heard the common question, "If God is so loving, why does He let bad things happen to good people?" This is asked from an immature perspective of God's character and our utter depravity. There are no *good* people. Every single human has sinned (ROM 3:23). We exhaust the Lord by saying, "I'm a good person" (MAL 2:17). In reality everyone deserves eternal damnation. If we truly grasped

You have wearied the LORD ... by saying, "All who do evil are good ..." MALACHI 2:17 NIV

this, we would ask, "If God is holy, why does He not totally destroy all of mankind?" He nearly did so once.

Within a thousand years of creation, man had become so wicked that "every inclination of the thoughts of his heart was only evil all the time" (GEN 6:5 NIV). For this reason the Lord determined to destroy mankind from the face of the earth. But He found one man who was righteous in his generation (GEN 6:7-9; 7:1). Noah walked with God. The Lord showed this godly man favor by establishing His covenant. God preserved Noah and his family while sending a flood to destroy the rest of life on the earth (GEN 6:8, 17-18). The Lord then promised never again to wipe out His creation with a flood. He set His rainbow in the sky as a reminder of this covenant (GEN 8:21; 9:11, 16).

> *Never again will I destroy all living creatures ...*
> GENESIS 8:21 NIV

If God knew the earth would become corrupt again, why did He not completely destroy every creature then? Why did He make a covenant not to destroy us now? Even after His chosen people, Israel, responded with generations of apostasy, why does He maintain His covenant with them? Our answer is found in His name: "God is Love" (1 JOHN 4:16). With great love He restrains His full manifestation of wrath. Sometimes the Lord releases a measure of judgment as mercy. This alerts people to repent because His Kingdom is coming to Earth. In mercy, God delays judgment giving us more opportunities to choose Him. In Noah's day, God delayed for a hundred years, each day a warning of His coming wrath. It is for the sake of God's amazing love that He does not eradicate humanity. Our Beloved keeps His promises even to an obstinate people.

Why does God deal harshly with some but kindly to others? Instead of striving to reconcile two seemingly incompatible attributes, we must understand God's perfectly consistent character. The Israelites did not recognize the cohesiveness of God's justice and mercy. They complained that the Lord was not fair. The Lord responded by questioning, "Are My ways unjust? Is it not your ways that are unjust?" (EZEK 18:29). We are unfair, not God. Our Beloved is totally *other than*. Nothing less than perfection can exist in His presence. When His presence is manifest, everything unholy and unrighteous is consumed. We must consider God's justice in the context of His love. God loves righteousness. He

Your throne,

O God,

is forever ...

You love

righteousness

and hate

wickedness ...

PSALM 45:6-7

hates wickedness (Ps 45:7). The Lord is just and true in everything He does (REV 15:3). He is holy. God cannot do anything contrary to His nature. He does not suspend one attribute while exercising another. These are not opposing characteristics. His justice demonstrates His love. In love He executes justice. Viewing God's judgment as a display of His love is not heretical. The difference between God's wrath and mercy lies in the response of individuals. Those who humble themselves and repent receive God's mercy. Those who refuse to turn from evil endure God's wrath. The Lord administers justice by punishing the wicked and vindicating the righteous. To the wicked God's judgment is death; to the righteous it is life.

The Lord is gracious. He is full of compassion. His anger is not quickly kindled. Our Beloved abounds in mercy (Ps 145:8-9). This is why the Father sent His Son to atone for our sin. Jesus paid the price so that all who believe in Him would have eternal life. At the Cross, He suffered the full wrath of God on behalf of those who would believe and accept

His sacrifice. Even so, this provision of mercy is only available to those who receive it. Those who reject Christ will be found guilty of iniquity and suffer the consequences.

God's justice requires atonement for sin, whether through Jesus' blood or the blood of the wicked. The Lord does not delight in the death of anyone but would rather all turn to Him and live (EZEK 18:23, 32). Jesus said, "Unless you repent, you will perish" (LUKE 13:3). Jeremiah prophesied, "Thus says the Lord God: 'Behold, My anger and My fury will be poured out on this place ... And it will burn and not be quenched" (JER 7:20). This is the blazing fire described in the Song as the Bridegroom's love, which "many waters cannot quench." His love is "strong as death" and His jealousy is "cruel as the grave" (SONG 8:6-7). God's *love* and *wrath* are synonymous. Both are unquenchable.

I learn about the attributes of this Perfect Man every time I enter the Prayer Room. Even now the worship team expresses His nature as they sing, "Consider His goodness. Consider His severity. It is goodness to those who are found in His name. It is severity for those who turn away. God is not mocked. Man will reap what he sows. The Lord is not slow about His promise as some count slowness. He wants all to come to repentance. This is His mercy. Be wise!"

Note then the kindness and the severity of God: severity toward those who have fallen, but God's kindness toward you, provided you continue in his kindness; otherwise you also will be cut off. —Romans 11:22 NRSV

The Lord has given us a window of mercy with time to repent before He pours out His fierce wrath. Our great High Priest has gone ahead to prepare a way for us to receive mercy before His throne of grace.

Let us therefore come boldly to the throne of grace, that we may obtain mercy and find grace to help in time of need.

–Hebrews 4:16

A day of vengeance is coming, but for a brief moment there is a window of mercy standing open. Today, if we hear His voice, let us not harden our hearts (HEB 3:15). Jesus' arms and hands are rods of gold. He will administer justice and establish His righteous Kingdom "on earth as it is in heaven" (MATT 6:10). Let us consider His kindness and severity.

BLOOD ON OUR HANDS

The issue of justice extends beyond us individually. God judges entire regions for sin. As the corporate Body of Christ, we stand guilty for ignoring the crime of abortion. We have blood on our hands because life is in the blood (LEV 17:11). Every time a baby is aborted, we are accountable for another murder in our land. According to our deeds the Lord will repay (IS 59:3, 18). The blood of over fifty million babies is crying out for justice. There is a day of reckoning in God's heart. He is coming to judge the earth. What will He find when He returns?

And shall God not avenge His own elect who cry out day and night to Him, though He bears long with them? I tell you that He will avenge them speedily. Nevertheless, when the Son of Man comes, will He really find faith on the earth?

–Luke 18:7-8

All of our Beloved's ways are just and true (REV 15:3). He is a God of justice. He will gird a sword on His side and ride forth (PS 45:3). In righteousness He will judge and make war (REV 19:11). His arms of gold are ready for battle. Vengeance is His. He will repay (ROM 12:19).

*And the LORD ... proclaimed, "The LORD, the LORD God,
merciful and gracious, longsuffering, and abounding in
goodness and truth, keeping mercy for thousands, forgiving
iniquity and transgression and sin, by no means clearing the
guilty, visiting the iniquity of the fathers upon the children and
the children's children to the third and the fourth generation."*

–Exodus 34:6-7

And yet, our Beloved is a God of mercy. Though He is holy and just, the Lord is slow to anger. There is no one like Him. He is full of compassion and abounding in love. He bows low to the weakest ones. He helps the needy. He defends the cause of the widow and orphan. He acts on behalf of everyone who loves Him.

As the Body of Christ it is our responsibility to weep between the porch and the altar by standing in the gap and pleading for mercy. Beloved Church, let us lift up our voice on behalf of those who have no voice and for those who are appointed to die.

*Open your mouth for the speechless, in the cause of all who
are appointed to die. Open your mouth, judge righteously,
and plead the cause of the poor and needy.   –Proverbs 31:8-9*

Abortion is not about politics. It is an issue of life verses death. Are we willing to break our agreement with a culture of death?

*I call heaven and earth as witnesses today against you,
that I have set before you life and death, blessing and cursing;
therefore choose life, that both you and your descendants
may live.   –Deuteronomy 30:19*

We have a choice to make. The Lord has set before us life and death, blessing and cursing. Will we endure His wrath? Or will we embrace His mercy? Let us contend for life that His will may be done.

> *Our Father in heaven, hallowed be Your name. Your kingdom come. Your will be done on earth as it is in heaven. Give us this day our daily bread. And forgive us our debts, as we forgive our debtors. And do not lead us into temptation, but deliver us from the evil one. For Yours is the kingdom and the power and the glory forever. Amen.* —Matthew 6:9-13

In the government of heaven, do we really think it is a woman's *choice* to kill the one God is knitting together in her womb?

> *For You formed my inward parts; You covered me in my mother's womb. I will praise You, for I am fearfully and wonderfully made … My frame was not hidden from You, when I was made in secret … Your eyes saw my substance, being yet unformed. And in Your book they all were written, the days fashioned for me, when as yet there were none of them.* —Psalm 139:13-16

His hands are divine instruments of perfection, forming each baby. He fashions each precious creation with great care. Even before this, our Beloved knew us. Every child has a God-ordained destiny, which was appointed before birth.

> *Before I formed you in the womb I knew you; before you were born I sanctified you; I ordained you a prophet to the nations.* —Jeremiah 1:5

Lou Engle penned this simple twenty-two word "LIFE" prayer to help us contend daily for the ending of abortion in our nation:

Jesus, I plead your blood over my sins and the sins of my nation. God, end abortion and send revival to America!

Lou Engle (www.bound4life.com)

Even now a chorus echoes through the House of Prayer, "End abortion. In our land, have mercy." Every day we pray for the altar of abortion to be demolished. As *one nation under God* we must turn from our wicked ways. We must seek His face in order to receive His mercy. If we humble ourselves and pray, He will hear our cry. Our Beloved will forgive our sins and heal our land.

If My people who are called by My name will humble themselves, and pray and seek My face, and turn from their wicked ways, then I will hear from heaven, and will forgive their sin and heal their land. —2 Chronicles 7:14

Beloved Church, let us turn to the Lord with fasting, weeping, and mourning. Let us pray for the Lord to tear down wickedness and raise up righteousness. Who knows if He may relent from pouring out His wrath and leave behind a blessing!

"Now, therefore," says the LORD, "Turn to Me with all your heart, with fasting, with weeping, and with mourning." So rend your heart, and not your garments; return to the LORD your God, for He is gracious and merciful, slow to anger, and of great kindness; and He relents from doing harm. Who knows if He will turn and relent, and leave a blessing behind

Him ... Blow the trumpet in Zion, consecrate a fast, call a
sacred assembly; gather the people ... Let the priests, who
minister to the LORD, weep between the porch and the altar;
let them say, "Spare Your people, O LORD ..."   *–Joel 2:12-17*

Jesus is our way. He is truth and life (JOHN 14:6). Our Beloved's very
name is Life. His life is our light (JOHN 1:4). He is our way forward. Let
us open our eyes to see His light and truth. Let us repent for the blood
on our hands, that we may have Life in our nation!

WELCOME HIS DISCIPLINE

We have considered the Lord's hand stretched forth with mercy to
deliver His people and in wrath to slay His enemies, but at times, what
seems like God's judgment is really His mercy. He may show us a small
glimpse of punishment to come in order to give
us time to repent. This is His loving discipline. *He who spares the*
The arm of the Lord works on our behalf using *rod hates his son,*
the least severe means necessary in order to give *but he who loves*
us the greatest opportunity to turn to Him. *him is careful*
We may not see every hidden variable, but we *to discipline him.*
can trust that, with tender compassion, God's *PROVERBS 13:24 NIV*
hands orchestrate every event in our lives. Paul
reminds us, "All things work together for good to those who love
God" (ROM 8:28). When tempted to respond to God with contempt
in difficult circumstances, we must keep a Scriptural perspective. God
diligently disciplines His children because He loves us (PROV 13:24).

My son, do not despise the LORD's discipline and do not resent
his rebuke, because the LORD disciplines those he loves, as a
father the son he delights in.   *–Proverbs 3:11-12 NIV*

Our Father's discipline demonstrates His love. Let us not despise His rebuke. Remember that the north winds of adversity and south winds of blessing are sent by the Lord in the right proportion necessary to bring forth a pleasing fragrance from our lives (SONG 4:16). Let us endure His chastening, that we may become holy and blameless.

> And you have forgotten the exhortation which speaks to
> you as to sons: "My son, do not despise the chastening of the
> LORD, nor be discouraged when you are rebuked by Him; for
> whom the LORD loves He chastens, and scourges every son
> whom He receives." If you endure chastening, God deals with
> you as with sons; for what son is there whom a father does
> not chasten? —Hebrews 12:5-7

God interacts with us as children by pouring His love into our hearts. Knowing this, Paul invites us to rejoice in our suffering. It produces endurance, character, and hope (ROM 5:3-5). James also encourages us to rejoice when we encounter various trials. Such testing of our faith develops perseverance that we may be mature and complete (JAS 1:2-4). His rod of correction actually brings comfort during our struggle.

> Yea, though I walk through the valley of the shadow of death,
> I will fear no evil; for You are with me; Your rod and Your staff,
> they comfort me. —Psalm 23:4

The Lord searches our hearts to see if there is any wicked way in us and leads us in the way everlasting (Ps 139:23-24). With tenderness He reveals hairline fractures in our earthen vessels, which would cause us to break in the higher fires of refinement. He helps us catch the little foxes of compromise that spoil our blossoming vineyards (SONG 2:15).

When we remain silent and do not confess our sins, His hand is heavy upon us (Ps 32:3-4). When we look to other things in this world to bring us satisfaction, our Beloved hedges us in with thorns. He blocks our paths so that we cannot find our false lovers. The Lord leaves us no better alternative than returning to Him (Hos 2:6-7).

Our Beloved allures us into the wilderness. In this place of desolation, He speaks tenderly to us, giving us a secret door of hope in our valley of despair (Hos 2:14-15). It is His merciful kindness leading each of us to repentance. He will not violate our free will. The choice is ours. Will we humble ourselves, pray, turn from our wicked ways, and seek His face? He promises that if we do, He will hear from heaven, forgive our sins, and heal our land (2 Chron 7:14). The Lord's chastisement is our invitation to repentance.

Those whom I love I rebuke and discipline. So be earnest, and repent. Here I am! I stand at the door and knock. If anyone hears my voice and opens the door, I will come in and eat with him, and he with me. —Revelation 3:19-20 NIV

If we open the door to our hearts, our Beloved will enter in. When we acknowledge our sins, He forgives us (Ps 32:5). If we repent He does not count our iniquity against us. How blessed we are to be covered by His blood (Ps 32:1-2).

I can see why David was so eager for the Lord to show him his hidden faults. He invited God's correction so that presumptuous sins would not have dominion over him. The psalmist knew the reward of living in a manner worthy of the Lord, holy and blameless. His desire was that the words of his mouth and meditations of his heart would be acceptable in the sight of his Redeemer (Ps 19:12-14). No wonder the

Shepherd's staff brought David comfort in the valley of death (Ps 23:4). Jesus preserves us from trouble. He instructs us in the way we should go. He counsels us with His eye upon us (Ps 32:7-8). He leads us in paths of righteousness (Ps 23:3). Beloved, let us receive His rebuke with thankful hearts and welcome His discipline.

DECLARE HIS WORKS

In the trials of life we may begin to think the Lord has forgotten us. Others may scorn us, saying, "Where is your God?" In the midst of the swirling tempest we can say, "Why are you downcast, Oh my soul? Put your hope in God. I will yet praise Him" (Ps 42:5). We can declare along with David, "Though war break out against me, I will be confident" (Ps 27:3). Our Beloved has our best interest in mind. Even if the Lord has allowed the enemy to sift us, we must refuse the advice of Job's wife to "curse God and die." Wisely did Job reply, "Shall we receive good from God and not evil?" In all this he did not sin (JOB 2:9-10).

> Will the Lord cast off forever? And will He be favorable no more? Has His mercy ceased forever? Has His promise failed forevermore? Has God forgotten to be gracious? Has He in anger shut up His tender mercies?   Selah
>
> And I said, "This is my anguish; but I will remember the years of the right hand of the Most High." I will remember the works of the LORD; surely I will remember Your wonders of old.
>
> —Psalm 77:7-11

No matter how devastating life may seem, we have this invitation to remember God's wonders. He shows Himself strong to those whose hearts are loyal to Him (2 CHRON 16:9). He moves on behalf of those who wait for Him (Is 64:4). He delivers His people from despair. Beloved, let us live to declare His works (Ps 118:17).

I WILL REMEMBER

This is my confession. When I consider the works of the Lord, I will remember His miracles in my life—how He reached down from on high and drew me out of deep waters. I will recall that He rescued me because He delighted in me (Ps 18:16-19). Yes, I will live and not die and declare the works of the Lord.

Who am I that God is mindful of me? Even when I am unaware, He gives His angels charge over me. His delight is in me. His desire is for me. How precious are all His thoughts toward me. If I tried to count them, they would be more than the sand (Ps 139:17-18). He loves me. He says I ravish His heart. And I believe it. Though I am dark, He calls me lovely. It is this reality infused into my heart that brings such freedom to my soul.

How precious also are Your thoughts to me, O God! How great is the sum of them!
PSALM 139:17

For though my sins were scarlet, they have been washed white as snow. I am forgiven. I am cleansed. Jesus does not count my iniquity against me. His blood covers me. I know my heart is desperately wicked. I know I have sinned and fall short of His glory. I know that all my righteous acts are like filthy rags. I know that I am poor, wretched, miserable, blind, and naked. But my Beloved has redeemed me. He now clothes me in white garments. Therefore, I will remember His divine activity. I will remember how Jesus works on my behalf. Though I have gone astray and turned to my own way, my Shepherd has come after me. I will remember His discipline and chastisement with gratitude. Yes, His rod and staff comfort me.

His arm is glorious. I will remember how His arm worked salvation. His hands are rods of gold. His left hand is under my head. His right hand embraces me (SONG 2:6). I will recall the years of the right hand of the Lord (PS 77:10). I will consider the works His left hand does in secret. I will remember both His discipline and tender affection.

> Praise the LORD,
> for His mercy
> endures forever.
>
> 2 CHRONICLES 20:21

I will recall how the Lord hides me under His wings and sends His angels to watch over me (PS 91:4, 11). I will reflect on the times He sets ambushes for my enemies when I lift my voice with songs of praise (2 CHRON 20:21-22). I will remember every time darkness tries to consume me and He delivers me. Over and over, when I am weak He shows Himself strong (2 COR 12:9). I will not forget any of His benefits. He heals me and forgives all of my sins.

I will remember how, when I keep silent, my bones waste away (PS 32). When I try to hide, His hand is heavy upon me. He hedges me in on every side. He walls me in and blocks my path so that I cannot find my way (HOS 2:6). He opposes me like the angel He sent to oppose Balaam whenever my way is perverse (NUM 22:32). When I finally acknowledge my sin, He forgives me. I will remember how quickly He covers my sin when I confess and repent. What joy this brings to my soul! I am blessed because I am forgiven. Like the women caught in the act of adultery, Jesus says to my accusers, "He who is without sin, throw the first stone." He does not condemn me but urges, "Go and sin no more" (JOHN 8:7-11). Yes, I will remember His mercy. Because I have been forgiven much, surely I will love much. With all my heart, soul, mind, and strength I will forever love and praise my Beloved, Jesus Christ. Yes, I will remember!

CONSIDER HIS DIVINE ACTIVITY

May this become our testimony every day. I have only expounded on a few aspects of the Lord's arm. His divine activity is entirely perfect. As Creator, He forms us in the wombs of our mothers. As Savior, He delivers us from our powerful enemy. His hand is stretched forth to heal all our diseases, provide all our needs, and protect us underneath His shelter. As Judge, He pours out wrath on His enemies. Our Beloved is full of zeal and strength (Is 63:15). There is so much more to say. Let us consider the many ways He reveals His hands as rods of gold. Even today, let us recall how He has acted on our behalf!

His *body* is *carved* ivory

inlaid with sapphires.

❦

Song 5:14

Chapter 10

His Body—Complete Salvation

ATTRIBUTE #7
His body: Jesus' tender *compassion*

PRAYER

Jesus, have mercy on me, a sinner. I acknowledge that I am wretched, pitiable, poor, blind, and naked (Rev 3:17). I have sinned against You. I am unworthy of sharing in Your glory (Rom 3:23). I confess my faults (Jas 5:16). I humble myself and pray; I turn from my wicked ways to seek Your face. Thank you for hearing from heaven, forgiving my sins, and healing my life (2 Chron 7:14). You paid the Bride price to purchase me at Calvary. I am ever grateful. Thank you for setting me as a beautiful jewel in Your side. Your mercy endures forever. How precious is the body of my Beloved. Let me be a vessel of honor equipped to carry your glory to the nations! Amen.

SKILLFUL MERCY

With tender compassion for fallen man, God designed a unique plan to save sinful people. The Father sent His only Son as a sacrifice to pay the penalty for our iniquity. Jesus came to the earth to rescue us from our sinful depravity. Christ died for our sins, was buried, and rose on the third day (1 Cor 15:3-4). The Light of the world poured out His light from heaven to shine on our darkness. He brought us to a place of safety because He enjoys us (Ps 18:19). With tender mercy, He forgives. Our Beloved removes our transgressions as far as the east is from the west (Ps 103:12). He is slow to anger and quick to love.

The LORD is slow to anger, abounding in love and forgiving sin and rebellion. Yet he does not leave the guilty unpunished; he punishes the children for the sin of the fathers to the third and fourth generation. —Numbers 14:18 NIV

His mercies never end. His compassions do not fail. They are new every morning (LAM 3:22-23). Have you ever had one of those days when you just did not want to get out of bed? It has been a sleepless night and your body aches from some kind of ailment. You long for anything to relieve the misery. Jesus has done just this. He bore the entire wrath of God on his own body. Not only did He pay the full price for our sins, He took on all our diseases. Beloved, do we comprehend the full implications of Jesus' death on the cross? His body is rare ivory. There is none other like Him. His body is pure because He is perfect. It is expensive because He alone could pay the Bride price. And yet it is carved with His sufferings. On His body Jesus bore our griefs, took up our infirmities, and carried our sorrows. He was wounded, pierced, bruised, and crushed because of our transgressions. The punishment that we deserve was inflicted upon Him so we could have peace. His very flesh was ripped apart as He endured intense scourging. By the stripes on His back we have obtained healing. His Father laid upon His body our iniquity. So disfigured was His entire frame that He could not even be recognized.

His appearance was so disfigured beyond that of any man and his form marred beyond human likeness ...

Surely he took up our infirmities and carried our sorrows … He was pierced for our transgressions, he was crushed for our iniquities; the punishment that brought us peace was upon him, and by his wounds we are healed. We all, like sheep, have gone astray … and the LORD has laid on him the iniquity of us all. —Isaiah 52:14; 53:4-6 NIV

If His body was so entirely mutilated, what are the sapphires? Beloved, these jewels are the reward of His suffering. It was for this joy that He endured such torture (HEB 12:2). There was a prize waiting at the end of His Via Dolorosa (Way of Suffering), the path He walked to His crucifixion. He saw a light at the end of this dark tunnel (Is 53:11). His wounds have become like precious stones. When Jesus came to the earth in perfection, He carried the beauty of the sapphire pathway from heaven to earth (EXOD 24:10). These are the same costly stones described in Aaron's breastplate, God's throne, and the foundation of the New Jerusalem (EXOD 28:17, 29; EZEK 1:26; 10:1; REV 21:19). As Jesus bore our iniquities, our Beloved's body was carved with affliction. We have been crucified with Christ so that we may take on the nature of this pure ivory. We have been joined to the Living God. Christ now lives in us!

> *After the suffering of his soul, he will see the light of life and be satisfied.*
> ISAIAH 53:11 NIV

I have been crucified with Christ; it is no longer I who live, but Christ lives in me; and the life which I now live in the flesh I live by faith in the Son of God, who loved me and gave Himself for me. —Galatians 2:20

For we know that our old self was crucified with him so that the body of sin might be done away with, that we should no longer be slaves to sin …   –Romans 6:6 NIV

If we are in Christ, our sinful nature is dead (2 COR 5:17). We are no longer enslaved to it. We are bright and sparkling jewels set in the body of our Beloved. Each sapphire stone set in His body is carried with Him to glory (HEB 2:10). With tender compassion, God made us alive in Christ so that we are seated with Christ in heavenly places.

But because of his great love for us, God, who is rich in mercy, made us alive with Christ even when we were dead in transgressions—it is by grace you have been saved. And God raised us up with Christ and seated us with him in the heavenly realms in Christ Jesus.   –Ephesians 2:4-7 NIV

Through His body, inlaid with precious jewels, our Beloved imparts His glory to human beings that we may be one with Him (JOHN 17:22). We are the valuable jewels, which Jesus asked of the Father to be given as His inheritance (Ps 2:8). Our Beloved purifies and mounts us in His own body with discernment and skillful mercy. We are now bound securely in the bundle of the living (1 SAM 25:29). Our bodies are temples of the Holy Spirit who lives within us. We are no longer our own (1 COR 6:19-20). From every people group all across the world, Jesus has purchased us for God with His own blood (REV 5:9).

> *And the glory which*
> *You gave Me*
> *I have given them,*
> *that they may be one*
> *just as We are one.*
>
> JOHN 17:22

PAID IN FULL

So what exactly did He purchase on Calvary's cross? Jesus' blood paid the price for our iniquities. His body took on our infirmities. He purchased *salvation*. Beloved, salvation is not limited to the forgiveness of sins; it includes everything. The Greek word for save is *sozo*. It means that we will be kept safe and made whole. It encompasses body, soul, and spirit. This extends to every facet of life both

> *Jesus took bread, blessed and broke it, and gave it to the disciples and said, "Take, eat; this is My body."*
> MATTHEW 26:26

on this side of eternity and in the age to come. The chastisement that was upon His body brought us peace for our entire beings. We do not have to wait for glorified bodies to begin receiving His benefits now. Every time we take communion we remember what He purchased. He says, "This is my blood of the covenant shed for your sins. Take and drink it. This is my body pierced through for you. Take and eat it." He tells us to take, eat, and drink (MATT 26:26-28).

> Jesus on the same night in which He was betrayed took bread; and when He had given thanks, He broke it and said, "Take, eat; this is My body which is broken for you; do this in remembrance of Me." In the same manner He also took the cup after supper, saying, "This cup is the new covenant in My blood. This do, as often as you drink it, in remembrance of Me."
> –1 Corinthians 11:23-25

Jesus' body was broken for our healing. His blood was poured out to pardon our transgressions. It pleased the Father to crush His Son that we might be saved (Is 53:10). Complete redemption has been bought at the price of our Beloved's body and blood. He desires that all would come to Him for salvation, healing, and deliverance. If we receive His full *sozo package,* we will be saved from disease, preserved from danger, rescued from destruction, and delivered from death.

This gift is ours. It is as if our Beloved gave us a voucher that He is waiting for us to redeem. Imagine someone paying for an expensive vacation at a luxurious resort. Every amenity imaginable is included. Dining, entertainment, room service, and a wide variety of exclusive activities nearby are merely a few of the benefits. Many do not believe the vacation is for real. These refuse the initial airline ticket. Others accept the vacation by traveling to the resort, but a large percentage do not get the full value offered to them. They stay at the hotel free of charge but spend their own money paying for food and entertainment. Unfortunately, most do not fully cash in on what has already been purchased. Very few take advantage of this gift entirely.

The same is true of salvation. Many will not receive God's free gift of forgiveness. They may believe in Jesus as Savior but do not receive the full measure of His mercy. There is much more available than we realize. We try to attain emotional, mental, and physical health in our own strength as if it were something we could buy. The cost of salvation has already been paid in full. We have a choice. Will we believe? Dear friends, let us not forget any of the Lord's great benefits!

> Bless the LORD, O my soul, and forget not all His benefits:
> Who forgives all your iniquities, Who heals all your diseases,
> Who redeems your life from destruction, Who crowns you
> with lovingkindness and tender mercies, Who satisfies your
> mouth with good things, so that your youth is renewed
> like the eagle's.   –Psalm 103:2-5

How marvelous are His benefits. How precious is His gift of total salvation. Jesus not only forgives our sins but also heals our diseases. What He accomplished on the cross was more than enough for our physical healing. His very wounds heal ours. He bore our sickness and carried our sorrows. He crowns each of us with loving-kindness and tender mercies. Surely our Beloved satisfies us with good things. Let us bless the Lord for all His benefits. Oh, the beautiful body of Christ inlaid with the prize of His inheritance. Oh, the enduring mercies that caused our Lord to take upon His body all of our diseases, all of our sorrows, and all of our punishment. Oh, the depth of the riches of God's wisdom (ROM 11:33). Rarely would anyone die for a righteous man, but Jesus gave it all. He demonstrated His love by laying down His life that we may live.

You see, at just the right time, when we were still powerless, Christ died for the ungodly. Very rarely will anyone die for a righteous man, though for a good man someone might possibly dare to die. But God demonstrates his own love for us in this: While we were still sinners, Christ died for us.

—Romans 5:6-8 NIV

Our Beloved surrendered His body. How great is His compassion, how endless His mercy. What tenderness and kindness He has extended to us. Although He was rich, He became poor. It was all for love's sake. No greater love has anyone than this Perfect Man who took upon His body everything we deserve (JOHN 15:13).

The sapphires that shine so brightly are carefully laid along the scars on our Beloved's body. Thomas touched these wounds where blood and water once flowed forth (JOHN 19:34; 20:27). By faith we too can reach our hands into Jesus' side to receive His enduring mercy. Jesus paid the full price to purchase us, that we might have access to healing, deliverance, and redemption. The question is, "Will we receive it?" He tells us to ask, seek, and knock. If we know how to give good gifts, how much more does He?

Ask, and it will be given to you; seek, and you will find; knock, and it will be opened to you. For everyone who asks receives, and he who seeks finds, and to him who knocks it will be opened. Or what man is there among you who, if his son asks for bread, will give him a stone? Or if he asks for a fish, will he give him a serpent? If you then, being evil, know how to give good gifts to your children, how much more will your Father who is in heaven give good things to those who ask Him!

–Matthew 7:7-11

He will give us whatever we ask in the Father's name (JOHN 15:16). This is the confidence we have. If we ask anything according to His will, He hears and grants our petitions.

Now this is the confidence that we have in Him, that if we ask anything according to His will, He hears us. And if we know that He hears us, whatever we ask, we know that we have the petitions that we have asked of Him. *–1 John 5:14-15*

Some question whether or not it is God's will to heal. The man with leprosy expressed this same concern when he approached the Lord. Jesus responded with compassion saying, "I am willing." Immediately the man was cured.

A man with leprosy came to him and begged him on his knees, "If you are willing, you can make me clean." Filled with compassion, Jesus reached out his hand and touched the man. "I am willing," he said. "Be clean!" Immediately the leprosy left him and he was cured.   *–Mark 1:40-42 NIV*

Beloved, God is willing. Jesus Christ gave Himself to deliver us from this evil age according to the will of our Father (GAL 1:4). It is the Lord's will to grant each of us healing and deliverance. He already has. It was finished at the Cross (JOHN 19:30)!

What was finished? Death was swallowed up in victory. The Father exalted Jesus to the highest place (PHIL 2:9). There He sat down at God's right hand (MARK 16:19). Our Beloved's enemies became His footstool (MATT 22:44). The last enemy to be conquered is death: to our bodies, our souls, and our spirits.

The last enemy that will be destroyed is death. For "He has put all things under His feet." … So when this corruptible has put on incorruption, and this mortal has put on immortality, then shall be brought to pass the saying that is written: "Death is swallowed up in victory." "O Death, where is your sting? O Hades, where is your victory?" The sting of death is sin, and the strength of sin is the law. But thanks be to God, who gives us the victory through our Lord Jesus Christ.
–1 Corinthians 15:26-27; 54-57

The afflictions Jesus suffered have delivered us from the sting of sin and death once and for all. Death no longer has mastery (ROM 6:9-11). Behold, our Beloved comes leaping on the mountains conquering all opposition (SONG 2:8). His Father has put all things under His feet.

"You have put all things in subjection under his feet." For in that He put all in subjection under him, He left nothing that is not put under him. But now we do not yet see all things put under him. But we see Jesus, who was made a little lower than the angels, for the suffering of death crowned with glory and honor, that He, by the grace of God, might taste death for everyone. For it was fitting for Him, for whom are all things and by whom are all things, in bringing many sons to glory, to make the captain of their salvation perfect through sufferings. … Through death He might destroy him who had the power of death, that is, the devil, and release those who through fear of death were all their lifetime subject to bondage.

—Hebrews 2:8-15

The One who tasted death for us is now Ruler over all. Our Captain of Salvation destroyed the power of death, releasing us from its bondage, that we might partake of His glory. The One dwelling in our hearts is greater than the one who is in the world (1 JOHN 4:4). The enemy is defeated. Death has no authority. We are covered in the precious blood of the Lamb. Sickness must go in the name of Jesus. He did not take His stripes in vain. The enemy has no ground. Our bodies are temples of the Holy Spirit. Satan has no territory. The spirit of death is pushed back. Pain must leave. It is finished. It is done! In Jesus' name there is fullness of healing: physical, spiritual, mental, and emotional. This is normal Christianity. Our Beloved purchased the whole package that we might be saved, healed, and delivered. Every good and perfect gift comes from Him (JAS 1:17). He delights in showing mercy.

Every good and every perfect gift is from above …

JAMES 1:17

*Who is a God like You, pardoning iniquity and passing over
the transgression of the remnant of His heritage? He does not
retain His anger forever, because He delights in mercy.*

—Micah 7:18

Let us then reach up toward heaven and grasp hold of these sapphire
stones. Let us lay aside every hindrance and run our race for the reward
that is before us (HEB 12:1-2). Let us press on to lay hold of that prize for
which He laid hold of us.

*Not that I have already attained, or am already perfected; but
I press on, that I may lay hold of that for which Christ Jesus
has also laid hold of me. Brethren, I do not count myself to
have apprehended; but one thing I do, forgetting those things
which are behind and reaching forward to those things which
are ahead, I press toward the goal for the prize of the upward
call of God in Christ Jesus.*   *—Philippians 3:12-14*

Will we appropriate God's blessings in their entirety: body, soul, and
spirit? Our Beloved is Jehovah Rophe. His name is *The Lord Who
Heals* (EXOD 15:26). His very identity equates spiritual, physical, and
emotional healing. The exact same power that raised Christ from the
dead is at work in us.

Those who dwell in the secret place of the Most High will hide under
His shadow. He is our refuge. We can trust Him to protect and deliver
us from deadly diseases. The terrors of night and the pestilence that
stalks in the darkness have no power over the Beloved of God. Ten
thousand may fall beside us, but no harm will come near us. Blessed is
the one who makes the Lord his trust (PS 40:4).

He who dwells in the secret place of the Most High shall abide under the shadow of the Almighty. I will say of the LORD, "He is my refuge and my fortress; My God, in Him I will trust." Surely He shall deliver you from the snare of the fowler and from the perilous pestilence. He shall cover you with His feathers, and under His wings you shall take refuge; His truth shall be your shield and buckler. You shall not be afraid of the terror by night, nor of the arrow that flies by day, nor of the pestilence that walks in darkness, nor of the destruction that lays waste at noonday. A thousand may fall at your side, and ten thousand at your right hand; but it shall not come near you. Only with your eyes shall you look, and see the reward of the wicked. Because you have made the LORD, who is my refuge, even the Most High, your dwelling place, no evil shall befall you, nor shall any plague come near your dwelling; for He shall give His angels charge over you, to keep you in all your ways. In their hands they shall bear you up, lest you dash your foot against a stone. You shall tread upon the lion and the cobra, the young lion and the serpent you shall trample underfoot. "Because he has set his love upon Me, therefore I will deliver him; I will set him on high, because he has known My name. He shall call upon Me, and I will answer him; I will be with him in trouble; I will deliver him and honor him. With long life I will satisfy him, and show him My salvation."

–Psalm 91

If Jesus Christ is our dwelling place, no plague can enter in. No evil will befall us. He will command His angels charge over us. They will guard us from disaster. We will tread upon lions and cobras. Jesus said we would pick up snakes with our hands. He told His disciples that when they drank deadly poison, it would not hurt them (MARK 16:18). When Paul laid a bundle of sticks on the fire and a viper fastened to his hand, he shook it off and suffered no harm (ACTS 28:3-5). The Lord promised the Israelites that if they would diligently keep His commandments none of the plagues of the Egyptians would come upon them.

If you diligently heed the voice of the LORD your God and do what is right in His sight, give ear to His commandments and keep all His statutes, I will put none of the diseases on you which I have brought on the Egyptians. For I am the LORD who heals you. —Exodus 15:26

Jesus is the Lord who heals. Why? Because He loves us. When we set our affections on our Beloved, He delivers us. When we set our love upon Jesus, we can have confidence in His name. He is our Healer, Provider, Protector, Savior, Deliverer, Judge, and so much more. We can call upon the name of the Lord. He will answer. He promises to deliver and honor us, to be with us in trouble, to satisfy us with long life, and to show us His salvation. What is His salvation? It is everything He purchased on the cross. Will we receive His salvation for the healing of our bodies, minds, emotions, and entire beings?

It is not for us to ask, "Why was this person not healed?" Instead we can pray, "Why not me? Why not now? Why not today?" The devil does not want us to have the good gifts, which our Father delights to give us through His Son. Our adversary prowls around like a hungry lion seeking someone to devour. We need to resist him (1 PET 5:8-9). This life is a battleground. We wrestle not against flesh and blood but against principalities and every evil spirit of this dark world. We must stand firm in the power of His might, clothe ourselves in the full armor of God, and fight for the manifestation of God's promises in our lives (EPH 6:10-18). The Lord has given each of us a governmental position. We are seated together with Him in heavenly places over all principalities and darkness (EPH 2:6). Let us take our place of authority in the spirit and call heaven to earth. Power to lift up righteousness and tear down wickedness is released through worship and intercession.

> *And God raised us up with Christ and seated us with him in the heavenly realms in Christ Jesus.*
>
> EPHESIANS 2:6 NIV

Our Beloved is enthroned on the praises of His people (PS 22:3). Let us thank Him for His blessings and make our requests known (PHIL 4:6). Let us praise Him for His enduring mercy and watch the Lord set ambushes for our enemy (2 CHRON 20:21-22). He will thunder from heaven and scatter our enemy (PS 18:13-14).

Jesus *can* and *will* heal. Even when He does not, we have victory over death. We will have glorified bodies. Our earthly bodies are perishable, but they will be raised imperishable. We will be raised in glory and power. Every time we pray, "Let Your Kingdom come and Your will be done," we are really asking for a down payment of what is to come.

The body is sown in corruption, it is raised in incorruption. It is sown in dishonor, it is raised in glory. It is sown in weakness, it is raised in power. It is sown a natural body, it is raised a spiritual body. There is a natural body, and there is a spiritual body. And so it is written, "The first man Adam became a living being." The last Adam became a life-giving spirit. However, the spiritual is not first, but the natural, and afterward the spiritual. The first man was of the earth, made

*of dust; the second Man is the Lord from heaven. As was the
man of dust, so also are those who are made of dust; and as
is the heavenly Man, so also are those who are heavenly. And
as we have borne the image of the man of dust, we shall also
bear the image of the heavenly Man. −1 Corinthians 15:42-49*

We will bear the image of this heavenly Man. He is a life-giving spirit.
We are strangers on the earth, just pilgrims on our way to Zion. Let us
look for the holy city whose builder and maker is God (HEB 11:10-16).
Behold, the New Jerusalem is coming to Earth (REV 21:2). Let us lift
our eyes to heaven and set our minds on things to come. Satan may
very well try to kill, steal, and destroy the very blessings God has laid
up for us, but the Good Shepherd gives life to His sheep. Christ has
purchased us that we may have life abundantly today.

*The thief does not come except to steal, and to kill, and to
destroy. I have come that they may have life, and that they
may have it more abundantly. "I am the good shepherd. The
good shepherd gives His life for the sheep."   −John 10:10-11*

Why do we turn so quickly to medicine and doctors? King Asa died
from a severe disease because he sought physicians instead of the Lord
(2 CHRON 16:12-13). How is it that we often wait until all else fails before
turning to Jesus? There is a time to seek medical help, but should we not
first ask the Lord to heal us in His name? If we ask, He will answer.

*Most assuredly, I say to you, whatever you ask the Father
in My name He will give you. Until now you have asked
nothing in My name. Ask, and you will receive, that your
joy may be full.   −John 16:23-24*

I never realized salvation was for my entire being until I encountered back and wrist injuries compiled on top of intense heartache and deep depression. My heart was sick, my body was in excruciating pain, and my mind was experiencing the effects. My soul was completely downcast. Salvation was no consolation when all hope for this life had seemed to vanish. The enemy was crushing me under his heavy weight of oppression until I cried to the Lord for help. My Beloved delivered me. This is why He says to those who are weary and heavily burdened, "Come to Me. My yoke is easy. I will give you rest" (MATT 11:28). Strength comes to those who wait on the Lord (IS 40:31). Our Beloved speaks to us in times of struggle, saying, "Come up from this wilderness leaning on your Beloved. Lean on My Body. It is your road to healing, recovery, and freedom. Take the position of authority I have given you in the spirit." In His name we can tell the devil, "This far and no further." By living according to His Spirit, our souls and bodies follow in alignment. When I discovered the fullness of freedom and healing available to all believers, I truly became alive to God (ROM 6:11).

> *But those who wait on the LORD shall renew their strength ...*
>
> ISAIAH 40:31

Let us go before the Judge who vindicates us. Do you recall the parable of the persistent widow who cried out for justice? The unjust judge avenged her merely to keep her from wearing him out. How much more will our Righteous Judge bring about justice to His elect who cry out to Him day and night? He will deliver justice speedily. Therefore, we ought to always pray and not lose heart.

Then He spoke a parable to them, that men always ought to pray and not lose heart, saying: "There was in a certain city a

*judge who did not fear God nor regard man. Now there was
a widow in that city; and she came to him, saying, 'Get justice
for me from my adversary.' And he would not for a while; but
afterward he said within himself, 'Though I do not fear God
nor regard man, yet because this widow troubles me I will
avenge her, lest by her continual coming she weary me.'"
Then the Lord said, "Hear what the unjust judge said. And
shall God not avenge His own elect who cry out day and
night to Him, though He bears long with them? I tell you
that He will avenge them speedily. Nevertheless, when the
Son of Man comes, will He really find faith on the earth?"*

–Luke 18:1-8

Will He find such faith in our hearts? He has given us these promises,
but we must believe and lay hold of them. The Lord heard Hezekiah's
plea and added fifteen years to his life.

*Go back and tell Hezekiah … "This is what the LORD, the God
of your father David, says: I have heard your prayer and seen
your tears; I will heal you … I will add fifteen years to your life.
And I will deliver you …"*   *–2 Kings 20:5-6 NIV*

We can question all day long, asking, "What about this person or that
situation?" But will we actually dare to believe He *might* heal *us*? The
woman who had a flow of blood for twelve years risked believing in the
Healer. She had already suffered many things from physicians and spent
all her money but only grew worse. With faith she pressed through the
crowds, believing that she would be made well if she could just touch
Jesus' clothes. When she reached for the hem of His garment, healing
power went out and instantly dried up her fountain of blood. What

was the Lord's response? "Daughter, your faith has made you well. Go in peace, and be healed of your affliction" (MARK 5:25-34). Her faith in the Healer made her well.

Likewise, the centurion believed the Lord could heal his paralyzed servant by simply speaking a word. Jesus marveled, saying, "I have not found such great faith, not even in Israel!" He said it would be done as the man had believed, and the servant was healed that same hour (MATT 8:5-13). Another man begged the Lord to heal his dying son. Jesus replied, "Go your way; your son lives" (JOHN 4:46-54). The royal official took Jesus at His word. While he was returning home, he heard the report that his son was living. Upon inquiring when the boy got better, he realized it was the exact time Jesus spoke to him. This caused his whole household to believe. Jesus healed all who were sick. With a word He commanded demons to flee. This reality is available today.

> When evening had come, they brought to Him many who were demon-possessed. And He cast out the spirits with a word, and healed all who were sick, that it might be fulfilled which was spoken by Isaiah the prophet, saying: "He Himself took our infirmities and bore our sicknesses."
> –Matthew 8:16-17

Before raising a young girl from the dead, Jesus said to the ruler of the synagogue, "Do not be afraid; only believe" (MARK 5:36). All things are possible to those who believe. If our faith is weak, let us cry out, "Lord, I believe. Help my unbelief" (MARK 9:23-24).

If we believe the Lord forgives our sins, why do we doubt His ability to heal our bodies? Is it easier for Him to say, "Your sins are forgiven," or to command, "Be healed"? When Jesus saw the faith of those who brought the paralytic to Him for healing He said, "Son, your sins are forgiven" (MARK 2:3-12). He perceived that some teachers of the law were thinking, "He's blaspheming! Who can forgive sins but God alone?" Proving His authority to forgive sins, Jesus told the paralytic to take up his mat and go home. And so he did. The crowd was amazed.

Our Beloved has authority to forgive *all* of our sins and heal *all* of our diseases. Let us stir up our faith to believe as we call upon the Lord. He may just tear the heavens open to come down. Watch as the mountains tremble at His presence. Let us call upon this One who can effortlessly overcome every obstacle (SONG 2:8). He declares His name to every adversary (Is 64:1-2). This Righteous Judge inclines His ear to our weak prayers. He confirms His Word with signs and wonders. He stretches out His hand to heal all our afflictions (ACTS 4:30). This Perfect Man judges cancer, mental disease, emotional trauma, and ailments that rise up against God. He demonstrates His power in order to manifest His glory. Our Beloved rides forth prosperously for the sake of truth, humility, and righteousness (Ps 45:4). God's Kingdom is in our midst. His will shall be done. We need only to receive Jesus' free gift. We have this freedom because our Beloved has been anointed to heal broken hearts and release prisoners (LUKE 4:18-21). His Spirit gives us freedom (2 COR 3:17). The law of the Spirit of Life liberates us from the law of sin and death (ROM 8:2). Let us remember that Christ dwells in our bodies; let us contend for healing. Our enemy devises our hurt saying a disease clings to us. Satan proclaims that we will never recover.

All my enemies whisper together against me; they imagine the worst for me, saying, "A vile disease has beset him; he will never get up from the place where he lies." –Psalm 41:7-8 NIV

Let us take our stand against our evil foe. His diagnosis concerning our bodies, minds, and spirits is false. Let us not so readily receive the enemy's curse of death upon our bodies. Often times he causes us to feel symptoms just to get us to give into sickness especially after we have already received a measure of healing. Satan is a liar. The Lord has given us a new verdict: *"Sozo!"* Let us lay hold of His truth. We have been saved completely. He has brought total salvation to every part of our beings. Our Beloved has loosed our chains. We are set free from the bondage of this fallen world in the name of Jesus. Let us contend for victory over death and call forth the promises of our Beloved. Death has been defeated. Every time Satan attempts to proclaim the curse of death upon our lives, let us silence him by proclaiming, "I will *not* die. I will live and declare the marvelous works of my Beloved!"

> *The voice of rejoicing and salvation is in the tents of the righteous ... I shall not die, but live, and declare the works of the LORD.* —Psalm 118:15, 17

Jesus said, "And do not fear those who kill the body but cannot kill the soul. But rather fear Him who is able to destroy both soul and body in hell" (MATT 10:28). Let us fear the Lord with holy reverence. Let us put our confidence in the Great Physician. He is our Healer, Savior, and Deliverer. Christ's body is our evidence. Let us praise our Beloved for His glorious body as we press on for our heavenly reward.

FREELY GIVE

Salvation is our free gift. When Jesus sent the twelve apostles to preach, He reminded them of the gift they had received, saying, "Freely you have received, freely give."

And as you go, preach, saying, "The kingdom of heaven is at hand." Heal the sick, cleanse the lepers, raise the dead, cast out demons. Freely you have received, freely give. Provide neither gold nor silver nor copper in your money belts …

—Matthew 10:7-9

What did He instruct His disciples to give? It was not money. He told them not to take any. He told them to preach His coming Kingdom and freely give the salvation they had received. He commissioned them to heal the sick, cleanse the lepers, raise the dead, and cast out demons. Would we recommend this set of guidelines to those evangelizing today? This is the way our Beloved teaches us to preach.

Peter and John did not have any money but gave the very gift they had been freely given. Peter said to the man who had been crippled from birth, "Silver and gold I do not have, but what I do have I give you: In the name of Jesus Christ of Nazareth, rise up and walk." The man leaped to his feet and praised God. All were filled with wonder and amazement (ACTS 3:1-10). The apostles performed many other miracles in Jesus' name as well. When the Lord appointed seventy others and sent them out two by two, He told them to go into every city and heal the sick. They returned rejoicing that even demons fled in His name.

> *Silver and gold I do not have, but what I do have I give you: In the name of Jesus Christ of Nazareth, rise up and walk.*
>
> *ACTS 3:6*

After these things the Lord appointed seventy others also, and sent them two by two … Then He said to them, "… Go your way … Heal the sick there, and say to them, 'The kingdom of

God has come near to you' … " Then the seventy returned with joy, saying, "Lord, even the demons are subject to us in Your name." And He said to them, "I saw Satan fall like lightning from heaven. Behold, I give you the authority to trample on serpents and scorpions, and over all the power of the enemy, and nothing shall by any means hurt you. Nevertheless do not rejoice in this, that the spirits are subject to you, but rather rejoice because your names are written in heaven."

—Luke 10:1, 9, 17-20

Jesus gives us authority to trample on serpents, scorpions, and all of the enemy's power (LUKE 10:19). These things are to be expected, but they are just a sign of something greater. It gets better! Humanity has been redeemed. One day all the demons will be gone. There will be no more death and we will still be alive. Our glory is in having our names written in the Lamb's Book of Life (REV 21:27). We are partnering with the Living God. Beloved, we are going to live forever. We will rule and reign with Jesus. This is truly something to rejoice about!

Do we believe that walking in supernatural power is Christianity 101? Jesus told His disciples to tarry in Jerusalem until they were endued with power from on high (LUKE 24:49). Our Beloved said we would receive power from the Holy Spirit to be His witnesses (ACTS 1:8). With a word, Jesus commanded demons to flee. Through the power of His Spirit, we will do greater works than He did.

He who believes in Me, the works that I do he will do also; and greater works than these he will do, because I go to My Father. And whatever you ask in My name, that I will do, that the Father may be glorified in the Son. —John 14:12-13

Jesus' testimony was accompanied with signs, wonders, miracles, and gifts of the Spirit (HEB 2:4). If we are to do greater works than these, how much more will He confirm His word through us? When the apostles were threatened by authorities, they asked the Lord for boldness to proclaim God's word with signs and wonders. After they prayed, their meeting place was shaken, they were filled with Holy Spirit power, and they confidently proclaimed the Word of God.

> "Now, Lord, look on their threats, and grant to Your servants that with all boldness they may speak Your word, by stretching out Your hand to heal, and that signs and wonders may be done through the name of Your holy Servant Jesus." And when they had prayed, the place where they were assembled together was shaken; and they were all filled with the Holy Spirit, and they spoke the word of God with boldness.
>
> −Acts 4:29-31

Do we comprehend the apostolic authority we have been granted? Jesus told His disciples, "All authority has been given Me ... Go therefore ..." He sends us to make disciples of all nations, baptizing them in His name, and teaching them to observe all He commanded.

> And Jesus came and spoke to them, saying, "All authority has been given to Me in heaven and on earth. Go therefore and make disciples of all the nations, baptizing them in the name of the Father and of the Son and of the Holy Spirit, teaching them to observe all things that I have commanded you; and lo, I am with you always, even to the end of the age." Amen.
>
> −Matthew 28:18-20

Chapter 10: His Body—Complete Salvation

God has given us His authority. There is power in the name of Jesus. There is power in the Blood of Christ. After Jesus had risen, He appeared to His disciples, rebuked their unbelief, and commanded them to preach the Gospel. These are the signs He said would follow: they would drive out demons, speak in new tongues, pick up snakes, drink deadly poison without harm, and heal the sick. And so they went. The Lord was with them everywhere they preached, confirming His word through these signs.

> Later He appeared to the eleven as they sat at the table; and He rebuked their unbelief and hardness of heart, because they did not believe those who had seen Him after He had risen. And He said to them, "Go into all the world and preach the gospel to every creature. He who believes and is baptized will be saved; but he who does not believe will be condemned. And these signs will follow those who believe: In My name they will cast out demons; they will speak with new tongues; they will take up serpents; and if they drink anything deadly, it will by no means hurt them; they will lay hands on the sick, and they will recover." So then, after the Lord had spoken to them, He was received up into heaven, and sat down at the right hand of God. And they went out and preached everywhere, the Lord working with them and confirming the word through the accompanying signs. Amen.
>
> —Mark 16:14-20

We are His disciples. He tells us to go in His name, to lay our hands on the sick, to cast out demons, and to raise the dead. I spoke with a pastor from Mozambique who has seen several people raised from the dead. So many people want to know his secret. They ask, "How is this possible? How did you do it?" He simply answers, "I look behind as I go. These signs just follow." If we have faith as small as a mustard seed, we will say to this mountain, "Move." It will go. Nothing will be impossible for us. Why could the disciples not cure the epileptic? Jesus told them, "Because of your unbelief." Faith is required.

> *And when they had come to the multitude, a man came to Him, kneeling down to Him and saying, "Lord, have mercy on my son, for he is an epileptic and suffers severely; for he often falls into the fire and often into the water. So I brought him to Your disciples, but they could not cure him." Then Jesus answered and said, "O faithless and perverse generation, how long shall I be with you? How long shall I bear with you? Bring him here to Me." And Jesus rebuked the demon, and it came out of him; and the child was cured from that very hour. Then the disciples came to Jesus privately and said, "Why could we not cast it out?" So Jesus said to them, "Because of your unbelief; for assuredly, I say to you, if you have faith as a mustard seed, you will say to this mountain, 'Move from here to there,' and it will move; and nothing will be impossible for you. However, this kind does not go out except by prayer and fasting."* —Matthew 17:14-21

We need faith to both receive and give. Add in prayer and fasting and nothing is impossible. Freely we have received. Let us freely give.

VESSELS OF GLORY

Our Beloved carried on His body all of our iniquities and infirmities. This Perfect Man became sin that we might be glorified (2 COR 5:21). The Father carved His Son's body as a holy vessel equipped to carry many sons to glory (HEB 2:10). His side was pierced to form a place for every person in the Body of Christ. This is what made a way for us to become one with Jesus and His Father (JOHN 17:24). By confessing Jesus as Lord, our guilt is pardoned. We are declared innocent because Christ endured our punishment. Our Beloved delivers us from every demonic stronghold. He heals our every disease. Salvation is just the beginning. God has made a way to bring us into union with Himself. He desires for the very ones who rebelled against Him to partner with Him for eternity. Through His earthly body, Jesus brought the glory of heaven to earth. The Son also brought glory to His Father in heaven by completing the work He was given to do (JOHN 17:4).

Jesus' carved body is inlaid with each precious jewel He purchased as His prized possession. We have been grafted as sapphires into Christ. As we partake of His body, we become new creations (2 COR 5:17). He promises us spiritual bodies that will bear the likeness of the Man from heaven (1 COR 15:49). Christ perfects what is lacking in our faith (1 THESS 3:10). We become like glorious jewels. It is the Body of Christ that carries His glory to the ends of the earth. It was prophesied, "The earth shall be filled with the knowledge of the glory of the Lord as the waters cover the sea" (HAB 2:14). Beloved, how can this be except that we would be fashioned as vessels for honorable use, set apart as holy, prepared for every good work (2 TIM 2:21)? Even now the Potter is forming vessels to send forth into the nations. The Word of the Lord will run swiftly and be glorified (2 THESS 3:1). We are the precious jewels that will carry His glory. In order to do so we must be purified. Only then will our true beauty shine forth. We

> *He will be a vessel for honor, sanctified and useful for the Master, prepared for every good work.*
>
> 2 TIMOTHY 2:21

must enter the fiery kiln that causes our glazed colors to radiate with the splendor of our Beloved. It is His body we represent. We are the sapphires who will display His majesty for every nation to behold.

Let us give to the Lamb the reward of His suffering. Let us surrender to the Flame that we may become His full possession. Let us continually remember His enduring love, forgetting none of His benefits, that we might receive His full gift of redemption. This is why His body was broken for us. Let us take and eat it for the wholeness of our bodies, minds, and spirits. Yes, let us partake of the precious body of Christ. Beloved, let us freely give in the same way we have freely received. We will lay our hands on the sick and see them recover. We will cast out demons and watch them flee. We will go forth into the nations. These signs will follow us. We will be vessels who carry our Beloved's glory!

His *legs* are

pillars of marble

set on bases of fine *gold* ...

❦

Song 5:15

Chapter 11

His Legs—Righteous Judgment

ATTRIBUTE #8
His legs: Jesus' *administration* of the Father's will

PRAYER

Jesus, You are perfect from head to toe. Your leadership, divine activity, and administration are finer than gold. I love all Your ways; they are just and true (Rev 15:3). Righteousness and justice are the foundation of Your throne (Ps 89:14; 97:2). Your throne, O God, endures forever. The scepter of Your Kingdom is the scepter of righteousness (Ps 45:6). Righteous Judge, release Your government in this world. Let Your Kingdom come and Your will be done in my life (Matt 6:10). In Your majesty, ride forth victoriously. Defeat every enemy of my heart (Ps 45:4). Amen.

THE RIGHTEOUS JUDGE

Jesus is perfect in His ability to administer His Father's will. Heaven and earth will come together when our Beloved returns to establish His Kingdom "on earth as it is in heaven" (Eph 1:10; Matt 6:10). Our Beloved will reign forever (Rev 11:15). There will be no end to the increase of His government.

For unto us a Child is born, unto us a Son is given; and the government will be upon His shoulder. And His name will be called Wonderful, Counselor, Mighty God, Everlasting Father, Prince of Peace. Of the increase of His government and peace there will be no end, upon the throne of David and over His kingdom, to order it and establish it with judgment and justice from that time forward, even forever. The zeal of the Lord of hosts will perform this.   *—Isaiah 9:6-7*

This Perfect Man who has authority over all things will complete the work He started. He said to His disciples, "My food is to do the will of Him who sent Me, and to finish His work" (JOHN 4:34). This work is a story that continues from eternity past, long before time began. Father and Son together created all things. The only begotten of the Father, fully God and fully Man, stepped into earth in our likeness. He became the perfect sacrifice and reconciled us to God through His death and resurrection. His Father then exalted Him to the highest place and gave Him the name above all names. He is King of all kings. And His Kingdom is coming to earth. He has already come as our Messiah, and He will come again. Jesus is seated at the right hand of the Father interceding for His inheritance. Our Beloved will return to claim the ends of the earth as His possession (PS 2:8). The earth and all its fullness belong to Jesus (PS 24:1). He will fulfill all things spoken of by the prophets. The Son will accomplish His Father's will. The knowledge of our Beloved's glory will cover the entire earth (HAB 2:14).

For the earth will be filled with the knowledge of the glory of the LORD, as the waters cover the sea.

HABAKKUK 2:14

When John peered through an open door in heaven, the Lord showed him what would soon take place (REV 4-5). In the right hand of the Father was a scroll sealed with seven seals. It was the *title deed* to the earth. A mighty angel proclaimed, "Who is worthy to open the scroll and loose its seals?" John wept because no one in all of heaven, earth, or under the earth was found worthy to open the scroll. One of the elders told John, "Do not weep. Behold, the Lion of the tribe of Judah, the Root of David, has prevailed to open the scroll and to loose its seven seals." When John looked, he saw a Lamb that had been slain. It was Jesus Christ. The Son of God came forth and took the scroll from His Father's hand. This compelled the elders and living creatures to fall down and worship Him. He is the One worthy to open the scroll.

> Now when He had taken the scroll, the four living creatures and the twenty-four elders fell down before the Lamb, each having a harp, and golden bowls full of incense, which are the prayers of the saints. And they sang a new song, saying: "You are worthy to take the scroll, and to open its seals; for You were slain, and have redeemed us to God by Your blood out of every tribe and tongue and people and nation, and have made us kings and priests to our God; and we shall reign on the earth." —Revelation 5:8-10

Only one fully God and fully Man is able to bring the Father's plan to completion. This is the Lamb of God who takes away the sin of the world (JOHN 1:29). He alone is worthy to loose the seals that will release God's end-time judgments. Our Beloved purchased this right with His blood. The Father entrusts all judgment to His Son (JOHN 5:22). He has given Jesus authority over His enemies.

> For David himself said by the Holy Spirit: 'The LORD said to my Lord, "Sit at My right hand, till I make Your enemies Your footstool."' —Mark 12:36

Chapter 11: His Legs—Righteous Judgment

Jesus is the righteous Judge over the whole earth (GEN 18:25; 2 TIM 4:8). He is perfect in His ability to administer His Father's purposes.

> *I can of Myself do nothing. As I hear, I judge; and My judgment is righteous, because I do not seek My own will but the will of the Father who sent Me.* —John 5:30

What will our Beloved's judgment be? Day and night the voices of martyrs arise before the Lamb in heaven as they cry out with a loud voice, "How long, Sovereign Lord, holy and true, until you judge the inhabitants of the earth and avenge our blood?" (REV 6:10 NIV). Along with those slain for the Word of God, add the blood of millions of innocent Jews and aborted babies. Approximately six million Jews were killed during the Holocaust. Including non-Jewish victims, the estimate totals eleven million. Still, these numbers cannot compare to those murdered in the *silent Holocaust*. Over fifty million babies have been slaughtered since the 1973 legalization of abortion in America. The numbers continue to rise. Have we ever considered this? There is a deafening cry for vengeance resounding through the courts of heaven.

I am struck with the realization that God feels indignation every day (PS 7:11). Jesus is coming with vengeance to judge the earth. We often regard Him as the slain Lamb, but He is also a roaring Lion. He will judge both the living and the dead (2 TIM 4:1). In Chapter 9, "His Hands: Divine Activity," we looked at the severity of His wrath. If it surprises us that He will trample nations with fury, we may be more awestruck to recognize the worship He will receive for executing justice.

> *Then the seventh angel sounded: And there were loud voices in heaven, saying, "The kingdoms of this world have become the kingdoms of our Lord and of His Christ, and He shall reign*

forever and ever!" And the twenty-four elders who sat before God on their thrones fell on their faces and worshiped God, saying: "We give You thanks, O Lord God Almighty, the One who is and who was and who is to come, because You have taken Your great power and reigned. The nations were angry, and Your wrath has come, and the time of the dead, that they should be judged, and that You should reward Your servants the prophets and the saints, and those who fear Your name, small and great, and should destroy those who destroy the earth."   —Revelation 11:15-18

They sing the song of Moses, the servant of God, and the song of the Lamb, saying: "Great and marvelous are Your works, Lord God Almighty! Just and true are Your ways, O King of the saints! Who shall not fear You, O Lord, and glorify Your name? For You alone are holy. For all nations shall come and worship before You, for Your judgments have been manifested."   —Revelation 15:3-4

Then I heard a loud voice from the temple saying to the seven angels, "Go and pour out the bowls of the wrath of God …" Then the third angel poured out his bowl on the rivers … they became blood. And I heard the angel of the waters saying: "You are righteous, O Lord, the One who is and who was and who is to be, because You have judged these things. For they have shed the blood of saints and prophets, and You have given them blood to drink. For it is their just due." And I heard another … saying, "Even so, Lord God Almighty, true and righteous are Your judgments."   —Revelation 16:1, 4-7

The elders fall on their faces, worshiping Jesus for the coming of His Kingdom and wrath. Saints rejoice at the manifestation of the Lord's judgments. An angel who pours out God's wrath praises the Righteous Judge, saying, "You are righteous, O Lord ... because You have judged ... And You have given them blood to drink. For it is their just due." In fact, a multitude in heaven celebrates when the *great harlot* is judged.

> *After these things I heard a loud voice of a great multitude in heaven, saying, "Alleluia! Salvation and glory and honor and power belong to the Lord our God! For true and righteous are His judgments, because He has judged the great harlot who corrupted the earth with her fornication; and He has avenged on her the blood of His servants shed by her." Again they said, "Alleluia! Her smoke rises up forever and ever!" And the twenty-four elders and the four living creatures fell down and worshiped God who sat on the throne, saying, "Amen! Alleluia!"* —Revelation 19:1-4

All of our King's judgments are worthy of praise. He will perfectly accomplish the Father's plan. His ways are just. His administration is true. Are we ready to stand in agreement with our Beloved when He slays His enemies? I am comfortable singing love songs to Jesus as my Savior, Messiah, Redeemer, and Friend. I enjoy praising the One we call Alpha, Omega, Lord of lords, King of kings, Emmanuel, and Prince of Peace. But somehow worshiping the Judge for executing people does not sound as inviting. Although the Scriptures abound with testimonies and prophesies of His judgments, I had never before thought about praising Him for the outpouring of His wrath. This is not the Jesus we typically learn about in Sunday school. For many, this attribute of our Beloved is a new concept.

It is essential to fully know this Perfect Man for this reason. We must believe He is Altogether Lovely, that He is entirely perfect. Otherwise, we will be offended when Jesus' actions do not match our view of His character. This is why many Jews rejected their Messiah. They were expecting a King, but He came as a humble Child. How do we anticipate He will return? Beloved friends, know for sure that He is returning as a Judge. Blessed are those who are not offended (MATT 11:6).

> *"And blessed is he who is not offended because of Me."*
> MATTHEW 11:6

WATCH AND PRAY

Jesus will return with a sword to establish His everlasting Kingdom. He rules over the kings of the earth. His throne is forever. He is the King of Glory who is mighty in battle (PS 24:8). In justice this warrior rides forth victoriously. His arrows pierce the hearts of His enemies.

> *Gird Your sword upon Your thigh, O Mighty One, with Your glory and Your majesty. And in Your majesty ride prosperously because of truth, humility, and righteousness; and Your right hand shall teach You awesome things. Your arrows are sharp in the heart of the King's enemies; the peoples fall under You. Your throne, O God, is forever and ever; a scepter of righteousness is the scepter of Your kingdom. You love righteousness and hate wickedness …*
> *–Psalm 45:3-7*

Our Beloved is a mighty Man of war. He loves righteousness and hates wickedness. His name is Faithful and True. Christ is going to return on a white horse covered in blood as He judges and makes war.

Now I saw heaven opened, and behold, a white horse.
And He who sat on him was called Faithful and True, and
in righteousness He judges and makes war.   –Revelation 19:11

Who will listen to this warning? Who will not find the word of the Lord offensive? The whole world will be crying, "Peace, peace," when there is no peace.

To whom can I speak and give warning? Who will listen to
me? Their ears are closed so they cannot hear. The word
of the LORD is offensive to them; they find no pleasure in it.
They dress the wound of my people as though it were not
serious. "Peace, peace," they say, when there is no peace.
*   –Jeremiah 6:10, 14 NIV*

On the Mount of Olives, Jesus' disciples asked Him about the sign of His coming and the end of the age. He did not say, "You don't need to know because nothing really bad will happen. You won't have to suffer. Go about your life. Don't be concerned about the end of the age because it's not going to happen for another 2,000 years anyway." No! He responded to their inquiry by describing the initial birth pangs. He warned them repeatedly against both deception and offense at God in the approaching time of tribulation.

And Jesus answered and said to them: "Take heed that no one
deceives you. For many will come in My name, saying, 'I am
the Christ,' and will deceive many. And you will hear of wars
and rumors of wars. See that you are not troubled; for all these
things must come to pass, but the end is not yet. For nation
will rise against nation, and kingdom against kingdom. And

there will be famines, pestilences, and earthquakes in various places. All these are the beginning of sorrows. Then they will deliver you up to tribulation and kill you, and you will be hated by all nations for My name's sake. And then many will be offended, will betray one another, and will hate one another. Then many false prophets will rise up and deceive many. And because lawlessness will abound, the love of many will grow cold. But he who endures to the end shall be saved. And this gospel of the kingdom will be preached in all the world as a witness to all the nations, and then the end will come ... See, I have told you beforehand."

—Matthew 24:4-14, 25

In that day, He says, many will be offended and the love of most will grow cold. Even the elect will be deceived if possible (MARK 13:22). The only hope Jesus offers is, "Endure tribulation and preach the Gospel." Why was it necessary to warn His disciples of the signs? Why is His counsel still relevant for us today? Our Beloved knew that awakening a sense of urgency would keep us steady. Having the knowledge of God and wholehearted love for Jesus will sustain us to the very end. He told us beforehand so that we would not be taken by surprise. He is coming quickly, if not in our generation, then in our children's or grandchildren's. The day of the Lord is close at hand.

Blow the trumpet in Zion; sound the alarm on my holy hill.
Let all who live in the land tremble, for the day of the LORD
is coming. It is close at hand.   *—Joel 2:1-3*

Just look at the sky. Interpret the signs (MATT 16:2-3). Birth pangs are intensifying. We can easily think, "This doesn't apply to me. Jesus said no one knows the *exact* time of His return." True, but we do know the season. We are not to live at ease. Rather, He tells us, "Keep watch, *because* you do not know the day or the hour" (MATT 25:13 NIV).

> *But of that day and hour no one knows, not even the angels in heaven, nor the Son, but only the Father. Take heed, watch and pray; for you do not know when the time is. It is like a man going to a far country, who left his house and gave authority to his servants, and to each his work, and commanded the doorkeeper to watch. Watch therefore, for you do not know when the master of the house is coming— in the evening, at midnight, at the crowing of the rooster, or in the morning—lest, coming suddenly, he find you sleeping. And what I say to you, I say to all: Watch!*   —Mark 13:32-37

This reminds me of what Jesus said to His disciples in the garden of Gethsemane before His crucifixion. When He found them sleeping, He said, "Could you not watch with Me one hour? Watch and pray, lest you enter into temptation" (MATT 26:40-41). Beloved, are we watching? When the Son of Man returns, will He find faith? Will we be found watching and praying? Or will we still be sleeping? The day of the Lord will come swiftly. It will be as in the days of Noah. Many will be saying, "Peace and safety," but there will be sudden destruction. While everyone is eating, drinking, and laughing, He will come like a flood. "Therefore," Jesus alerts us, "Watch! *Because* you do not know the day, be ready! I am coming at an hour you do not expect."

> *But of that day and hour no one knows, not even the angels of heaven, but My Father only. But as the days of Noah were, so also will the coming of the Son of Man be.*

For as in the days before the flood, they were eating and drinking, marrying and giving in marriage, until the day that Noah entered the ark, and did not know until the flood came and took them all away, so also will the coming of the Son of Man be. Then two men will be in the field: one will be taken and the other left. Two women will be grinding at the mill: one will be taken and the other left. Watch therefore, for you do not know what hour your Lord is coming. But know this, that if the master of the house had known what hour the thief would come, he would have watched and not allowed his house to be broken into. Therefore you also be ready, for the Son of Man is coming at an hour you do not expect.

–Matthew 24:36-44

What was it like in the days of Noah? For a hundred years this faithful man built a boat. People thought he was crazy because there had never been rain before. His very life prophesied for a century. Those who scorned were all swept away in the flood. Noah diligently prepared not knowing what day or hour the flood would come, but God told him seven days in advance (GEN 7:4). It will be like this when the Son of Man returns. Our Beloved will come suddenly, like a thief in the night. We are instructed to live soberly. Attentive preparation is of utmost importance. We do not know the hour, but Jesus has given us signs to know when the day is near. We must watch so we will not be swept away. Peter, who denied Jesus when Satan sifted the disciples, reminds believers of the urgency to remain watchful.

Knowing this first: that scoffers will come in the last days, walking according to their own lusts, and saying, "Where is

the promise of His coming? ... But, beloved, do not forget
this one thing, that with the Lord one day is as a thousand
years, and a thousand years as one day. The Lord is not slack
concerning His promise ... But the day of the Lord will come
as a thief in the night ... Therefore ... what manner of persons
ought you to be ... hastening the coming of the day of God ...
Therefore, beloved, looking forward to these things, be diligent
to be found by Him in peace, without spot and blameless; you
therefore, beloved, since you know this beforehand, beware
lest you also fall from your own steadfastness, being led
away with the error of the wicked; but grow in the grace and
knowledge of our Lord and Savior Jesus Christ.   –2 Peter 3:3-18

As it was in Noah's time, many scoffers will say, "Where is the so-called *Reign* you say is supposed to come? Where is your promised King?" Many will scorn the name of Jesus Christ. Beloved, beware lest we fall from our own steadfastness. He has shown us beforehand what will take place. The only way we will remain faithful is by diligently seeking the Lord and growing in the knowledge of Him.

For this reason we ... ask that you may be filled with
the knowledge of His will in all wisdom and spiritual
understanding; that you may walk worthy of the Lord,
fully pleasing Him, being fruitful in every good work and
increasing in the knowledge of God.   –Colossians 1:9-10

We must continually increase in our knowledge of God. Studying the Scriptures should never become merely a religious ritual. It is unto something greater. Bible study is a doorway into relationship with our Beloved. It is our window into the knowledge of His nature. A time is coming when people will reject the truth. They will only listen to teaching that suits their own desires.

> For the time will come when men will not put up with sound doctrine. Instead, to suit their own desires, they will gather around them a great number of teachers to say what their itching ears want to hear. They will turn their ears away from the truth and turn aside to myths. —2 Timothy 4:3-4 NIV

Already people refuse sound doctrine and turn away from the truth. I spoke with a woman who claimed that she used to be a Christian missionary in Russia. She is now agnostic. Unfortunately, she has been led astray by the false teachings of our society. Seeking the knowledge of God day after day is essential. We cannot only study portions of Scripture that seem pleasant. We must seek the Lord's entire counsel (Jer 23:18). It is imperative that we perceive our Beloved's Words from Genesis to Revelation. This includes eschatology, which is the study of the end-times. The *Omega Course* curriculum provides an introduction for individuals desiring a foundational understanding of the last days (see "Road Maps: Tools for Your Journey").

Let us seek the Lord while He may be found (Is 55:6). This is how we can remain watchful. The day of the Lord is coming. He is not slack concerning His promise. Though it has been two thousand years, let us look for and hasten the day of His return.

> For the grace of God that brings salvation has appeared to all men, teaching us that, denying ungodliness and worldly lusts, we should live soberly, righteously, and godly in the present age, looking for the blessed hope and glorious appearing of our great God and Savior Jesus Christ. —Titus 2:11-13

Beloved, Jesus is coming quickly. Therefore, we should live soberly and eagerly anticipate His appearing. Let us watch and pray.

> *And behold, I am coming quickly, and My reward is with Me, to give to every one according to his work.* —Revelation 22:12

UNMOVABLE AND UNSHAKABLE

A day is coming when Jesus will shake everything, not only the earth, but also heaven. Only what cannot be shaken will remain.

> *See that you do not refuse Him who speaks. For if they did not escape who refused Him who spoke on earth, much more shall we not escape if we turn away from Him who speaks from heaven, whose voice then shook the earth; but now He has promised, saying, "Yet once more I shake not only the earth, but also heaven." Now this, "Yet once more," indicates the removal of those things that are being shaken, as of things that are made, that the things which cannot be shaken may remain. Therefore, since we are receiving a kingdom which cannot be shaken, let us have grace, by which we may serve God acceptably with reverence and godly fear. For our God is a consuming fire.* —Hebrews 12:25-29

Will we remain unshakable in that day? When Jesus shakes heaven as He shook the earth, how will we stand firm? In order to withstand the storm, we must build our lives on the Rock of Jesus Christ (1 COR 10:4). Every other ground is sinking sand. His Kingdom is unshakable.

> *Therefore whoever hears these sayings of Mine, and does them, I will liken him to a wise man who built his house on*

the rock: and the rain descended, the floods came, and the
winds blew and beat on that house; and it did not fall, for
it was founded on the rock. But everyone who hears these
sayings of Mine, and does not do them, will be like a foolish
man who built his house on the sand: and the rain descended,
the floods came, and the winds blew and beat on that house;
and it fell. And great was its fall.   –Matthew 7:24-27

The foolish one, whose home is built upon the sand, will be swept away by floodwaters. The wise one, whose foundation is the Rock of Christ, will not be shaken. When many are being deceived, we will resist the enemy only if we are in perfect agreement with our Beloved. If we make our dwelling in the tabernacle of the Most High, we will be unmovable. God will help us. He is the one who fights for us (JOSH 23:10).

There is a river whose streams shall make glad the city of God,
The holy place of the tabernacle of the Most High. God is in
the midst of her, she shall not be moved; God shall help her,
just at the break of dawn.   –Psalm 46:4-5

Jesus prepared His disciples for the shaking they would endure. Before they were scattered and persecuted for His name's sake, He asked, "Who do you say that I am?" Confidence in the name of God would be their anchor. Peter replied to Jesus, "You are the Christ, the Son of the living God."

He said to them, "But who do you say that I am?" Simon
Peter answered and said, "You are the Christ, the Son of the
living God."   –Matthew 16:15-16

Our Beloved asks us the same question. So who do *we* say that He is? Yes, He is Christ, God's own Son, but He is so much more. He is our Maker and our Husband. He is our Master and our Friend. He is our Savior, Provider, Deliverer, and Healer. Jesus is the King of Glory. He is the Almighty God, the Everlasting Father, the Prince of Peace. He is the spotless Lamb. He is God Transcendent. There is no one like Him. His name is infinite. But do we say He is Judge of the earth?

> *O God, to whom vengeance belongs, shine forth! Rise up,*
> *O Judge of the earth; render punishment to the proud.*
> *–Psalm 94:1-2*

We must know His name. Knowledge of this One who is Altogether Lovely is what keeps us steady. It is only through His name that we can stand with confidence in the face of great trouble. Those who love His name rejoice and take refuge in Him (Ps 5:11). The name of the Lord is our strong tower (Prov 18:10). In His name there is safety. We must be firmly rooted and grounded, established in His love (Eph 3:17). Our roots must go deep in the knowledge of His Word. Beloved, these few pages are merely a brief introduction to Jesus' nature, personality, and character. This must be our lifelong pursuit: to ever increase in the knowledge of God. A.W. Tozer offers profound insight in *Knowledge of the Holy*.

> *The name of the LORD is a strong tower; the righteous run to it and are safe.*
> Proverbs 18:10

There will be a generation who sees the Lord. It may be ours. The issue is not whether or not we will see His appearing. What matters is that we prepare ourselves and the next generation. We are His Bride. Let us make ourselves ready (Rev 19:7). Let us loose our grasp on temporal things (ECCLES 1:14) and press on for the prize of the upward call in Christ Jesus (PHIL 3:14). Let us live with our eyes and our hearts fixed on eternity (2 COR 4:18; ECCLES 3:11). And let us train up our children in the way they should go (PROV 22:6). Jesus sternly warned His disciples to watch and be ready. Just because it seems He has delayed in coming for two millennia, is His Word any less relevant? No, but all the more. The time is near. If the Kingdom of God was at hand then, how much more is it now?

For the wedding of the Lamb has come, and his bride has made herself ready.

REVELATION 19:7 NIV

Are we ready? We are quick to say, "I will not deny Christ." Is this not the same response Peter gave? He knew Jesus personally. He saw the signs and wonders first-hand. He swore that he would not deny Jesus. Why should he say anything less? Peter's confidence in his ability to stand firm until the end can be easily justified.

Then Jesus said to them, "All of you will be made to stumble because of Me this night, for it is written: 'I will strike the Shepherd, and the sheep will be scattered' ... Peter said to Him, "Even if all are made to stumble, yet I will not be." Jesus said to him, "Assuredly, I say to you that today, even this night, before the rooster crows twice, you will deny Me three times." But he spoke more vehemently, "If I have to die with You, I will not deny You!" And they all said likewise. —Mark 14:27-31

So who are we to say that we will not deny the Lord when we encounter such severe testing? How will we respond when false prophets arise and the Antichrist shows up on the scene? What will we do when all are required to have the mark of the beast to buy or sell (REV 13:17)? These are serious questions. The pressure will be far greater than we can imagine. God's people are ruined for lack of knowledge (HOS 4:6).

> *"Watch and pray,*
> *lest you enter*
> *into temptation.*
> *The spirit indeed*
> *is willing, but*
> *the flesh is weak."*
>
> MATTHEW 26:41

What Peter failed to comprehend was the depravity of his own heart. Only God truly knows the depth of our capacity to sin. Jesus told Peter that he would deny Christ not just once but three times. He warned them that although the spirit is willing, the flesh is weak. This is why He told His disciples to watch and pray. He knew that if their spirits were not continually strengthened in fellowship with God they would fall into temptation (MATT 26:41). Jesus has given us the same warning beforehand so that we may be prepared.

Those who were imprisoned in Nazi concentration camps probably never dreamed of experiencing such suffering. I have heard that out of fear many Christians refused to help the Jews. Churches would sing hymns louder and louder to drown out the screams of prisoners from passing trains. *The Heavenly Man* is Brother Yun's astonishing account of the tribulation he suffered for giving leadership to the movement of underground Churches in China. Most people who live in Western cultures are sheltered from the horrific tortures inflicted upon Christians across the globe. How could we possibly be ready?

Though we are weak, God knows our willingness to suffer persecution for His name's sake. This is the *dark but lovely* paradox (SONG 1:5). When we discover our true darkness, it is scandalous to our hearts. In order to endure until the end, we must face this crisis. Peter had not begun his ministry when he denied the Lord three times. Such failure caused him to give up completely. After Jesus rose from the grave and appeared to His disciples, Peter returned to fishing (JOHN 21:3-17). How could he preach? This trial was necessary to prepare him for the fiery ordeals he would face later when Jesus was no longer by his side. When Jesus came to Peter in the midst of his discouragement, what did He say? He asked Peter three times, "Do you love me?" He did not rebuke him or talk to him about his ministry. Jesus addressed the one thing that mattered. Was Peter lovesick? Jesus already knew the answer. He perceives the *Yes* in our spirits even when we do not. Though we see our darkness, He views us as *lovely* through the lens of His grace. Peter was not so sure. He was still surprised by his sin. No wonder Jesus inquired of his love three times. Peter needed to hear the declaration of his affections for the Lord in place of each time he had denied them. This is the only way to be ready for trouble, persecution, famine, danger, and all kinds of tribulation. Watching and waiting begins with our hearts. We have to stay near the Lord. Our hearts are prepared only through diligent pursuit of the Perfect Man, Christ Jesus.

Contemplate the parable of the ten virgins (MATT 25:1-13). When the Bridegroom was delayed, they all fell asleep. The foolish virgins had failed to buy oil while they had time. When the Bridegroom returned, they went in search for more oil and missed their chance to enter in. Will we be like them, consumed with the things of this world? Or will we take time now to gather oil like the wise virgins? Will we make ourselves ready for our Bridegroom? Are we spending time cultivating intimacy with Jesus, diligently seeking Him, and studying His Word so that we may be well acquainted with His ways? Do we spend our time on what really matters? We may well build on a solid foundation, but the material we use will be tested by fire (1 COR 3:12-14). Only eternal things remain. When all else fades away, all we have is Jesus.

I am a
stranger
on earth;
do not
hide your
commands
from me.

PSALM
119:19 NIV

Beloved, this world is passing away. It is not really our home. We are strangers passing through (PS 119:19). Are we engrossed in our culture? Will we be surprised when our Beloved comes like a thief? We must stay alert. For this reason He said we would not know the day or hour. If we are not watchful, the customs of our society will lull us to sleep. Let us watch and pray so that we will not fall into temptation. Let us seek the knowledge of God so that we may not be moved. Let us build our lives with silver and gold, the only things that last for eternity. We are living for another age!

While we live in captivity in this foreign land, let us set our hearts like Daniel. Let us purpose not to defile ourselves with the delicacies of our world's culture (DAN 1:8). Let us walk worthy of our Lord's calling, set apart for His glory (EPH 4:1). Only those with clean hands and pure hearts may ascend the hill of the Lord (PS 24:3-4). Let us purify our hearts and go to the mountain of the Lord, that He may teach us His ways (IS 2:3). We are beginning to learn them even now. He has given us pillars called the Beatitudes to strengthen our structure. Jesus says, "Blessed are the poor in spirit, those who mourn, the meek, those who hunger and thirst for righteousness, the merciful, the pure in heart, the peacemakers, and all of those who are persecuted for righteousness (MATT 5:2-12). We make ourselves ready for our Beloved's coming by living according to His Word. Let us recognize our sinful depravity. Let us lament over our sins and repent. Let us hunger for the Living Word and thirst for the Fountain of Life. When we endure persecution for the sake of righteousness, let us gaze into heaven to behold the glory of God (ACTS 7:55-56). Jesus' entire Sermon on the Mount teaching is full of strong pillars. Let us build our lives on the One whose legs are pillars of marble set on bases of fine gold. The Lord will be with us in the wilderness as a pillar of cloud by day to show us the way and a pillar of fire by night to give us His light.

And the LORD went before them by day in a pillar of cloud to lead the way, and by night in a pillar of fire to give them light, so as to go by day and night. —Exodus 13:21

I pray that we may approve what is excellent, that we may be sincere and without offense until the day of Christ (PHIL 1:10). At His coming, may we be found watching and waiting. Let not our hearts be weighed down by the cares of this life. Let us stay awake and alert. Let us seek the One who is able to keep us steadfast by His name.

To him who is able to keep you from falling and to present you before his glorious presence without fault and with great joy—to the only God our Savior be glory, majesty, power and authority, through Jesus Christ our Lord, before all ages, now and forevermore! Amen. —Jude 1:24-25 NIV

God's Kingdom is coming to Earth. Everything will be shaken when Jesus returns. If we are established on our Beloved's foundation, we can have confidence. He is our strength (Is 41:10). Let us stand in agreement with this Perfect Man as He administrates His Father's will. When our Judge brings justice to the earth, let us praise Him for His righteous judgments. His administration is perfect. May His will be done (MATT 6:9-10). Let us declare, "Lord, You are just and true. Come with Your Kingdom. Beloved, have Your way!"

Your kingdom come. Your will be done on earth as it is in heaven.
MATTHEW 6:10

His

countenance

is like *Lebanon,*

excellent as the cedars.

❦

Song 5:15

Chapter 12

His Countenance—Consuming

ATTRIBUTE #9

His countenance: Impartation of Jesus' *nature*

PRAYER

Jesus, I long to behold Your face. This is my only desire, that I may gaze upon Your beauty all the days of my life (Ps 27:4). Why should I be as one who is veiled beside the flocks of Your companions (Song 1:7)? Shine the light of Your countenance on my heart (Num 6:25-26). If I have found favor in Your sight, show me Your ways that I may know You. Lord, please show me Your glory (Exod 33:13, 18). Amen.

LIGHT MANIFEST

Jesus' countenance is more majestic than the snow-capped mountains of Lebanon. His radiance is more magnificent than the sun shining in all of its strength (Rev 1:16). The Lord longs to impart His nature to our hearts with power. Are we seeking to behold His face? Are we asking this glorious One to impart His nature? This is something we often take for granted. If we have grown up in Christian homes attending Church regularly, we can easily think we *know* God. In reality, we merely know *about* Him and very little at that. What does it mean to know God?

His countenance was like the sun shining in its strength.

REVELATION 1:16

Who is this One shining like the sun who sits enthroned above the circle of the earth? Do we truly know the One who created the universe and made the starry hosts by the breath of His mouth? Who is this One who knew us before He formed us in our mothers' wombs? Who is this One: infinite, omnipotent, omniscient, omnipresent, transcendent, and incarnate? Who is He as the triune God: Father, Son, and Holy Spirit? Who is Jesus as the Lamb slain from before the foundations of the earth, the One worthy to take the scroll from the Father's hand and execute justice on the earth? Who is the Word made flesh? Who is this One with eyes like flames of fire? Who is this One, glorious in majesty, blazing like a fire with intensity far greater than the sun? What causes elders to cast their crowns and living creatures to cry, "Holy"? Who is the One whose splendor elicits joyful praise through all of heaven? Why does every knee bow and tongue confess He is Lord? Who is this One before whose radiant presence clouds move forth? Why does heaven tremble and the earth quake? Who is this Majestic God? Beloved, we have just begun to touch the surface of the knowledge of God. But this hope we have: if we search for the Lord with all of our hearts we will find Him.

Then you will call upon Me and go and pray to Me, and I will listen to you. And you will seek Me and find Me, when you search for Me with all your heart. I will be found by you, says the LORD ... —Jeremiah 29:12-14

It is our Beloved's pleasure to reveal Himself. No one has ever seen God, but we have beheld the glory of His countenance. The One who is at the Father's side has made Him known.

*No one has ever seen God, but God the One and Only, who is
at the Father's side, has made him known.* —John 1:18 NIV

The true Light stepped out of heaven into darkness. The knowledge of
God's glory burns brightly in the face of Jesus Christ.

*For it is the God who commanded light to shine out of
darkness, who has shone in our hearts to give the light of
the knowledge of the glory of God in the face of Jesus Christ.*
—2 Corinthians 4:6

The Father pronounced His glory through our Messiah. He is our Light
and Salvation (Ps 27:1). The only begotten Son who is in the Father's
bosom made His tabernacle among us. The Word of God became flesh
(Lev 26:11; John 1:14, 18). The Faithful Witness declared God's name.
If we have seen Jesus, we have seen the Father. He displayed the Father's
mercy and compassion, His grace and truth, and His perfect Justice.
Every healing, deliverance, exhortation, and rebuke was according to
His Father's character. Every act of obedience, humility, kindness, and
forgiveness expressed His Father's heart. He did only what He saw His
Father doing. Jesus is the exact representation of God's nature.

*God, who at various times and in various ways spoke in time
past to the fathers by the prophets, has in these last days
spoken to us by His Son, whom He has appointed heir of all
things, through whom also He made the worlds; who being
the brightness of His glory and the express image of His
person, and upholding all things by the word of His power,
when He had by Himself purged our sins, sat down at the
right hand of the Majesty on high.* —Hebrews 1:1-3

Chapter 12: His Countenance—Consuming

God has revealed the brightness of His glory through this Perfect Man. When the Lord was transfigured before Peter, James, and John, light radiated from His face and garments.

> Jesus took with him Peter, James and John the brother of James, and led them up a high mountain by themselves. There he was transfigured before them. His face shone like the sun, and his clothes became as white as the light. Just then there appeared before them Moses and Elijah, talking with Jesus. —Matthew 17:1-3 NIV

> He took Peter, John, and James and went up on the mountain to pray. As He prayed, the appearance of His face was altered, and His robe became white and glistening. And behold, two men talked with Him, who were Moses and Elijah ... —Luke 9:28-30

After Christ's resurrection, the Lord appeared to His disciples and more than five hundred others (1 COR 15:5-6). At the tomb two women beheld His countenance like bolts of lightning and His clothes like shimmering snow (MATT 28:3). On a path that led to Emmaus, Jesus appeared and conversed with two of His disciples. These men later recalled their hearts burning within. While they recounted the story to others, Jesus again stood in their midst (LUKE 24:13-43). These have seen and testified of the Light made manifest.

Beloved, we have seen the Light of the world and yet have heard barely a whisper of His majesty. Moses longed to behold God's glory. When he inquired, the Lord responded by proclaiming His name.

"I will make all My goodness pass before you, and I will proclaim the name of the LORD before you. I will be gracious to whom I will be gracious, and I will have compassion on whom I will have compassion." But He said, "You cannot see My face; for no man shall see Me, and live." And the LORD said, "Here is a place by Me, and you shall stand on the rock. So it shall be, while My glory passes by, that I will put you in the cleft of the rock, and will cover you with My hand while I pass by. Then I will take away My hand, and you shall see My back; but My face shall not be seen." … And the LORD passed before him and proclaimed, "The LORD, the LORD God, merciful and gracious, longsuffering, and abounding in goodness and truth, keeping mercy for thousands, forgiving iniquity and transgression and sin, by no means clearing the guilty, visiting the iniquity of the fathers upon the children and the children's children to the third and the fourth generation."

–Exodus 33:19-23; 34:6-7

As Moses stood within the rock, the Lord revealed His very nature. He overwhelmed him with His beauty. This is how we too will know our Beloved. God tells us who He is. Why should we remain as those who are veiled (SONG 1:7)? The Israelites were blinded, but the veil is removed through Christ (2 COR 3:14-16). The Lord will shine the light of His countenance on us. He will cause His goodness to pass before our eyes, but we have to ask for it. When Mary sought Him at the tomb, He said, "Woman, why are you weeping? Whom are you seeking?" He then called her by name (JOHN 20:15-16). He enjoys revealing Himself to those who search. If we ask, He will answer.

CONSUMING FIRE

Are we desperate for the Lord's presence? David's desire to know God intimately was so intense that he proclaimed it to be his only desire in life. This king set his heart to pursue the knowledge of God.

One thing I have desired of the LORD, that will I seek: that I may dwell in the house of the LORD all the days of my life, to behold the beauty of the LORD, and to inquire in His temple.
—Psalm 27:4

So what does it mean to gaze on the beauty of the Living God? How does the Lord shine the light of His countenance? He first showed Himself to Moses as a flame of fire.

And the Angel of the LORD appeared to him in a flame of fire from the midst of a bush. So he looked, and behold, the bush was burning with fire, but the bush was not consumed.
—Exodus 3:2

Why did the Lord appear this way? He was proclaiming His name: *Consuming Fire.* He blazes hotter and brighter than the sun. When Moses went to the mountain of God, the Israelites saw God's glory like a raging fire (EXOD 24:17). After being in God's presence, Moses' face was so radiant he wore a veil (EXOD 34:35). The sun is millions of miles from Earth, but staring at it could impair our vision. Any matter that comes near it disintegrates. How then can we consider gazing upon the Eternal Flame? Would not His Presence forever blind us? Would we not be entirely consumed? Even the soldiers who threw Shadrach, Meshach, and Abed-Nego into the fiery furnace were burned up. How did the fire not destroy these three men of God?

Then Nebuchadnezzar was full of fury ... He spoke and commanded that they heat the furnace seven times more than it was usually heated. And he commanded certain mighty men of valor ... to bind Shadrach, Meshach, and Abed-Nego, and cast them into the burning fiery furnace. Then these men ... were cast into the midst of the burning fiery furnace. Therefore, because the king's command was urgent, and the furnace exceedingly hot, the flame of the fire killed those men who took up Shadrach, Meshach, and Abed-Nego. And these three men ... fell down bound into the midst of the burning fiery furnace. Then King Nebuchadnezzar was astonished; and he rose in haste and spoke, saying to his counselors, "Did we not cast three men bound into the midst of the fire?" They answered and said to the king, "True, O king." "Look!" he answered, "I see four men loose, walking in the midst of the fire; and they are not hurt, and the form of the fourth is like the Son of God." Then Nebuchadnezzar went near the mouth of the burning fiery furnace and spoke, saying, "Shadrach, Meshach, and Abed-Nego, servants of the Most High God, come out, and come here." Then Shadrach, Meshach, and Abed-Nego came from the midst of the fire ... They saw these men on whose bodies the fire had no power; the hair of their head was not singed nor were their garments affected, and the smell of fire was not on them.   *–Daniel 3:19-27*

The furnace had been heated seven times more than usual! What kept these three men alive? Consuming Fire was in their midst. The Lord appeared as the fourth Man walking among them.

Chapter 12: His Countenance—Consuming

There are two kinds of fire. Either lusts of our flesh can burn inside or we can be consumed by God's holy fire. The furnace could not kill these men because they had not kindled worldly fire. They did not live according to their culture. Neither did they bow down to its customs. When the king commanded them to worship his idol, they refused. The Fire of God had so entirely consumed the lives of these men that earthly afflictions had no power over them. The Living Flame rendered a man-made fire powerless over these ones whose hearts were faithful to Him. When we catch a vision of living for the age to come, we are untouchable. God's seal of love upon our hearts guards us.

Set me as a seal upon your heart, as a seal upon your arm;
for love is as strong as death, jealousy as cruel as the grave;
its flames are flames of fire, a most vehement flame. Many
waters cannot quench love, nor can the floods drown it ...
—Song of Solomon 8:6-7

Beloved, God's love is like flashes of fire. The light of Jesus' countenance is more vehement than any other flame. Our Beloved's name is *Jealous Jealousy*. He loves righteousness and hates wickedness. The Lord makes His name known to His adversaries the same way wildfire spreads in a forest (Is 64:2). His fire is unquenchable; it burns away everything that is not love. Mountains melt like wax in His presence.

The LORD reigns ... A fire goes before Him, and burns up
His enemies round about. His lightnings light the world; the
earth sees and trembles. The mountains melt like wax at the
presence of the LORD, at the presence of the Lord of the whole
earth. The heavens declare His righteousness, and all the
peoples see His glory.   *—Psalm 97:1-6*

Fire devours all of God's enemies. When the Israelites complained against the Lord in the wilderness, His fire burned among them and consumed some in the outskirts of camp (Num 11:1). Another time two hundred and fifty leaders questioned the authority of Moses and Aaron. A fire came out from the Lord and consumed this rebellious congregation (Num 16:35). His fierce anger was aroused over and over. The fire of the Lord burned among His people and consumed them. When God proclaims His name, whatever is righteous remains, but everything wicked is destroyed. The zeal of the Lord breaks in like an explosion of light consuming darkness entirely.

HOLY FEAR

It is not surprising that the children of Israel were afraid when God made a covenant with them in Horeb. When the Lord spoke with the Israelites face to face from the fire, Moses had to stand as a mediator declaring the Ten Commandments.

> The LORD our God made a covenant with us in Horeb …
> The LORD talked with you face to face on the mountain from
> the midst of the fire. I stood between the LORD and you …
> to declare to you the word of the LORD; for you were afraid
> because of the fire … —Deuteronomy 5:1-5

What are these commandments? In summary, the Lord said, "Do not have any other gods, do not worship idols, do not misuse the Lord's name, keep the Sabbath holy, honor your father and mother, do not murder, do not commit adultery, do not steal, do not lie, and do not covet." On two stone tablets God gave the children of Israel this basic code of morality (Deut 5:6-22). They heard God's voice, saw His glory, and lived, but refused to hear His voice any further lest they die.

So it was, when you heard the voice from the midst of the darkness, while the mountain was burning with fire, that you came near to me … And you said: "Surely the LORD our God has shown us His glory and His greatness, and we have heard His voice from the midst of the fire. We have seen this day that God speaks with man; yet he still lives. Now therefore, why should we die? For this great fire will consume us; if we hear the voice of the LORD our God anymore, then we shall die … You go near and hear all that the LORD our God may say, and tell us all that the LORD our God says to you …"

–Deuteronomy 5:23-27

They begged Moses to listen to God and relay the message for fear that His fire would consume them. The Lord knew the wickedness in their hearts and agreed with their evaluation. He longingly spoke to Moses: "Oh, that they had such a heart in them that they would fear Me and always keep all My commandments, that it might be well with them and with their children forever" (DEUT 5:28-29).

Only those with clean hands and pure hearts may ascend God's holy hill to behold His glory (Ps 24:3-4). Do we really desire to see Him face to face? IHOP–KC is located in the *Show Me State*. Like Moses, we constantly pray, "Lord, show me Your glory. Let Your goodness pass before me, right before my eyes." We sing, "Let the light of your face shine on my heart. Let me feel it."

The LORD bless you and keep you; the LORD make His face shine upon you, and be gracious to you; the LORD lift up His countenance upon you, and give you peace.

–Numbers 6:24-26

Do we know what we are asking? What would happen if God actually lifted up His countenance on us? This Jealous Flame of Love would consume every area of darkness in our lives.

The Israelites were well aware that anyone who saw the Lord face to face would die. Are we ready for this? We are inviting the Living Flame to ignite our hearts, consume our darkness, and set us ablaze. The Father of glory has transferred us from the power of darkness into the Kingdom of the Son of His love (COL 1:13). We are asking this Son to

> *He has delivered us from the power of darkness and conveyed us into the kingdom of the Son of His love.*
>
> COLOSSIANS 1:13

rise and shine in our hearts that we may be holy as He is holy. We are saying, "Lord, touch my lips with Your fiery coal. Cleanse me from all unrighteousness" (Is 6:5-6).

God is a Refiner's Fire. He purifies. Our Beloved does not tolerate iniquity. He searches our hearts to see if there is any perverse way in us. Nothing is hidden from His fiery eyes. He knows the thoughts and intentions of our hearts. His burning gaze wipes away every wicked thing that quenches love. True Light penetrates our wickedness, deceitfulness, and depravity. The fire of God burns away evil desires, motives, intentions, addictions, habits, anger, adultery, murder, malice, covetousness, hatred, envy, strife, sexual immorality, compromise, disobedience, apathy, perversion, lethargy, complacency, and every sinful practice. This is the light of His countenance. This is the way He imparts His nature. He ignites our hearts and infuses us with passion. We cannot just stop, drop, and roll to put out His fiery love. It does not work that way. His love is unrelenting. His passion for our souls is unyielding as the grave. The greatest floods cannot quench God's love (SONG 8:6-7). We cannot escape the heat of His gaze. Try as we may to chase other lovers, they perish in the furnace of His affections. God is after our hearts. He stops at nothing until He possesses us entirely.

If we could only see this Perfect Man and His eyes like flames of fire (REV 1:14). Our Beloved is all-consuming. Jealousy is His fury. When we see Him face to face, we burn. He does not relent until we become His pure and spotless Bride. Oh, dear friends, that we would fear the Lord and always obey His commandments!

> *The fear of the LORD is the beginning of wisdom, and the knowledge of the Holy One is understanding.* –Proverbs 9:10

Let us be wise and serve our Lord with holy fear. This is the beginning of wisdom. Let us tremble before the *All-Consuming Fire.*

> *Now therefore, be wise, O kings; be instructed, you judges of the earth. Serve the LORD with fear, and rejoice with trembling. Kiss the Son, lest He be angry, and you perish in the way, when His wrath is kindled but a little. Blessed are all those who put their trust in Him.* –Psalm 2:10-13

Let us honor the Son, lest He become angry and we perish when His wrath is kindled. His Word is like a double-edged sword (HEB 4:12). It burns like a fire and breaks the rocks like a hammer (JER 23:28-29). His voice splinters the cedars.

> *The voice of the LORD breaks the cedars, yes, the LORD splinters the cedars of Lebanon.* –Psalm 29:5

Who can stand before the Lord? The God of glory thunders (PS 29:3). From His throne proceed lightnings, thunderings, and voices. Before

His throne burn seven Spirits (REV 4:5). How do we escape from being consumed by worldly fire? We must receive the impartation of God's Consuming Fire, which includes: the Spirit of the Lord, wisdom, understanding, counsel, might, knowledge, and the fear of the Lord.

> *The Spirit of the LORD shall rest upon Him, the Spirit of wisdom and understanding, the Spirit of counsel and might, the Spirit of knowledge and of the fear of the LORD. His delight is in the fear of the LORD …* —Isaiah 11:2-3

Beloved, let us delight in the fear of the Lord. Let us enter the Refiner's kiln, that we may forever be changed. Let us position our cold hearts before the Jealous Flame of Love so that all our goals, desires, and dreams melt into His. Let us lift our faces to behold His glory. May He give us the fear of the Lord that we might burn with holy passion!

SET ABLAZE

We need divine illumination to set us on a different course. Paul's encounter with this brilliant Light blinded him to worldly pursuits and caused a complete turn-around. Gazing on God's beauty brings a reorientation to our lives. It sets us into our eternal calling and causes us to carry our hearts differently. When God's light breaks in, we begin to live like men and women of faith of whom the world is not worthy (HEB 11). We need His fire burning on the inside!

Our Beloved is just waiting for us to ask. Jesus greatly desires to shine the light of His countenance. He wants to consume us entirely so we can love Him with all of our hearts, all of our souls, all of our minds, and all of our strength. This will happen as we gaze upon His glory. How can we stand before the Eternal Burning One and not be changed? How can we come before Him and not be transformed? His light transforms our thoughts, emotions, values, and actions. Let us say like Moses, "I will not go without Your Presence. Lord, show me Your glory" (EXOD 33:14-18). We cannot discern our errors. We need His light to show the way so we can see clearly.

> The commandment of the LORD is pure, enlightening the eyes … Moreover by them Your servant is warned … Who can understand his errors? Cleanse me from secret faults. Keep back Your servant also from presumptuous sins; let them not have dominion over me. Then I shall be blameless, and I shall be innocent of great transgression. −Psalm 19:8-13

Only the Lord can disclose the secrets sins of our hearts. His Word is light. It illuminates the hidden fault lines and then burns them away. He shifts our thoughts and changes our emotional chemistry.

We are asking Him to consume all our senses. We need His light to flood our thoughts, time, emotions, activities, desires, vision, hearing, speech, and entire lives. The Lord deposits the light of His Kingdom in our hearts. This is the inner strength for which Paul prays (EPH 3:16). Without it we are like flickering wicks, easily snuffed out. Fortunately, our Beloved does not extinguish dimly burning candles but instead ignites us with His power and light (IS 42:3). The light of the Living God allows us to shine like blazing torches. His Holy Spirit oil keeps our hearts burning brightly.

Why then do we hide our light under a bush? Are we ashamed of the Gospel? Why should we shrink back? We are the light of the world. A city on a hill cannot be hidden, so neither should we.

You are the light of the world. A city that is set on a hill cannot be hidden. Nor do they light a lamp and put it under a basket, but on a lampstand, and it gives light to all who are in the house. Let your light so shine before men, that they may see your good works and glorify your Father in heaven.

—Matthew 5:14-16

God imparts His countenance to fill our eyes with heavenly light. If the light in our hearts is darkness, how great is that darkness?

The lamp of the body is the eye. If therefore your eye is good, your whole body will be full of light. But if your eye is bad, your whole body will be full of darkness. If therefore the light that is in you is darkness, how great is that darkness!

—Matthew 6:22-23

Nothing should hinder our light from shining. For this reason, we gaze upon Jesus as those with unveiled faces. We welcome His purification that we may ascend the mountain to see His face. His fire burns up the chaff, purges the dross, and purifies us into vessels that are worthy to carry His glory. If darkness tries to consume us, it cannot because His light lives within. Even darkness is as light to Him and the night shines like the day (Ps 139:11-12). We are reflections of the true Light of the world. The Lord permeates our beings with His glory so that our whole bodies are full of light. If we follow Him we do not walk in darkness but have the light of life.

I am the light of the world. He who follows Me shall not walk in darkness, but have the light of life. *—John 8:12*

In the heavens, God has set a tabernacle for the sun, which is like a bridegroom coming forth from his chamber (PS 19:4-5). Still, in all its brightness this star cannot dispel the darkness of night. But God is Light. In Him there is no darkness (1 JOHN 1:5). His light is limitless. The New Jerusalem will be full of light. There will be no night. It has no need of the sun. God's glory illuminates it (REV 21:22-25). Truly He is the Bridegroom coming forth. And so we rejoice because we see His light. The Morning Star shines in our hearts (2 PET 1:19). We are transformed from glory to glory to look like Him. As we gaze upon His beauty, we shine brighter.

And we, who with unveiled faces all reflect the Lord's glory, are being transformed into his likeness with ever-increasing glory, which comes from the Lord, who is the Spirit.
—2 Corinthians 3:18 NIV

The light of our Beloved's countenance sets us ablaze. It causes us to burn with holy fire. Is not His Word like a fire shut up in our bones (JER 20:9)? Do not our hearts burn within us (LUKE 24:32)? The Light of the world illuminates our hearts so we shine like stars in this perverse generation (PHIL 2:15-16). The Lord makes our righteousness shine like the dawn and our justice like the noonday sun (PS 37:6). Like John the Baptist, we are like burning and shining lamps preparing the way of our Beloved's return (JOHN 5:35).

Burning men and women impact every sphere of society. When the Lord takes full possession of our hearts we are utterly transformed. We are filled with the knowledge of His will. His ways are so much higher than ours. His thoughts are far superior. When God takes hold of us completely, our hearts are set on fire with His desires. We begin to know His yearnings, to love righteousness and hate wickedness, to walk worthy of His calling, fully pleasing, and continually bearing good fruit. This is the light that tears down altars of abortion and every evil practice. Are we close enough to be consumed by the fire of His love? Can we feel our hearts beating to the rhythm of His?

What would happen if the Body of Christ were set ablaze with passion for Jesus? The Church would go forth like a mighty forest fire. No one would be able to ignore such intensity. This kind of burning sets whole nations on fire. We are like cities at the top of hills all across the world giving light to our communities. The Lord sends us forth as messengers of light running swiftly through our land to glorify His Word. We light up our governments, our schools, our businesses, our media, our families, and our social systems. And so we let our light shine that others may see and glorify God. With blazing hearts God's people can start a revolution.

Why should we be like dying stars shining in our own strength until we burn out? We need His zeal to consume us. We need desperation for the One who is Light. We must surrender to the Flame of Love. Let us go before this Burning Man who alone sets our hearts on fire. Let us stare into His eyes of fire and behold His glory every day. It is His Spirit that blazes within. He is the One who said, "Let there be light." Jesus Christ shines through each one of us so that those who walk in darkness may see His radiant light (MATT 4:16). Just one glimpse of His countenance is enough to reform hearts and revolutionize societies. He is fascinating! Such terrifying beauty causes the seraphim to shield their faces and feet. When one of them

> *The people who sat in darkness have seen a great light ...*
> MATTHEW 4:16

*Holy, holy, holy is
the LORD
Almighty; the
whole earth is
full of his glory!*

Isaiah 6:3 NIV

declares His transcendence to another it shakes the whole temple (Is 6:1-4). This is the result of gazing. Our Beloved's beauty is overwhelmingly stunning. His majesty thrills our hearts. We can do nothing less than proclaim, "Holy, holy, holy is the Lord. The earth is full of His glory!" When this message resounds across the nation, it will shake our entire culture.

I pray this would become the cry of our hearts: to gaze upon the beauty of the Lord and *burn*. Let us draw nearer to God that we might see Him face to face. We may be consumed but we will not die. We will become even more alive. May everything die that is not from Him. Let us live to declare His goodness, His beauty, and His passion. The only thing worth living and dying for is knowing our Beloved and making Him known. Let us seek His face that we may be burning and shining lamps in this dark world. Oh, that we might see the face of God.

Let us call out to Him, "Lord, shine the light of Your countenance on my heart. Let me feel Your jealous flame consuming all my senses. I long to be near You and feel Your Presence. Take full possession of my heart. Let me see Your face. Transform me into Your image. Jesus, make me a burning and shining lamp in my generation, in my home, my family, my community, my ministry, my workplace, my post office, my grocery store, my recreation center. Everywhere I go, let me radiate Your majestic splendor. Let me see the light of Your face. Come, Lord Jesus. Show me Your glory!"

As we gaze upon this One who is Altogether Lovely, His unquenchable fire sets us ablaze. Our Beloved consumes our darkness so we can shine forth His glory. May His fire ever burn in our hearts!

His *mouth*

is most *sweet* ...

❧

Song 5:16

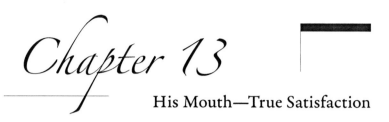

Chapter 13

His Mouth—True Satisfaction

ATTRIBUTE #10

His mouth: *Intimacy* with Jesus

PRAYER

Jesus, I feel like I'm in the desert. I am hungry and thirsty for heavenly manna (Ps 63:1). Kiss me with Your Word (SONG 1:2). Revive my soul (Ps 119:25). Where else can I go? My Beloved, only You have the Words of eternal life (JOHN 6:68). You alone are the Bread of Life and the Living Water (JOHN 6:35; 4:10). Your Word is sweeter than honey; I desire it more than fine gold (Ps 19:10). I treasure the Words of Your mouth more than my necessary food (JOB 23:12). I will meditate on Your Truth day and night (Ps 1:2). You are the Vine; I set my heart to abide in You daily (JOHN 15:5). Impart the deep things of Your heart to mine. Come satisfy my thirsty soul (Ps 145:16). Lord, write Your Word upon my heart, in Your precious name! Amen.

BREAD OF HEAVEN

In the beginning was the Word; and the Word, who is God, became flesh (JOHN 1:1, 14). Jesus Christ is the Living Word. This Word brings true nourishment to our souls. He is the Bread of Life. Those who feed upon His Word are never hungry. Those who partake of the Bread of Heaven live forever (JOHN 6:32-35; 48-51).

To whom shall we go? You have the words of eternal life.

JOHN 6:68

This reality must take hold of our lives. We do not get spiritual sustenance from natural food. Our souls and spirits feed upon the Lord. We live by every Word that proceeds from the mouth of our Beloved (DEUT 8:3). Only His Word supplies what we need. Where else can we go? He alone has the Words that give eternal life (JOHN 6:68). His Living Word gives us daily provision. Even as we would die of starvation in a famine, our spirits will waste away without the Word of God. We must store His Word in our hearts, otherwise we will go hungry in times of drought.

"The days are coming," declares the Sovereign LORD, "when I will send a famine through the land—not a famine of food or a thirst for water, but a famine of hearing the words of the LORD." —Amos 8:11 NIV

ONE THING NEEDED

How do we partake of this manna from heaven? How do we receive the divine kisses of His mouth (SONG 1:2)? How do we abide in the Vine that we might live according to His Word (JOHN 15:5-10)? One thing is needed. Jesus identifies it as the greatest commandment. In fact, God's entire law hinges on two commandments (MATT 22:37-40).

"And you shall love the LORD your God with all your heart, with all your soul, with all your mind, and with all your strength." This is the first commandment. And the second, like it, is this: "You shall love your neighbor as yourself." There is no other commandment greater than these. —Mark 12:30-31

Our Beloved is the Vine. If we abide in Him, we will bear much fruit.

> I am the vine, you are the branches. He who abides in
> Me, and I in him, bears much fruit; for without Me you can
> do nothing … As the Father loved Me, I also have loved
> you; abide in My love. If you keep My commandments,
> you will abide in My love, just as I have kept My Father's
> commandments and abide in His love.   —John 15:5, 9-10

To abide in the Vine is to abide in His Word. To abide in His Word is to abide in His *love*. To abide in His love is to obey His commands. To obey our Beloved's commands is to love Him with all of our time, emotions, thoughts, money, energy, and entire lives. His love is the most excellent way. Without it we have nothing (1 COR 12:31; 13:1-3). Truly we have no good apart from Him (PS 16:2). This is the one thing needed. It is the one thing David earnestly sought (PS 27:4). This one thing is the prize Paul pressed on to apprehend (PHIL 3:13-14). Mary of Bethany likewise chose this one thing.

> He entered a certain village; and a certain woman named
> Martha welcomed Him into her house. And she had a sister
> called Mary, who also sat at Jesus' feet and heard His word.
> But Martha was distracted with much serving, and she
> approached Him and said, "Lord, do You not care that my
> sister has left me to serve alone? Therefore tell her to help me."
> And Jesus answered and said to her, "Martha, Martha, you
> are worried and troubled about many things. But one thing is
> needed, and Mary has chosen that good part, which will not
> be taken away from her."   —Luke 10:38-42

One thing is
needed ...
it will not
be taken ...
LUKE 10:42 NIV

Mary sat at the feet of Jesus listening to what He said. She heard His Word and waited upon the Lord in undistracted devotion. Mary chose the good part, the one thing necessary. When Martha complained that Mary was not helping her, Jesus said to Martha, "You are worried and upset about many things, but only one thing is needed. Mary has chosen what is better, and it will not be taken away from her" (LUKE 10:41-42 NIV). He was not telling Martha that work was not important but that sitting at His feet was essential at the moment. The preparations could wait. Intimacy comes before activity. This is our ultimate priority in light of eternity. The single most critical activity we must embrace is cultivating intimacy with Jesus. All other activity revolves around this primary goal. Fruitfulness in ministry to people can only flow out of individual communion with the Living God.

We are all so busy—a frantic pace being the norm for most—spending time with God often becomes another item on our list of things to do. Intimacy with God is not something we can do in fifteen to thirty minutes a day and then check off before rushing to the next item on our agenda. He has instructed us to be still and wait (Ps 46:10; 27:14). We must dwell daily in His presence and nourish our souls by feeding on His faithfulness. We must rest and wait upon our Beloved.

Trust in the LORD, and do good; dwell in the land, and feed on His faithfulness. Delight yourself also in the LORD, and He shall give you the desires of your heart. Commit your way to the LORD, trust also in Him ... He shall bring forth your righteousness as the light, and your justice as the noonday. Rest in the LORD, and wait patiently for Him ... –Psalm 37:3-7

This is our cry, "Let Him kiss me with His Word" (SONG 1:2). We long for our Beloved to communicate the deep things of His heart to ours. Let us search for hidden treasure as we discover the mysteries of God (MATT 13:44). God's Word is a lamp for our feet (Ps 119:105). Without oil, a lamp quickly burns out. Like the wise virgins, we must take oil with our lamps (MATT 25:4). Let us make time to gather the oil of intimacy before our Bridegroom returns. We face burnout every time we go about doing all the tasks at hand thinking we have enough oil to last. Every wise traveler ensures there is enough oil and gas in their vehicle before taking a long trip. Our life on the earth is a journey. We cannot go very far without daily refueling. We get too busy to spend time in the secret place with Jesus and find ourselves running on fumes. If this is the case, we are too busy. We must stop chasing all the other loves in this life and return to our *First Love.*

> *She will chase her lovers, but not overtake them; yes, she will seek them, but not find them. Then she will say, "I will go and return to my first husband, for then it was better for me than now."* —Hosea 2:7

Communion with our Beloved is the one thing that is necessary in life. Intimacy with Jesus is not an item on a checklist. It is ongoing dialogue with the Lord through fellowship with His indwelling Spirit. Intimacy is unceasing; it never ends. This is why we are exhorted to pray at all times (1 THESS 5:17). We can actually have continual conversation with our Beloved while doing mundane daily tasks. Intimacy is much more than time set aside each day for Bible study and prayer. Though these practices are fundamental disciplines, they are just an initial taste of our Beloved's goodness (Ps 34:8).

FAST TO FEAST

Time in the secret place is one morsel of the banquet the Lord has prepared for us. In the middle of life's storms, our Good Shepherd sets a table before us (Ps 23:5). There is so much more than we can perceive. His love sustains us.

> *He brought me to the banqueting house, and his banner over me was love. Sustain me with cakes of raisins, refresh me with apples, for I am lovesick.* —Song of Solomon 2:4-5

Five thousand people ate and were satisfied when only five loaves and two fish were available. Twelve baskets of bread were gathered up as leftovers (MATT 14:16-21). Who could feed this multitude except Jesus? The Fountain of Life invites us to partake of His abundance.

> *They feast on the abundance of your house; you give them drink from your river of delights. For with you is the fountain of life …* —Psalm 36:8-9 NIV

We have been invited to His feast! Can you imagine stuffing yourself with all kinds of junk food before sitting down to an exquisite dinner? You would have no appetite. This is what happens if we try to satisfy our cravings with earthly pleasures. When spiritual boredom sets in, we do not hunger for God.

This is why fasting is beneficial. It causes us to encounter true hunger. We discover that the lesser pleasures in life actually spoil our appetites for spiritual things. The Israelites fasted unintentionally. They were completely dependent on the Lord to feed them with bread from heaven during their wilderness journey.

So He humbled you, allowed you to hunger, and fed you
with manna which you did not know nor did your fathers
know, that He might make you know that man shall not
live by bread alone; but man lives by every word that proceeds
from the mouth of the LORD.   *–Deuteronomy 8:3*

So why would we fast purposefully? According to the Lord, it humbles us. Physical hunger reminds us that our spiritual nourishment comes through God's Word alone. We fast to gain a spiritual appetite.

Fasting is also a spiritual discipline, which was commanded by God in the Bible. The Lord established both yearly fasts and feasts. Throughout Scripture, we read about various kinds of corporate and individual fasts. Jehoshaphat set himself to seek the Lord and proclaimed a fast in all Judah (2 CHRON 20:3). Esther proclaimed a fast to intercede for the deliverance of her people (ESTH 4:16). The word of the Lord came to Joel instructing him to consecrate a fast and call a sacred assembly because of the coming day of the Lord (JOEL 1:14-15; 2:1, 15). When taken into captivity, Daniel and his friends abstained from eating the king's delicacies (DAN 1:8). At another time, after fasting for three weeks, Daniel saw a vision and was encouraged through an angelic visitation (DAN 10). Even a pagan king was compelled to fast on behalf of this godly man (DAN 6:18). Twice Moses went forty days and forty nights without food and water. The Lord called Moses to the mountain of the Lord to receive the Ten Commandments. Upon returning to camp, he found the Israelites worshiping a golden calf. So he went up to the Lord for a second forty-day fast (EXOD 24:18; 34:28). Elijah fasted forty days before hearing the Lord's quiet whisper on the mountain of God (1 KINGS 19:7-12). Jesus also fasted forty days in the wilderness while being tempted by Satan (MATT 4:1-2).

Isaiah 58 describes the Lord's chosen fast. It is a day to feed the hungry, set prisoners free, and loose the bonds of wickedness. It is a time set aside to delight in the Lord rather than in self-gratification. When we fast, we must be sincere and fast for Him, not ourselves (ZECH 7:5). In His Sermon on the Mount Jesus gives instruction on what to do *when* we fast not *if* we fast (MATT 6:17). Jesus' disciples did not fast because He was with them. We fast now in the absence of our Bridegroom.

And He said to them, "Can you make the friends of the bridegroom fast while the bridegroom is with them? But the days will come when the bridegroom will be taken away from them; then they will fast in those days."   *–Luke 5:34-35*

This is why we have the *Bridegroom Fast* at IHOP–KC. The first Monday through Wednesday of every month is our corporate fast. Many people also schedule specific days to fast on a weekly basis. Individuals or communities might enter into longer fasts for various reasons. Although I grew up attending Church and reading the Bible, I never had a concept of fasting. Before I moved to Kansas City, some friends at church challenged me to fast with them once a week. It was not until much later that I understood the importance of fasting.

My fasting journey began with the elections in 2000 when I joined others in prayer for our nation. Since then I have purposed to fast regularly. This has taken various forms over the years. I usually fast food by skipping a meal, not eating for a day, or going several days at a time with a specific plan. This may involve eating certain kinds of food or drinking only water. I remember when removing sugar and caffeine from my diet was a huge sacrifice. The focus of each fast is to feed upon God's Word. For this reason I try to read more Scripture, memorize verses, journal, and increase spiritual disciplines while abstaining from food. At times I also eliminate distractions and comforts like entertainment, media, technology, make-up, sleep, and even speech. As I fast, my walk with the Lord is transformed. Spiritual dullness and lethargy give way to spiritual hunger and passion. My intimacy with Jesus and knowledge of His Word increase exponentially.

I write even now during an extended fast. By not talking, my attention is focused on God's Word. It forces me to listen and consider the words I would speak. Jesus' Words are spirit and life (JOHN 6:63). Our words have the power to give life or destroy (PROV 18:21). Sin abounds in a multitude of words. We are wise when we spare our words and restrain our lips (PROV 17:27; 10:19). Even a fool who remains

The words that I speak to you are spirit, and they are life.

JOHN 6:63

silent is considered discerning (PROV 17:28). We will all give account for the idle words we speak (MATT 12:36). What comes out of our mouths proceeds from our hearts (MATT 15:18). Jesus said those who are pure in heart will see God (MATT 5:8). This is why David prayed for the words of his mouth and meditations of his heart to be pleasing in the Lord's sight (PS 19:14). During this *silent fast,* I am unable to freely express all my thoughts. Occasionally, I communicate through writing, but mostly I refrain. This is giving me a greater appreciation for our Beloved's silence in front of His accusers (MATT 27:12). It is also causing me to face my own spiritual boredom. I realize how often I fill my time conversing with people rather than with my Beloved. And so I calm and quiet my soul waiting silently for God (PS 131:2; 62:5). I withhold my speech that I may receive the kisses of His Word. As a result, the Lord is giving me utterance to compose this book.

Living a fasted lifestyle is truly rewarding. *The Rewards of Fasting* is a great introduction (see "Road Maps: Tools for Your Journey"). If you have never fasted, I encourage you to begin. Fasting is between you and God. IHOP–KC has a "Don't ask; don't tell" policy to discourage competition, but it is advisable to have accountability for spiritual and health reasons. You may simply start by cutting out unnecessary things like television and sweets. One time I asked the Lord what to fast and the thought crossed my mind, "the color blue." For a week I painted using every color except blue. Believe it or not, Jesus used this to draw me closer to Him. Fasting enlarges our capacity to receive more of God. It causes us to value His Word more than our daily meals.

> *I have not departed from the commandment of His lips;*
> *I have treasured the words of His mouth more than my*
> *necessary food.*   *–Job 23:12*

While fasting is intended to accompany intercession for a specific focus, our primary goal is to increase hunger for Jesus. We fast in order to feast upon His goodness. Sometimes we have to start by simply asking the Lord for a desire to hunger. He promises that those who hunger and thirst will be filled!

> *Blessed are those who hunger and thirst for righteousness,*
> *for they shall be filled.*   *–Matthew 5:6*

TRUE SATISFACTION

Our Beloved has created each of us with deep longings in our hearts that only He can fulfill (see "Road Maps: Tools for Your Journey"). We often attempt to satisfy our desires with natural things. This is

not limited to sinful activity. There are plenty of
pleasures on the earth, which are not blatantly *sin,*
though if these consume our time, thoughts, and
emotions more than God, they become idolatry.
Still, there are legitimate pleasures in God. He
blesses us in areas of finance, health, relationship,

Your love is
better
than wine.
Song 1:2

and influence. The Father delights to give us good gifts (Jas 1:17). Even
so, circumstantial blessings cannot begin to compare with the superior
spiritual pleasures we receive from our Beloved. His love is more
exhilarating than the wine of this world (Song 1:2). There is no higher
pleasure in life than communion with the Living Word. His mouth is
most sweet. His words are more delightful than honey. They are more
desirable than fine gold (Ps 19:10).

> I have not departed from your laws, for you yourself have
> taught me. How sweet are your words to my taste, sweeter
> than honey to my mouth!   –Psalm 119:102-103 NIV

Paul knew the benefit of spiritual pleasures. He prayed for the Ephesians
to experience the width, length, depth, and height of God's love.

> For this reason I bow my knees to the Father of our Lord Jesus
> Christ ... that He would grant you, according to the riches
> of His glory, to be strengthened with might through His Spirit
> in the inner man, that Christ may dwell in your hearts through
> faith; that you, being rooted and grounded in love, may be
> able to comprehend with all the saints what is the width and
> length and depth and height— to know the love of Christ
> which passes knowledge; that you may be filled with all
> the fullness of God.   –Ephesians 3:14-19

In Your presence
is fullness of joy;
at Your right
hand are pleasures
forevermore.

Psalm 16:11

Christ dwells within our hearts. His love surpasses anything we know naturally. True intimacy is the indwelling Spirit continually imparting God's Word to our hearts. This is more enjoyable than living with blessed circumstances. In the presence of our Beloved we experience joy fully (Ps 16:11). The Word of God has power to touch our emotions and transform our hearts. I can see why loving God is the greatest commandment. This is the one thing needed. Intimacy with Jesus must be our primary desire in life. When this becomes our utmost priority, we view life from an entirely new perspective. We begin to hunger and thirst for righteousness (Matt 5:6). We discover true satisfaction. Our spirits become vibrant. We live for God not because we *have to* but because we *want to*. We actually begin to partner with our Beloved. Our ministry or career should never be first priority. If our dreams are mainly set on increase in ministry or business, we are in danger. It will be difficult to avoid seduction by the cares of this world (Mark 4:19). Why should we run after these things that the world pursues? This is why Jesus said, "Seek first the Kingdom of God!"

> For the pagans run after all these things, and your heavenly Father knows that you need them. But seek first his kingdom and his righteousness, and all these things will be given to you as well.   –Matthew 6:32-33 NIV

LIVING WATER

Why do we spend our efforts pursuing things that do not bring true satisfaction? Our Beloved has invited us to eat what is good.

*Ho! Everyone who thirsts, come to the waters; and you who
have no money, come, buy and eat. Yes, come, buy wine and
milk without money and without price. Why do you spend
money for what is not bread, and your wages for what does
not satisfy? Listen carefully to Me, and eat what is good, and
let your soul delight itself in abundance. Incline your ear, and
come to Me. Hear, and your soul shall live . . .* —Isaiah 55:1-3

We have the privilege of delighting in His wealth of supply. This is
better than "the richest of foods" (Ps 63:5 NIV). Let us come to Him so
our souls may live. The Lord has awakened desire in my heart to drink
from this well of Living Water. My soul thirsts for the Living God.

*O God, You are my God; early will I seek You; my soul thirsts
for You; my flesh longs for You in a dry and thirsty land where
there is no water.* —Psalm 63:1

*As the deer pants for the water brooks, so pants my soul for
You, O God. My soul thirsts for God, for the living God. When
shall I come and appear before God?* —Psalm 42:1-2

Centered in the Rose Garden at Loose Park is a fountain surrounded
by beauty. This is one of my favorite outdoor places to commune with
the Lord in Kansas City. One day it struck me that from spring to fall
every year the waters from this fountain never cease to flow. What a
prophetic picture of the Holy Spirit dwelling inside of us! Jesus told
the woman at the well that if she had asked Him for a drink, He would
have given her Living Water.

Jesus answered ... "If you knew the gift of God, and who it is who says to you, 'Give Me a drink,' you would have asked Him, and He would have given you living water." ... Whoever drinks of the water that I shall give him will never thirst. But the water that I shall give him will become in him a fountain of water springing up into everlasting life." —John 4:10, 14

This Perfect Man said that whoever drinks the water He gives would never thirst. If we drink this water it will become a fountain springing up to eternal life. Our Beloved is a Fountain of Blessing!

Come, Thou Fount of every blessing, tune my heart to sing Thy grace; streams of mercy, never ceasing, call for songs of loudest praise. Teach me some melodious sonnet, sung by flaming tongues above. Praise the mount! I'm fixed upon it, mount of Thy redeeming love.

Sorrowing I shall be in spirit, till released from flesh and sin, yet from what I do inherit, here Thy praises I'll begin; here I raise my Ebenezer; here by Thy great help I've come; and I hope, by Thy good pleasure, safely to arrive at home.

Jesus sought me when a stranger, wandering from the fold of God; He, to rescue me from danger, interposed His precious blood; how His kindness yet pursues me mortal tongue can never tell, clothed in flesh, till death shall loose me I cannot proclaim it well.

O to grace how great a debtor daily I'm constrained to be! Let Thy goodness, like a fetter, bind my wandering heart to Thee. Prone to wander, Lord, I feel it, prone to leave the God I love; here's my heart, O take and seal it, seal it for Thy courts above.

*O that day when freed from sinning, I shall see Thy lovely
face; clothed then in blood washed linen how I'll sing Thy
sovereign grace; come, my Lord, no longer tarry, take my
ransomed soul away; send thine angels now to carry Me
to realms of endless day.*

Robert Robinson, 1758; appeared in his A Collection of Hymns
Used by the Church of Christ in Angel Alley, Bishopgate, 1759.

Our hearts are prone to wander and often leave our Beloved, yet His
streams of mercy never cease. How faithfully He has sought us and now
in kindness still pursues us. He seals our hearts with His fire of love
(Song 8:6). Oh, that we may ever drink from this Eternal Fountain!

*His delight is in the law of the LORD, and in His law he
meditates day and night. He shall be like a tree planted by the
rivers of water, that brings forth its fruit in its season, whose
leaf also shall not wither; and whatever he does shall prosper.*
                                                    –Psalm 1:2-3

David and Jeremiah both describe the righteous "like a tree planted by
the river." Those who meditate on the Law of the Lord day and night
bring forth fruit in season. Their leaves do not wither. They prosper in
everything they do.

*Blessed is the man who trusts in the LORD, and whose hope
is the LORD. For he shall be like a tree planted by the waters,
which spreads out its roots by the river, and will not fear when
heat comes; but its leaf will be green, and will not be anxious
in the year of drought, nor will cease from yielding fruit.*
                                                    –Jeremiah 17:7-8

I long to be like a tree firmly planted by the Stream of Living Water. Those who trust in the Lord are firmly established. They are rooted and grounded in the love of God (EPH 3:17). These ones are not anxious in times of drought nor do they ever cease from yielding fruit. Even when heat comes, their leaves are green. How is this possible? Everywhere the river flows there is life (EZEK 47:9). If we drink from the river that flows from the sanctuary we will never cease to bear fruit.

Along the bank of the river, on this side and that, will grow all kinds of trees used for food; their leaves will not wither, and their fruit will not fail. They will bear fruit every month, because their water flows from the sanctuary … –Ezekiel 47:12

Beloved, we have access to this Living Water. The Eternal Fountain of God is Christ within! Unlike an earthly fountain that must be turned off during the winter, we can drink from the River that flows from the sanctuary and bear fruit during every season of our souls. If we truly abide in the Vine, we will bear much fruit (JOHN 15:5).

Can you imagine how our lives would look if everything we put our hands to prospered? I have begun to experience this in a small capacity through creativity. Every time I place intimacy before activity, the Lord blesses me with increased creative expression. I had always wanted to write a song. After an extended fast, the Lord blessed me with lyrics that expressed my longing for the kisses of His Word upon my heart. With the help of a few worship leaders, musicians, and singers, I was able to combine my simple melody with music to record my first song. This is such a testimony of the Lord's faithfulness to bring forth fruit from our lives as we abide in Him. Those whose roots are deeply established in Christ are forever flourishing (Ps 92:14).

Living Water

Parched is my heart and weary my soul
I need Your Word, Lord, to make me whole
Speak to my heart and come end this strife
For You have the Words of eternal life

So come and sustain me refresh me
'Til You flow from my heart like a River
Come and sustain me refresh me
Living Water, sustain me forever

I'm gonna feed on Your Word
I'm gonna drink of Your Truth
'Til You flow from my heart like a River
I'm gonna feed on Your Word
I'm gonna drink of Your Truth
Living Water, sustain me forever

'Cause I don't wanna be cracked and dry
Revive me in Your Truth
I don't wanna be barren, Lord
But bringing forth much fruit

For there is nothin' that I can do
Unless I am found abiding in You
So let me be like a tree
Firmly planted by the Stream

Living Water, sustain me!
Living Water, refresh me!

Send me Manna from heaven
I need my Daily Bread

I'm not gonna be barren, Lord
I'm gonna feed on You instead

Out of my heart will flow rivers
Out of my soul will pour streams
Out of my heart will flow rivers
With springs of Living Water

Living Water, spring up from my soul
Living Water, flow like a River

Living Water—Copyright © 2007
Chérie Blair and Jon Thurlow

Living Water flows out of our hearts when we drink from the River. It literally springs up from our souls! This is my prayer. I desire unceasing fellowship with the Holy Spirit. I long to be refreshed by the Eternal Fountain that never runs dry. I want Jesus to fill my cup so that it may continually overflow with His love (Ps 23:5).

Jesus stood and cried out, saying, "If anyone thirsts, let him come to Me and drink. He who believes in Me, as the Scripture has said, out of his heart will flow rivers of living water."
–John 7:37-38

DRINK DEEPLY

This abundance is not merely for our own enjoyment. Our Beloved likewise enjoys a feast. He eats the pleasant fruits produced from our lives of communion with Him. Whereas we once likened His love to the intoxicating effects of wine, He now pronounces our love as better than wine. The Eternal Fountain drinks from the streams that pour forth from our lives.

*How fair is your love, my sister, my spouse! How much better
than wine is your love … Your lips, O my spouse, drip as
the honeycomb; honey and milk are under your tongue …
A garden enclosed is my sister, my spouse, a spring shut up,
a fountain sealed. Your plants are an orchard … with pleasant
fruits … a fountain of gardens, a well of living waters, and
streams from Lebanon. Awake, O north wind, and come,
O south! Blow upon my garden, that its spices may flow out.
Let my beloved come to his garden and eat its pleasant fruits.*
                              –Song of Solomon 4:10-16

While we abide in God's Word, our vineyards begin to bud. Our fruit
is stored up for Him. He gives us the kisses of His Word that we may
give our love to Him in return. The King is enthralled with our beauty.
His desire is for us. He is pleased with our delights. We are gardens
preserved for His pleasure.

*A king is held captive by your tresses. How fair and how
pleasant you are, O love, with your delights! … The fragrance
of your breath like apples, and the roof of your mouth like
the best wine. The wine goes down smoothly for my beloved …
I am my beloved's, and his desire is toward me … Let us get
up early to the vineyards; let us see if the vine has budded …
There I will give you my love. The mandrakes give off a
fragrance, and at our gates are pleasant fruits, all manner,
new and old, which I have laid up for you, my beloved.*
                              –Song of Solomon 7:5-13

Our Beloved may keep us hidden for a season so that He alone may
take pleasure in His enclosed garden. It seems I have lived in this *secret*

garden for quite some time. Whenever I express anything creatively, it is mostly for His enjoyment. Sure others may catch a glimpse of the fruit He brings forth, but I have yet to be poured out like a fragrant aroma to His friends.

A dream I had expressed this. I was quite frustrated with a leader who did not recognize my ability in a certain area. I tried to communicate what I could do but was unable to speak because of my silent fast. Through numerous hand gestures and charades I was finally able to convey, "I don't want anything." This is exactly opposite of what I meant to say. My intent was to get this person to recognize my gifting and allow me to use it. The Lord used this to remind me what being poured out is really all about. Our Beloved invites us to go still lower.

Why is it so surprising when God humbles us? Jesus spent thirty years in obscurity before beginning His earthly ministry. Eventually we will be used to refresh others, but ministering to our Beloved takes precedence. Jesus first enters His garden, gathers His spices, eats His honey, and drinks His wine before inviting others to partake.

> *I have come to my garden, my sister, my spouse;*
> *I have gathered my myrrh with my spice; I have eaten*
> *my honeycomb with my honey; I have drunk my wine*
> *with my milk. Eat, O friends! Drink, yes, drink deeply,*
> *O beloved ones!* —Song of Solomon 5:1

Others can drink deeply only if our vineyards are cultivated. When we take time to make the *first commandment* first place in our lives, the second naturally follows. The north and south winds produce a plentiful harvest causing our fragrance to spread abroad. Others taste of His goodness through our lives. Our hearts overflow with His good theme. We speak concerning our King (Ps 45:1). From the overflow of our hearts we proclaim the majestic splendor of our Beloved.

Out of the abundance of the heart the mouth speaks.
A good man out of the good treasure of his heart brings
forth good things …   *–Matthew 12:34-35*

I can already smell a fragrance arising from the intimacy I share with my Beloved. The day before my forty-day silent fast ended, I dreamt that my roommate and I were in a coffee shop on day thirty-nine. Unlike other cafés, this one served wine. A gentleman asked why we were not having any. My friend replied, "We've found something that's so much better!" He asked *me* to tell him about it. We knew I was supposed to break my silence to declare the splendor of our Beloved. As I began to speak a crowd gathered, but then quickly became uninterested. We left to talk somewhere else. This time I was overcome with unction from the Holy Spirit and dramatically expressed the Bride's proclamation. "What is my Beloved more than another? He is dazzling and excellent. He is Chief among ten thousand. He is fairer than the sons of men." A friend confirmed my words as we both declared, "There is no one like Him." I continued, "He is fully God and fully Man. You wanna know what is better than wine? His love is more exhilarating!" Everyone was on the edge of their seats. A backslidden Christian picked up a guitar to play love songs to Jesus. When our hearts are filled with His love song we express it in extraordinary ways.

Where has your
beloved gone …
that we may seek
him with you?
Song 6:1

This dream reminds me of the time I was sitting in an airport waiting for my flight. I was silently reading my Bible when my thoughts drifted to a skit I had recently performed. Suddenly I found myself acting out this prayer for the kisses of His Word.

Why so cold, O heart of mine? Why refuse such Love Divine? Come, O Lord, and tenderize this hardened heart that's bought the lies, "He loves you not; you're filthy and poor. You can't even earn it; just look at your score!" But You tell me how I have stolen Your heart, when all I have done is a dance and some art. I'm not even worthy; can't You see that I'm dirty? Don't stare at me; I'm dark. You'll see a bruise, a scar, a mark—where I once let love in but was wounded by men. Yet, I long to know this Love of One who calls me His dove. Why should I hide behind a veil? Must I remain locked in this cell? Come quickly my Lover; do not delay. Kiss me with Your Word and take me away. Your love to me is more delightful than wine. Oh, satisfy my heart with the fruits of Your Vine. —Chérie Blair

This led to a couple of encouraging conversations. One gentleman asked if the drama was from the Bible so I was able to share some of my journey into intimacy with Jesus. On the flight I visited with the CEO of a company. He was inspired to heed the Spirit's prompting and boldly proclaim the Word of God in his workplace.

Our Beloved commissioned us to preach His Word (MARK 16:15). The testimony of our relationship with Jesus causes people to ask, "Where has your Beloved gone?" Our sweet aroma provokes others to pursue Him wholeheartedly (SONG 6:1). Beloved, the Fountain of Life invites us to drink from His River of delights (Ps 36:8-9). His mouth is most sweet. It is more enjoyable than the pleasures of this world. Let us drink deeply of His love. May Living Water spring up from our souls!

Yes, *he is* altogether *lovely*...

Song 5:16

Chapter 14

Altogether Lovely—Full of Love

ALTOGETHER LOVELY:
Jesus' comprehensive *beauty*

PRAYER

Jesus, my heart overflows with a good theme. It's the revelation of Your beauty. I recite my composition, Oh King. No one loves better than You. Thank you for giving Your life that I might be one with You (JOHN 17:21-22). Thank You for directing my steps and leading me perfectly (PROV 16:9). Thank You for revealing Your Father's nature. Thank You for making me the object of Your affections. Thank You for delighting my heart with Your fragrance (PROV 27:9). You endured suffering like no other. I marvel at the gracious words upon Your lips (LUKE 4:22). I remember Your miracles. Thank You for orchestrating every event in my life to glorify Your name. Thank You for saving, healing, and delivering me. Just and true are Your ways. Thank You for shining Your countenance and transforming my heart. Thank You for sustaining me with Your Words of eternal life. My Beloved, You are Altogether Lovely. Amen.

TOTALLY OTHER THAN

Everything about Jesus is entirely perfect. His head, His hair, His eyes, His cheeks, His lips, His hands, His body, His legs, His countenance,

Your name is like perfume poured out. No wonder the maidens love you!

and His mouth—every attribute represents His Father precisely. Our Beloved is white and ruddy, dazzling and excellent, Chief among ten thousand, the most excellent among men. His head is finest gold. His leadership is perfect. His locks are wavy and black as a raven. He is the Faithful Witness who has shown us the Father's glory. His eyes are like doves by the rivers of water, washed with milk and fitly set. He keeps us as the apple of His eye and washes us with the water of His Word. His cheeks are like beds of spices, banks of sweet smelling herbs. His diverse emotions reveal His character like a sweet fragrance poured forth (SONG 1:3). His lips are lilies dripping liquid myrrh graciously inviting us to partner in His suffering. He is anointed to preach the Gospel to the poor, to proclaim freedom to the captives, to comfort those who mourn, and to proclaim the day of vengeance of our God (Is 61:1-2). The Lord's hands are rods of gold set with beryl. His divine activity in our lives is marvelous. His body is carved ivory inlaid with sapphires. He is our Savior, Healer, and Deliverer. His tender compassion is new every morning (LAM 3:22-23). His legs are pillars of marble set on bases of fine gold. He is the Righteous Judge who perfectly administrates His Father's purposes. His countenance is like Lebanon, excellent as the cedars. He is the Eternal Flame who consumes all of our darkness. His fire sets us ablaze from the inside out. His mouth is most sweet. His Word is like honey. It satisfies our souls more than the choicest of foods. In every way our Beloved is Altogether Lovely!

This Perfect Man is the Word of God. The Father could not have said more. And yet He did not consider equality with God as something to be used to His advantage. He made Himself nothing. He became a curse by hanging on a tree. And He did it all for us, all for love. The Son revealed His Father's glory and then poured out His life unto death. What kind of love is this? Words cannot begin to articulate the excellence of our Beloved. I have attempted to recite my composition concerning our King. These weak words can only offer an introduction to God's comprehensive beauty. There is far more to explore.

And there are also many other things that Jesus did, which if they were written one by one, I suppose that even the world itself could not contain the books that would be written …
–John 21:25

The Bible presents a foretaste of what we will behold in the age to come. No utterance can describe this Majestic One. Only one word can come close to ascribing the honor due His name. It was revealed to John in his vision of heaven: "Holy!" He saw elders casting their crowns and living creatures full of eyes with their gaze fixed upon the One seated on the throne (REV 4). Night and day they never stopped saying, "Holy, holy, holy, is the Lord God Almighty, Who was and is and is to come!" How else could we describe Him? Jesus Christ is fully God and fully Man. He is totally *other than*. Our God is unlike any other. He is the only one who is holy. Our Beloved is set apart!

LOVE MANIFEST

Jesus Christ is Altogether Lovely. This is His very name. God is *Love*. Everything He does is for love, by love, through love, and in love. It is His nature. Our Beloved is Love Manifest.

God is Love? What does that mean? In writing about our Beloved's comprehensive beauty, I was struck with how little I really know. We know God loves us. Most people can easily quote John 3:16, "For God so loved the world that He gave His only begotten Son, that whoever believes in Him should not perish but have everlasting life."

> In this the love of God was manifested toward us, that God has sent His only begotten Son into the world, that we might live through Him. In this is love, not that we loved God, but that He loved us and sent His Son to be the propitiation for our sins.
> —1 John 4:9-10

God's love is manifest not by our love for Him but through His love for us. This is how God demonstrated His love. Christ died for sinners (ROM 5:8). Jesus showed the greatest love by laying down His life so we can live (JOHN 15:13). The Lord chose us before the foundations of the world (EPH 1:4). Perfect love between Father and Son brought forth the creation of heaven and earth. We have heard this all before. Still I scarcely comprehend that I am the object of His affection. God is in love with me. I am my Beloved's and His desire is for me (SONG 7:10).

I am my beloved's, and his desire is toward me.
SONG 7:10

His desire is for me? What do I have that the Lord wants? Does not the All-Powerful, All-Knowing, Ever-Present Being have everything? Who am I that God is mindful of me? I am but dust, a momentary vapor, just a wanderer passing through the earth. And He wants me to be His Bride? His jealousy for my heart is unyielding as the grave? One Man gave the wealth of His house for this love and was utterly scorned? I have no clue what this means. I like to say, "Jesus gave it all for love." It is a catchy phrase. But when I insert my name in place of love, my mind short circuits. "Jesus gave it all for Chérie?" How in the world is this possible? Beloved, we need God to reveal His unending, enduring, eternal, and infinite love. What are His affections for you and me individually? How does He love each of us? When we pray, "Lord, show me Your glory," we are also asking, "Lord, show me You love me!" We could look up all the verses and describe the ways God loves us, but until His love becomes a heart reality, it is just head knowledge. We need Love Himself to encounter our hearts. It is so easy to think, "I already know God loves me." But has this truth impacted the core of our beings? We may know the Scriptures but has His love become more than a concept? Do we personally grasp that God is in love with *me*, not just with *us*? Our Beloved is Love Manifest. It is His pleasure to reveal His affections personally.

ALTOGETHER IN LOVE

Our Beloved delights to *wow* us with His abounding love. God is the Lover of our souls. His love is better than life. This reality must take hold of us. His love is priceless, limitless, immeasurable, and all consuming. He loves with an everlasting love (JER 31:3). The Living God loves with all His heart, His soul, His mind, and His strength. His desire is toward human beings. He is moved with compassion for each of us. His thoughts about us outnumber the sand (PS 139:17-18). He restrained all of His strength to endure the Cross. And still Jesus loves us more than this. The omniscient, omnipotent, omnipresent God loves every individual with all of His wisdom, all of His power, and all of His presence. In the same way the Father loves Him, so He loves us (JOHN 15:9). God has abandoned Himself to His people with extravagant love. How

As the Father loved Me, I also have loved you; abide in My love
JOHN 15:9

prone we are to forget. We need to be reminded constantly. For this reason, our Beloved invites us to abide in Love. He repeatedly declares His affections. Day after day He pours His love into our hearts. Night after night He displays His love through all creation (Ps 19:1-2). Jesus *altogether loves* you and me. He continually demonstrates this love. Through sunsets and rainy days, through birds chirping and children at play, every night and all through the day our Beloved is saying over and over, "I love you!" Are we listening?

His head is like the finest gold: Jesus is the Counseling Shepherd. His sovereign leadership is perfect. We can trust Him without question. Our way is not hidden from Him. He is intimately acquainted with every detail of our lives. Like a magnificent conductor He orchestrates each moment. He arranges each season to produce a pleasing fragrance and a harvest of fruit. In both difficult and refreshing circumstances He is saying, "I love you!"

His locks are wavy, and black as the raven: Jesus is the Faithful Witness. Our Beloved is dedicated to revealing His Father's nature to the Church. His will is in complete submission to His Father's. He did not take advantage of His equality with God but laid aside His splendor to be clothed in skin. He was obedient even unto death on the cross. God's only Son lived on the earth as a Man to tell us that His Father is saying, "I love you!"

His eyes are like doves by the rivers of waters, washed with milk, and fitly set: Jesus is the God Who Sees. His undistracted vision is steadily focused on us. He is searching the whole earth to find hearts that are loyal to Him. With perfect discernment His eyes guide us along the path of righteousness. When He washes us with the water of His Word, He is saying, "I love you!"

His cheeks are like a bed of spices, banks of scented herbs: Jesus is the Suffering Servant. His emotions arise like a sweet fragrance. He was despised and rejected, a Man of sorrows, and acquainted with grief. When accused He did not retaliate. For the joy of having us as His Bride, He endured the Cross. To the very ones who spit in His face and struck Him on the cheek, He is saying, "I love you!"

His lips are lilies, dripping liquid myrrh: Jesus is the Lord God Gracious. His lips offer us an invitation to share in His sufferings. With gracious words He calls out, "Rise up, My love. Take up your cross. Follow Me." His voice beckons, "Open to Me." He awakens our desire to pursue Him into the night. Upon touching His affliction, we find His presence departed. His silence is saying, "I love you!"

His hands are rods of gold set with beryl: Jesus is the Almighty God. His divine activity is perfect. He extends mercy to the righteous and executes wrath upon the wicked. With mighty miracles He acts on behalf of those who love Him. He rescues us because He delights in us. Even His rod of correction brings us comfort. When He disciplines us we know He is saying, "I love you!"

His body is carved ivory inlaid with sapphires: Jesus is the God of Salvation. With tender compassion He forgives our sins and heals our diseases. The punishment that brought us peace was upon Him. He has paid the price for our total redemption, healing, and deliverance. Death no longer has dominion over our bodies, souls, or spirits. By purchasing us as His inheritance, He is saying, "I love you!"

His legs are pillars of marble set on bases of fine gold: Jesus is the Righteous Judge. He administrates the Father's will perfectly. Just and true are all His ways. In righteousness He judges and makes war against His adversaries. All of His judgments are worthy of praise.

His Kingdom is coming to earth and He will reign forever. When He returns to vindicate His Bride He will be saying, "I love you!"

His countenance is like Lebanon, excellent as the cedars: Jesus is the Consuming Fire. He imparts to us the nature of His glory. True light penetrates our hearts burning away every impurity. His jealous flame consumes our lives and ignites us to burn with holy passion. As we gaze upon His beauty, we behold Love like flashes of fire. From the midst of this most vehement flame, He is saying, "I love you!"

His mouth is most sweet: Jesus is the true Bread of Heaven. We have intimate communion with Him through His abiding Word. He causes us to hunger for true spiritual food. Only the kisses of His Word can satisfy our hearts. He has prepared a banquet that we may forever feast upon His abundance. With roots firmly established we never cease to bear fruit. Every time we partake of His fresh heavenly manna He is saying, "I love you!"

Jesus is *Altogether In Love* with us! Every attribute imparts the Lord's love to our hearts. In every event of our lives let us rejoice and remember His love (SONG 1:4). Our Beloved is *in love.* He is forever saying, "I love you!" Every time God heals, delivers, provides, protects, forgives, affirms, disciplines, vindicates, or does anything at all, He pronounces His love. Each attribute is defined by this one word: "Love." This is His nature. God is Love. He is Altogether Lovely.

LIVE FOR LOVE

True intimacy is found both in receiving God's love and loving Him. The God who created the universe is in love with weak and broken people. He left His Father's house for love's sake and now asks us to do the same. He beckons, "Consider and incline your ear. Forget your

people and your father's house. Leave it all behind. Come after Me!"
Are we willing to forget this world in which we are living?

> *Listen, O daughter, consider and give ear: Forget your people*
> *and your father's house. The king is enthralled by your beauty;*
> *honor him, for he is your lord.* —Psalm 45:10-11 NIV

A rich ruler inquired about what he must do to inherit eternal life.
When Jesus reminded him of the commandments, the young man
proudly reported keeping them all since he was a boy. Jesus lovingly
replied, "One thing you lack. Go sell all you have and follow me."

> *Now as He was going out on the road, one came running,*
> *knelt before Him, and asked Him, "Good Teacher, what shall*
> *I do that I may inherit eternal life?" So Jesus said to him, "Why*
> *do you call Me good? No one is good but One, that is, God.*
> *You know the commandments: 'Do not commit adultery,'*
> *'Do not murder,' 'Do not steal,' 'Do not bear false witness,'*
> *'Do not defraud,' 'Honor your father and your mother.'"*
> *And he answered and said to Him, "Teacher, all these things*
> *I have kept from my youth." Then Jesus, looking at him, loved*
> *him, and said to him, "One thing you lack: Go your way, sell*
> *whatever you have and give to the poor, and you will have*
> *treasure in heaven; and come, take up the cross, and follow*
> *Me." But he was sad at this word, and went away sorrowful,*
> *for he had great possessions.* —Mark 10:17-22

Great is the cost of following Jesus. Are we willing to give up what is
dear to us in this life? Mary of Bethany did. She sacrificed an expensive
perfume that was "worth a year's wages" (JOHN 12:5 NIV). Think about

this. The equivalent for someone with an average income today could be thirty to forty thousand dollars. Some thought pouring such a costly fragrance on the Lord's feet was a waste. But Jesus did not rebuke this young lady. Instead He praised her extravagant offering. It was rightly done to anoint Him for burial.

> *Then Mary took about a pint of pure nard, an expensive perfume; she poured it on Jesus' feet and wiped his feet with her hair. And the house was filled with the fragrance of the perfume.* —John 12:3 NIV

The fragrance of Mary's perfume filled the entire house. This is what happens when we give ourselves in extravagant devotion to the Lord. The aroma of our lives fills the throne room of heaven. Will we pour our earthly inheritance at His feet for the sake of love? Mary did not even consider the cost, nor did she see it as a waste. She was captivated by love for Jesus. Her sacrifice was an overflow of loving devotion. Jesus' love is enough to satisfy. It is better than life. Will we leave the pleasures of life behind and live extravagantly for our Beloved?

A poor widow did the same thing. While rich people gave of their wealth into the temple treasury, this woman put in two small coins (LUKE 21:1-4). Why did Jesus say she gave more than anyone else? Out of her poverty she gave her entire livelihood. Are we willing to make this kind of extraordinary sacrifice?

Jesus likewise gave everything to purchase us. We are His pearls. He paid the greatest price. His love is extravagant. He poured out His life unto death as a fragrant offering. No one has love greater than the love of our Beloved (JOHN 15:13). He died for us that we might live for Him. Will we live for Love Himself?

*And He died for all, that those who live should live no
longer for themselves, but for Him who died for them
and rose again.*   *−2 Corinthians 5:15*

Our Beloved laid down His life for us. His abandonment is so much
higher than ours. Will we lay down our lives for Him? Are we willing
to surrender everything: our plans, our dreams, our ambitions, and
even the *promises* God has given us? We have found the Pearl of Great
Price. Will we abandon all to gain Him? He is worth it. Paul lived with
such lovesick abandonment.

*But whatever was to my profit I now consider loss for the sake
of Christ. What is more, I consider everything a loss compared
to the surpassing greatness of knowing Christ Jesus my Lord,
for whose sake I have lost all things. I consider them rubbish,
that I may gain Christ and be found in him.*
                                    −Philippians 3:7-10 NIV

This man lost everything for Christ's sake but did not consider it a
sacrifice. His heart was overcome with love for Jesus. To him earthly
things seemed like trash compared to knowing the Lord. Let us forget
our earthly homes and live for Love alone. Doing so fulfills God's two
highest commandments: 1.) Love God. 2.) Love people.

*"And you shall love the LORD your God with all your heart,
with all your soul, with all your mind, and with all your
strength." This is the first commandment. And the second, like
it, is this: "You shall love your neighbor as yourself." There is no
other commandment greater than these.*   *−Mark 12:30-31*

Chapter 14: Altogether Lovely—Full of Love

Love is who God is. It is what He does. It is what He commands us to do. He longs for us to be one with Him. If we are to be united with the Godhead we must become Love. This is why Paul prays that the Church would abound still more and more in love.

> *And this I pray, that your love may abound still more and more in knowledge and all discernment, that you may approve the things that are excellent, that you may be sincere and without offense till the day of Christ, being filled with the fruits of righteousness which are by Jesus Christ, to the glory and praise of God.*　—Philippians 1:9-11

If we have any question about our purpose in life, the answer is "Love." This is the currency of God's Kingdom. When we stand before the Lord at the end of this age, He will have one question: "Have you learned to love?" This is what it all comes down to.

Life is really about love. It is the only thing that remains at the end of our lives. Everything else will just burn up. John reminds us not to love the world nor the things in it. We cannot serve both God and mammon (MATT 6:24). If we love the things of this world, God's love is not in us. The lust of the flesh, the lust of the eyes, and the pride of life are not of God. These will all pass away.

> *Do not love the world or the things in the world. If anyone loves the world, the love of the Father is not in him. For all that is in the world—the lust of the flesh, the lust of the eyes, and the pride of life—is not of the Father but is of the world. And the world is passing away, and the lust of it; but he who does the will of God abides forever.*　—1 John 2:15-17

Everyone who does the will of God lives forever. What is His will? It is His Greatest Command: love God entirely. It matters not what we accomplish in our brief earthly existence. So what if we have the most successful business, the furthest reaching ministry, or the greatest fame? Just like the flowers of the field all this will fade into nothing.

> *All men are like grass, and all their glory is like the flowers of*
> *the field. The grass withers and the flowers fall, because the*
> *breath of the LORD blows on them. Surely the people are*
> *grass. The grass withers and the flowers fall, but the word of*
> *our God stands forever.* —Isaiah 40:6-8 NIV

Only the Word stands for all eternity. His name is Love. We could have more wisdom than Solomon, suffer greater persecution than the apostles, do more charitable deeds than Mother Teresa, or win more souls than Billy Graham. But without Love, this life is just a bunch of noise. God's love is all we have. It is all we need. If we do not have Love, we have nothing; we gain nothing.

> *And now I will show you the most excellent way. If I speak*
> *in the tongues of men and of angels, but have not love,*
> *I am only a resounding gong or a clanging cymbal. If I have*
> *the gift of prophecy and can fathom all mysteries and all*
> *knowledge, and if I have a faith that can move mountains,*
> *but have not love, I am nothing. If I give all I possess to the*
> *poor and surrender my body to the flames, but have not love,*
> *I gain nothing.* —1 Corinthians 12:31; 13:1-3 NIV

Love is the most excellent way. There is nothing greater. Whatever we do without Love does not count in eternity. Do we not recall that all our righteous acts are like filthy rags (Is 64:6)? We must have the Living Flame called Love burning inside our hearts. Many will say to the Lord on that day, "Didn't you see all I did in your name? Look at the amazing things I accomplished!" He will respond bluntly, "I never knew you. Get away from me. You only practice wickedness."

> Not everyone who says to me, "Lord, Lord," will enter the kingdom of heaven, but only he who does the will of my Father who is in heaven. Many will say to me on that day, "Lord, Lord, did we not prophesy in your name, and in your name drive out demons and perform many miracles?" Then I will tell them plainly, "I never knew you. Away from me, you evildoers!" —Matthew 7:21-23 NIV

All of our mighty exploits do not equate to relationship with Jesus. James tells us that if we befriend the world we make ourselves enemies of God (Jas 4:4).

> Whoever confesses that Jesus is the Son of God, God abides in him, and he in God. And we have known and believed the love that God has for us. God is love, and he who abides in love abides in God, and God in him. —1 John 4:15-16

Love is the pathway to fellowship with God. Whoever abides in Love abides in Him. This is how we know God's love. Our Beloved wants us to be filled with the same love He and the Father shared. God is looking for those who will live with wholehearted abandonment to Him. Let us make this our aim, to live for Love!

Love's Response

How do we love God? It is through the movements of our hearts that we declare to Jesus, "I love You!" We love Him the same way He loves us because He loved us first. Our Beloved initially loved us with all of His heart, His soul, His mind, and His strength. Love's response is simply to return His love with all of our hearts, our souls, our minds, and our strength. Are we doing so? Do we demonstrate our love for Him in our actions?

We love Him because He first loved us.
1 JOHN 4:19

Through emotions and attitudes, through words we speak and everything we think, with each response in every circumstance are we saying, "I love You"? He is listening!

His head is like the finest gold: To the Counseling Shepherd we can say, "Your leadership is perfect. I trust You completely. Thank You for being intimately acquainted with every detail of my life. I love the way You orchestrate each moment. Thank You for arranging every circumstance for my good and for Your glory." In both difficult and refreshing circumstances, are we saying, "I love You"?

His locks are wavy, and black as the raven: To the Faithful Witness we can say, "Thank You, Lord for revealing Your Father's nature. I am overwhelmed by Your complete submission to His will. Thank You for humbling Yourself even unto death on the cross." In response to His declaration of the Father's love, are we saying, "I love You"?

His eyes are like doves by the rivers of waters, washed with milk, and fitly set: To the God Who Sees we can say, "Your undistracted vision is steadily focused on me. When You search the earth, Lord, find my heart faithful to You. Thank You for discerning my ways and guiding me with Your eye that I may walk righteously. Your eyes are full of mercy. Thank you for cleansing me." When He washes us with the water of His Word, are we saying, "I love You"?

His cheeks are like a bed of spices, banks of scented herbs: To the Suffering Servant we can say, "Jesus, Your emotions arise like a sweet fragrance. Thank You for suffering rejection and sorrow for my sake. I confess, I am guilty of crucifying my Lord. But You have shown me such kindness. Thank You for enduring the Cross that I may become Your Bride." Though we struck our own Beloved on the cheek, are we now saying, "I love You"?

His lips are lilies, dripping liquid myrrh: To the Lord God Gracious we can say, "Your lips invite me to share in Your sufferings. My heart leapt at the gracious words You spoke, beckoning me to take up my cross and follow You. When I touched Your affliction, You had already departed, but I am not offended. I will go into the dark night in search of You." Even while He is silent, are we saying, "I love You"?

His hands are rods of gold set with beryl: To the Almighty God we can say, "Your divine activity is perfect. Your mercy and Your wrath are worthy of praise. I will remember Your miracles, how You acted on my behalf. Thank You for rescuing me because You delight in me. Even Your rod of correction brings me comfort." When He disciplines us, are we saying, "I love You"?

His body is carved ivory inlaid with sapphires: To the God of Salvation we can say, "With tender compassion You forgave my sins and healed my diseases. Thank You for taking the punishment I deserved so that I could have peace. I receive the entire package You bought that I might have total redemption, healing, and deliverance. Death no longer has dominion over my body, soul, or spirit." With gratitude for purchasing us as His inheritance, are we saying, "I love You"?

His legs are pillars of marble set on bases of fine gold: To the Righteous Judge we can say, "You administrate the Father's will perfectly. Just and true are all Your ways. Thank You for making war against Your adversaries. I love Your judgments. Thank You for establishing Your Kingdom on earth and reigning forever." When He returns with justice to vindicate us, will we be saying, "I love You"?

His countenance is like Lebanon, excellent as the cedars: To the Consuming Fire we can say, "Let the light of Your face shine on my heart. Impart to me the nature of Your glory. I will gaze upon Your beauty that I might be transformed. Thank You for burning away every impurity. Consume my life. Your love is like flashes of fire. Set me ablaze with holy passion." From the midst of His most vehement flame of love, are we saying, "I love You"?

His mouth is most sweet: To the Bread of Heaven we can say, "I will abide in Your Word. Thank You for causing me to hunger for spiritual food and kissing me with Your Word. You alone satisfy. I will forever feast upon the abundant banquet You have prepared for me. Thank You for causing my roots to go deep that I might always bear fruit." Whenever we taste His heavenly manna, are we saying, "I love You"?

Jesus is *Altogether Worthy of Love!* Every attribute is deserving of our lovesick response. Each time God heals, protects, provides, brings forth justice, or does anything, do we express our gratitude for His love? In every season of our souls, are we saying, "I love You"? He is worthy of our affections. He is Altogether Lovely. This is love's response.

BROTHERLY LOVE

The second greatest commandment is like the first. Because God so loves us, we should also "love one another" (1 JOHN 4:11).

Beloved, if God so loved us, we also ought to love one another.

1 John 4:11

How do we love one another? We love people by loving God! The way in which we respond to others is actually our response to the Lord. Our love is shown every time we give someone a drink, invite a stranger in, or care for one who is sick. Whatever we do for the least of His brethren, we do unto Jesus (MATT 25:35-40). By extending love to our brothers and sisters we are saying, "I love You, Jesus!"

By this we know love, because He laid down His life for us. And we also ought to lay down our lives for the brethren.
—1 John 3:16

This is how we know Love. Our Beloved laid down His life for us. We respond with love by laying down our lives for His friends. If we do not love our brothers, we are *not* saying, "I love You, Jesus!"

If someone says, "I love God," and hates his brother, he is a liar; for he who does not love his brother whom he has seen, how can he love God whom he has not seen? And this commandment we have from Him: that he who loves God must love his brother also.
—1 John 4:20-21

Without obedience to the second we cannot fulfill the first. So how do we know that we love God's friends? If we love God we keep His commands (JOHN 14:15, 21).

By this we know that we love the children of God, when we love God and keep His commandments. For this is

the love of God, that we keep His commandments. And
His commandments are not burdensome.   *—1 John 5:2-3*

These two laws are not burdensome. The Lord draws us near to Himself in intimacy through the first commandment. The second naturally follows from the overflow of our hearts. This is why we pray, "Draw me after You and we will run together" (SONG 1:4). As we freely receive God's love and give Him our love, it becomes a joy to partner with our Beloved in ministry to others.

Feeding on God's Word teaches us to love as He loves. His Sermon on the Mount defines how to walk in love (MATT 5-7). We demonstrate love for God by following this road map. The Beatitudes are attitudes of the heart, which determine our actions. Godly reactions come forth from the treasure stored up in our hearts (LUKE 6:45). In each situation where we respond rightly, we are saying, "I love You, Jesus!"

Jesus affirms us, "Blessed are you who are poor in spirit. Because you recognize the depravity of your sin, I give you Kingdom authority. Blessed are you who mourn. Because you weep over the darkness of your heart, I comfort you. Blessed are you who are meek. Because of your humility and repentant heart, the earth is your inheritance. Blessed are

> *Out of the*
> *abundance of*
> *the heart his*
> *mouth speaks.*
> LUKE 6:45

you who hunger and thirst for righteousness. Because You long to be made perfect in love and transformed into My image, I am filling you. Blessed are you who are merciful. Because you forgive others, I show you mercy. Blessed are you who are pure in heart. Because you confess your sins, I wash you with My blood. You will see My glory. Blessed are you who make peace. Because you reconcile with those you sin against, I call you My child. Blessed are you when others misunderstand and mistreat you. It is for the sake of righteousness because I am purifying your heart. I am removing everything that hinders My love to prepare you as a Bride in My Kingdom. Blessed are you when people insult you, persecute you, and falsely accuse you. It is for My sake. I am jealous for your heart. Rejoice and be glad. I have a great reward stored up for you in heaven. Beloved, you prosper spiritually because these momentary trials are working in you an eternal glory." When our actions flow from these heart attitudes, the Lord hears us saying, "I love You, Jesus!"

> Blessed are the poor in spirit, for theirs is the kingdom of heaven. Blessed are those who mourn, for they shall be comforted. Blessed are the meek, for they shall inherit the earth. Blessed are those who hunger and thirst for righteousness, for they shall be filled. Blessed are the merciful, for they shall obtain mercy. Blessed are the pure in heart, for they shall see God. Blessed are the peacemakers, for they shall be called sons of God. Blessed are those who are persecuted for righteousness' sake, for theirs is the kingdom of heaven. Blessed are you when they revile and persecute you, and say all kinds of evil against you falsely for My sake. Rejoice and be exceedingly glad, for great is your reward in heaven, for so they persecuted the prophets who were before you.
>
> –Matthew 5:3-12

Loving our brothers and sisters naturally flows from our love for Jesus. But this is the easy part. Loving those who are loving is not a chore. It becomes more difficult to have the right heart attitudes with those who are not so kind. Even if we have nothing against someone else, if our brother is angry with us we must first be reconciled before we can offer our gift of love to God at the altar (MATT 5:24). If we keep the royal law found in Scripture, we will not stop at loving our neighbor. Jesus instructs us to love our enemies, bless those who curse us, and pray for those who spitefully use us (MATT 5:43-48). Think about the incredible misunderstandings and mistreatment our Beloved endured to show His great love. Just as Christ loves us, we must also love one another. When someone cuts us off in traffic, will we respond in love? When thieves break in and steal, will we pray for their salvation? When we are misunderstood, treated unjustly, or emotionally wounded, will we respond with love?

Each day we have limitless opportunities to express love to our Beloved by exhibiting love for others. If we confess our faults, repent, and choose to forgive, we are saying, "I love you!" Whenever we turn the other cheek, we are saying, "I love you!" If we quickly agree with our adversary, we are saying, "I love you!" Each time we drop a matter before a dispute breaks out, we are saying, "I love you!" When we refrain from gossip or slander, we are saying, "I love you!" Every time we obey our parents or those who have authority over us, we are saying, "I love you!" If we dress modestly in order to keep others from stumbling, we are saying, "I love you!" When we abstain from complaining, we are saying, "I love you!" In all this we are saying, "I love You, Jesus!"

But suppose someone is in need. What good is it if we say, "I love you" to our brothers and sisters or bless them with kind words but do nothing with our actions?

Suppose a brother or sister is without clothes and daily food. If one of you says to him, "Go, I wish you well; keep warm and well fed," but does nothing about his physical needs, what good is it?   *—James 2:15-16 NIV*

If we love one another, God abides in us, and His love has been perfected in us.

1 John 4:12

When we give to those who ask of us and do not turn away from those who want to borrow, we are saying, "I love you!" If someone demands our shirt and we give up our coat as well, we are saying, "I love you!" When people interrupt our plans but we gladly listen, help, or pray with them, we are saying, "I love you!" Every time we go the extra mile, we are saying, "I love you!" If we loose people from bondage to wickedness, we are saying, "I love you!" When we encourage the fainthearted and help the weak, we are saying, "I love you!" If we look after orphans and widows in distress, we are saying, "I love you!" As we shine like stars by sharing the Gospel in our communities, we are saying, "I love you!" If we give generously from our hearts, we are saying, "I love you!" When we serve others and bear their burdens, we are saying, "I love you!" By interceding in fervent prayer for others' needs, we are saying, "I love you!" The times we do good things in secret that go unnoticed except by the Lord, we are saying, "I love you!" Whatever we do in word or deed as unto Him, we are saying, "I love You, Jesus!"

Whenever we are patient or kind, we are saying, "I love you!" If we do not envy others or exalt ourselves, we are saying, "I love you!" When we take the low road of humility, not thinking of ourselves more highly than we ought, we are saying, "I love you!" Every time we show compassion instead of behaving rudely, we are saying, "I love you!" When we look out for the interests of others and not merely our own, we are saying, "I love you!" If we are quick to listen, slow to speak, and slow to become angry, we are saying, "I love you!" Whenever we overlook an offense, keeping no account of the wrong suffered, we are saying, "I love you!" Every time we say "No" to wickedness and "Yes" to righteousness, we are saying, "I love you!" With each thought taken captive and each glance turned away from lust, we are saying, "I love you!" Every time we are protecting, trusting, hoping, and persevering, we are saying, "I love You, Jesus!"

In every way we choose to imitate Christ, we are saying, "I love You, Jesus!" This is the fullness of love that Paul prayed we would know (EPH 3:16-19). It is the most excellent way of love he has shown us.

> *Love is patient, love is kind. It does not envy, it does not boast, it is not proud. It is not rude, it is not self-seeking, it is not easily angered, it keeps no record of wrongs. Love does not delight in evil but rejoices with the truth. It always protects, always trusts, always hopes, always perseveres. Love never fails ... These three remain: faith, hope and love. But the greatest of these is love.* —1 Corinthians 13:4-8, 13 NIV

We know the One whose name is Love by loving God and by loving people. We love as He loved by keeping His two greatest commands and by doing what He did.

> *Now by this we know that we know Him, if we keep His commandments. He who says, "I know Him," and does not keep His commandments, is a liar, and the truth is not in him. But whoever keeps His word, truly the love of God is perfected in him. By this we know that we are in Him. He who says he abides in Him ought himself also to walk just as He walked.* —1 John 2:3-6

God's love is perfected in us when we love one another (1 JOHN 4:12). If we genuinely love God, His love abides in us. We cannot help but love others. It is natural to spend our time, energy, resources, and emotions on God's friends. Beloved, this is how we love the Lord our God with our entire beings! Through humility, surrender, forgiveness, repentance, and acts of kindness we are saying, "I love You, Jesus!"

VOLUNTARY LOVE

The only thing God does not have is our love. The only thing we can give God is the very thing He gave us. He is searching for those who will give themselves in voluntary love.

This life is just a trial. As students in this earthly internship we have been given an open-Book exam. How will our hearts respond? We have the answer staring us in the face. It is in the Bible. Why would we choose to fail a test when we have been given the answer key? Jesus even tells us that the only way to pass the test is to use His Book. He says, "Abide in Me. Abide in Love. Abide in My Word. Read it. Meditate on it." This is how we love, by obeying His commands. They are all summed up with this one word: "Love." Life is not primarily about our careers, our vehicles, our houses, our families, our relationships, our businesses, our ministries, our reputations, or any aspiration. Our activities in this world are all about one thing. Life is not about how great an offering we present to God through our talents and abilities. The one purpose under heaven and only thing of any significance is love. Will we learn to love?

> *God is love, and he who abides in love abides in God, and God in him.*
> *1 JOHN 4:16*

Let us open the Book to find His answer. Let us surrender our plans and allow Him to consume us completely. Let us love Him with all of our hearts, souls, minds, and strength. By simply opening the Bible and reading His Words of Life, we are saying, "I love You!" Each time we gaze upon Him, set our hearts on a pilgrimage, purpose to run to win the prize, and live like strangers on the earth by not participating in common practices of our culture, we are saying, "I love You!" By living fasted lifestyles, denying our flesh, and ever increasing in hunger for God, we are saying, "I love You, Jesus!"

When we pray, "Lord, catch the foxes that spoil my vine, those little areas of compromise. Search me and try me. See if there is any wicked way in me. I surrender to Your jealous flame of love. Consume all my darkness. I yield to the Potter. Fashion me into a vessel of honor. Make me holy, as you are holy. Wash me with the water of Your Word. Send Your north winds of adversity. Blow Your south winds of blessing. Do whatever it takes to bring forth a pleasing fragrance from my garden. Yes, I will take up my cross and follow you to the mountain of myrrh and the hill of frankincense. I give up everything for the sake of knowing you," we are actually saying, "I love You, my Beloved!"

God is Love. We are called according to His name. Let us then make Love our lifelong pursuit. Jesus loves us with His whole heart, soul, mind, and strength. Let us therefore seek to love Him entirely: heart, soul, mind, and strength. Let us live for Love because He is worth it. Our Beloved is *Altogether Lovely!*

This is my *beloved* and this is my *friend*, O daughters of Jerusalem!

Song 5:16

Chapter 15

Beloved and Friend—Partnership

BELOVED AND FRIEND:
Jesus is our eternal *Husband* and *Companion*

PRAYER

Jesus, You are my Beloved Husband and my intimate Friend. Continue to awaken my heart with Your enduring love. Draw me in ever increasing intimacy with You (SONG 1:4). Help me not to lean on what I perceive as my own ability (PROV 3:5). I want to come up from this wilderness leaning upon You (SONG 8:5). Thank You for calling me Your friend (JOHN 15:15). I love how Your power is displayed through my weakness! Thank You for sending Your Holy Spirit to lead me into the knowledge of who You are (JOHN 14:26). Make me ready to be Your holy Bride. Cause me to run together with You in partnership. Amen.

BELOVED BRIDEGROOM

As Beloved, Jesus Christ is our eternal Bridegroom. Everything in this life is preparation for our Wedding Day. Right now we are in a divine courtship. He is returning soon to take us as His glorious Bride. This is why the Song of Solomon is called a love song. It is our Beloved's song declaring His love for us. In the end we come up from the wilderness leaning upon Him.

Trust in the LORD with all your heart, and lean not on your own understanding.

PROVERBS 3:5

With perfect wisdom our Beloved knows how to cause each of our hearts to rest in Him. His divine strategy in this season of my life has been this writing assignment. It seemed like such a marvelous idea when I first began. I really had no idea what I was getting myself into. I have found there is no other option but trusting the Lord with all my heart (PROV 3:5). Over and over again I face my inability to form a single sentence. And I thought I encountered writer's block when trying to complete college term papers. Never before have I undertaken such an enormous challenge. In desperation I keep fervently asking the Lord to give me the words He desires to express. Whenever I have absolutely nothing to say, He continually amazes me. When I need a break, I lie down to rest and dialogue with Him. Within moments I find myself jotting down a few brief thoughts. I am always astounded to see them expand into multiple pages. How our Beloved delights to reveal His nature and affections! Searching the Scriptures day and night is awakening my heart with greater longing for Him. This is how we come forth leaning. We find victory by pressing into His Word. I am beginning to learn what it means to be completely dependent on my Beloved. Writing can be emotionally exhausting, especially when doing so extensively during a focused period of time while fasting. My physical and mental weariness is quite evident, which forces me to trust in God's might. Every time I set my heart, my soul, my mind, and my strength to the task at hand, He sustains me.

Jesus often asks us to do things we could never do in our own capacity. Usually He puts a thought in our minds so we take the initiative. Peter said to the Lord, "Command me to come to You on the water." So Jesus told Peter to come and he did (MATT 14:28-29). With our eyes fixed on the Lord we find ourselves doing the impossible. This is how God demonstrates His power. His ability is perfected in our deficiency.

But he said to me, "My grace is sufficient for you, for my power is made perfect in weakness." Therefore I will boast all the more gladly about my weaknesses, so that Christ's power may rest on me. That is why, for Christ's sake, I delight in weaknesses, in insults, in hardships, in persecutions, in difficulties. For when I am weak, then I am strong.

–2 Corinthians 12:9-10 NIV

The Lord's grace is sufficient. This is the only thing we can boast in. Weakness is a blessing. It motivates us to run into the strength of our Beloved. He says, "I know the load is too heavy for you to carry alone. Come to me. My burden is light. Do not lean on your own talents or knowledge. Trust in Me. I will complete the good work I started. Just keep leaning" (MATT 11:28-29; PROV 3:5-6; PHIL 1:6). In a recent dream I was on a long voyage. In the final stages of my expedition I came to a large cove where people were swimming. Something unusual caught my attention. Large portions of ice bobbed up and down with the swell of the waves. It was glacier water. I needed to get across this foreboding expanse. The lifeguard saw me. Sensing my apprehension, the young man encouraged me, "Go for it!" I jumped in.

The icy waves were quite heavy. The northerners all cheered on the girl from Missouri. Somehow I made it to the other side with ease and in record time. I continued on to finish my journey. God's power works in us to accomplish what may seem insurmountable. With His help we can oppose

I can do all things through Christ who strengthens me.

PHILIPPIANS 4:13

the fiercest army and scale the highest wall (Ps 18:29). Through Christ we can do all things (PHIL 4:13). The Lord becomes our support as we cling to Him. He is our strong tower (PROV 18:10). Nothing is impossible for this Perfect Man. Jesus has already come up from the wilderness victoriously.

> Who is this coming out of the wilderness like pillars of
> smoke, perfumed with myrrh and frankincense, with all the
> merchant's fragrant powders? Behold, it is Solomon's couch,
> with sixty valiant men around it, of the valiant of Israel.
> –Song of Solomon 3:6-7

This is our Beloved! Christ came to earth and conquered the grave. His resurrection power is at work in our lives. He upholds those who are weak. The Everlasting God never grows weary.

> Have you not known? Have you not heard? The everlasting
> God, the LORD, the Creator of the ends of the earth, neither
> faints nor is weary. His understanding is unsearchable. He
> gives power to the weak, and to those who have no might He
> increases strength. Even the youths shall faint and be weary,
> and the young men shall utterly fall, but those who wait on
> the LORD shall renew their strength; they shall mount up with
> wings like eagles, they shall run and not be weary, they shall
> walk and not faint.   –Isaiah 40:28-31

When we have no might of our own, He increases our strength. As we wait upon the Lord, He revives us. We begin to soar above the clouds of discouragement. Our lengthy marathon turns into nothing more than a brief jaunt. Whereas we once might have easily fainted,

He gives us new vitality to press on. This is what happens when we give ourselves in extravagant devotion to Jesus. We come up from the wilderness leaning on Him! This is our Beloved! No longer our Master, but our Husband He is called. Our Beloved has allured us into the desert, but it is in

Who is this coming up from the wilderness, leaning upon her beloved?

SONG 8:5

this place where He gives us back our vineyards. This valley of trouble actually becomes a door of hope as we emerge from our barrenness.

> *"Therefore, behold, I will allure her, will bring her into the wilderness, and speak comfort to her. I will give her her vineyards from there, and the Valley of Achor as a door of hope; she shall sing there, as in the days of her youth, as in the day when she came up from the land of Egypt. And it shall be, in that day," says the LORD, "that you will call Me 'My Husband,' and no longer call Me 'My Master.' "*
>
> *–Hosea 2:14-16*

He blesses all who put their strength in Him. Wars may rage on every side while we rest. His perfect love removes all fear (1 JOHN 4:18). If God is for us, who can be against us? Absolutely nothing can separate us from His unfailing love. Through this love we are more than conquerors (ROM 8:31-39). Our confidence is found in beholding His beauty and cultivating intimacy.

> *The LORD is my light and my salvation; whom shall I fear?*
> *The LORD is the strength of my life; of whom shall I be afraid?*
> *… Though an army may encamp against me, my heart*
> *shall not fear; though war may rise against me, in this*

I will be confident. One thing I have desired of the LORD ...
that I may dwell in the house of the LORD all the days of
my life, to behold the beauty of the LORD, and to inquire
in His temple ...   *—Psalm 27:1-4*

Our goodness is nothing apart from the Lord (Ps 16:2). Those who are poor in spirit know this reality. Not by our own might or power do we accomplish anything; it is only through His Holy Spirit (ZECH 4:6). Once we recognize this truth, Jesus is our life's source of vitality.

For in the time of trouble He shall hide me in His pavilion; in
the secret place of His tabernacle ... And now my head shall
be lifted up above my enemies all around me ... When You
said, "Seek My face," My heart said to You, "Your face, LORD,
I will seek." ... I would have lost heart, unless I had believed
that I would see the goodness of the LORD in the land of the
living. Wait on the LORD ... and He shall strengthen your
heart; wait, I say, on the LORD!   *—Psalm 27:5-14*

As the Lord's mature Bride, it has become our practice to run into the secret place of His tabernacle in times of trouble. Our own vineyard is ever before us (SONG 8:12). Under the apple tree His love awakens us. Every time we sit beneath this shade, His fruit is sweet to our taste. His banner of love guards us. His Word sustains us (SONG 2:3-5). We eagerly anticipate the arrival of our Bridegroom. Like the five wise virgins, we gather the oil needed to keep our lamps burning brightly until He returns (MATT 25:4). Our hearts are energized with the first commandment in first place. His love imparts strength. We set ourselves on a journey of knowing the Lord. In so doing, our Beloved exalts us above our wicked foe. Even in the presence of our enemies,

He prepares a banquet. We dwell in His house (Ps 23:5-6). This is our assurance: we will see the Lord's goodness in the land where we live. And so we wait. Even in desolate times our Beloved brings refreshment. As we pass through the valley of hardship, He makes it an oasis.

> *Blessed is the man whose strength is in You, whose heart is set on pilgrimage. As they pass through the Valley of Baca, they make it a spring; the rain also covers it with pools. They go from strength to strength …* —Psalm 84:5-7

We arise from wilderness seasons with greater confidence in His perfect leadership and increased security in His divine activity. His love carries us. The Everlasting Arm escorts us from strength to strength as we lean. Those enormous mountains of opposition no longer weigh us down. We begin to skip and leap beside our Beloved. This partnership leads us into conquest over every enemy of our souls. Such victory over sin sends terror into the devil's camp. Satan trembles when he sees Christ's Bride marching forth like a magnificent army, triumphant in battle. This is our identity as His victorious Bride! He has chosen the weak things of the world to confound the wise. At the end of the day we will be found leaning upon our Beloved Bridegroom. Our song will be what He has done.

Who is she who looks forth as the morning, fair as the moon, clear as the sun, awesome as an army with banners?
Song 6:10

FRIEND OF SINNERS

As Friend, Jesus is our Brother. God became a Man that He might be well acquainted with our weakness. I am appalled by what I have learned about horrific abuses inflicted on people because of racial hatred. Our Messiah suffered such persecution from His own people. He was mocked, ridiculed, scorned, and rejected with intense disdain by the very ones created in His image. Our Beloved joined Himself to human beings by dwelling among us as God in flesh. But we treated Him like the scum of the earth. As if this were not enough, we then handed the Son of Man over to be tortured and executed.

> *He came to His own, and His own did not receive Him. But as many as received Him, to them He gave the right to become children of God, to those who believe in His name: who were born, not of blood, nor of the will of the flesh, nor of the will of man, but of God.*   *–John 1:11-13*

In spite of all we did, He responds by giving us sonship. The Lord is not ashamed to call us His brethren. When we accept Jesus Christ as Lord, we gain the right to be called His children. We are reborn, not by flesh but through God. This means God's Son is our sibling. Our companionship is with Christ crucified. We lean upon His mercy. This is our glory. He is the Great High Priest who made a way for us to share in His inheritance.

How could this be? This Man has every right to utterly despise all mankind. Furthermore, Christ has power to hand us over to eternal torment. Would we not ourselves consider thoughts of retaliation? Jesus can sympathize with our human frame because He took it upon Himself. He was tempted in every way we have been but did not sin.

> *For we do not have a High Priest who cannot sympathize with our weaknesses, but was in all points tempted as we are, yet without sin.*   *–Hebrews 4:15*

This is our Friend! Instead of retribution, He gives redemption. In place of bitterness, He chooses forgiveness. We rejected Him, but He accepts us. He became poor that we might be rich. He became a slave that we might go free. This Perfect Man became a sacrifice for our sins. He is the Mediator of the New Covenant. He has gone before us to make a way for us to enter the holy of holies. He is the Great Intercessor, always interceding before the Father on our behalf.

What kind of love is this? Our Lord has befriended sinners. Jesus tells us that if we confess Him before men, He will confess us before His Father (MATT 10:32). If we forgive those who sin against us He will also forgive our sins (MATT 6:14-15). Though He is King of kings and Lord of lords, He does not consider us His servants. Our Beloved made Himself nothing for us. He stepped across the line of segregation to associate with weak and broken human beings. No longer Master, but our Friend He has become. True friendship is realized in loyalty to God's commands: loving Jesus and loving others. By obeying His commandments, we ally ourselves with the Living God. We choose to be on His side. This is how we befriend Jesus.

*You are My friends if you do whatever I command you.
No longer do I call you servants, for a servant does not
know what his master is doing; but I have called you
friends, for all things that I heard from My Father I have
made known to you.*   *–John 15:14-15*

Servants do not know their master's business, but the Lord of creation calls us into partnership. He says, "Come up here. I will show you what must soon take place" (REV 4:1). What kind of ruler would share such matters with his subjects? What royal king would walk the streets with commoners? So great is the mystery concerning the Gospel of salvation for which Christ suffered that even angels long to peer into the matter (1 Pet 1:3-12). Only this Friend of sinners would bow so low.

Jesus invites the lowly to know His affairs. He welcomes the destitute to dine at His table. In a season when God's presence was withdrawn Job lamented the loss of such friendship with the Lord.

> *How I long for the months gone by, for the days when*
> *God watched over me, when his lamp shone upon my head*
> *and by his light I walked through darkness! Oh, for the days ...*
> *when God's intimate friendship blessed my house ...*
> —Job 29:2-4 NIV

God walked in the Garden of Eden in the cool of the day with Adam and Eve before they sinned (Gen 3:8). Christ died and rose again to restore this intimate fellowship to all who believe.

This is our Friend! He is the One on whom we lean. "He knows our frame; He remembers that we are dust" (Ps 103:14). And so He became one of us. God became a stranger on the earth. Through the power of His resurrection, Christ has made a way to carry each of us to His eternal home in glory. He gives weak human beings authority over demonic forces in the heavenly realms. Those who love Him are appointed to rule and reign by His side forever. Our Beloved Friend draws us into eternal union with the Godhead. This is our destiny. God has chosen us as His eternal companions.

Faithful Companion

The question we face on this side of eternity is one of confidence in the nature of our Friend. When all odds seem stacked against us, will we still hope in God? When He delays so long in answering our prayers will we trust Him? This is what it means to be a true friend of God. This is why Abraham was called God's friend (2 CHRON 20:7; Is 41:8). He was given credit for being a righteous man because he believed God (JAS 2:23). Even in his old age Abraham trusted in God's promise to make him the father of many nations. He took the Lord at His Word. By faith he and his wife walked out God's divine plan, leaving all they knew to live in a foreign land. Even though Sarah was beyond the age of child-bearing, she gave birth to their only son. They did not lose hope. Such is the faith of God's friends (HEB 11).

> *"Abraham believed God, and it was accounted to him for righteousness." And he was called the friend of God.*
> JAMES 2:23

By faith Abraham obeyed when he was called to go out to the place which he would receive as an inheritance. And he went out, not knowing where he was going. By faith he dwelt in the land of promise as in a foreign country, dwelling in tents with Isaac and Jacob, the heirs with him of the same promise; for he waited for the city which has foundations, whose builder and maker is God. By faith Sarah herself also received strength to conceive seed, and she bore a child when she was past the age, because she judged Him faithful who had promised. Therefore from one man, and him as good as dead, were born as many as the stars of the sky in multitude ...
—Hebrews 11:8-12

The Lord proved His faithfulness. He made Abraham's descendents as numerous as the stars in the sky and innumerable as the sands by the sea. Again, God tested his faith even after Abraham received the promise of a son. With confidence in the Lord, he offered his only son on the altar reasoning that God could raise him from the dead.

> *By faith Abraham, when he was tested, offered up Isaac, and he who had received the promises offered up his only begotten son, of whom it was said, "In Isaac your seed shall be called," concluding that God was able to raise him up, even from the dead, from which he also received him in a figurative sense.* —Hebrews 11:17-19

After waiting patiently, Abraham finally received the Lord's promise. God cannot lie. His assurance is our anchor in storms (HEB 6:15-19).

Now faith is being sure of what we hope for and certain of what we do not see.
HEBREWS 11:1 NIV

Faith is the tangible substance we hope for. It is the evidence we cannot see (HEB 11:1). In the desert of shattered dreams and unfulfilled promises will our Friend find faith in our hearts? Will we still find refuge in the secret place of communion with our Beloved? Even when we lack faith, God is faithful. He cannot and will not deny His nature (2 TIM 2:13). Our Beloved Friend is Faithful and True.

This is why I have poured out my heart proclaiming His name. Like Paul, I believe that knowing Jesus' Excellence is the most powerful motivation for a life of obedience and sacrifice (PHIL 3:8). Of course, I still have unfulfilled dreams, but my highest pursuit is knowing this Perfect Man. He is trustworthy. He tells us to delight in Him that He may grant our heart's desires.

> *Delight yourself also in the LORD, and He shall give you the desires of your heart.* —Psalm 37:4

Jesus Christ is my deepest heart's desire. I am overcome with desire for my Beloved. Though things may not always work out like I want, I am not offended at Him. Even in the wilderness seasons I remind myself of His faithfulness. My life is surrendered to His perfect leadership. He is able to surpass my wildest imagination. He has done so even in the composition and design of this book. For this I give Him glory!

Now to Him who is able to do exceedingly abundantly above all that we ask or think, according to the power that works in us, to Him be glory in the church by Christ Jesus to all generations, forever and ever. —Ephesians 3:20-21

Let us continue to trust in the Lord's faithfulness. He is in complete control. His ways are so much higher than ours. Our Beloved will bring us up from this life leaning upon Him. He is our Faithful Companion. Dear friends, let us continue along this journey *together* that we may run into the knowledge of God. And please remember: "If you find my beloved ... tell him I am lovesick!" (SONG 5:8).

FRIEND OF THE BRIDEGROOM

Until that glorious Day when our Beloved splits the sky, we have His Holy Spirit dwelling inside. The Father has sent this Helper to prepare us for our Bridegroom's return. He reminds us of everything Jesus said. We cannot flee from His presence. Everywhere we go God's Spirit is there (Ps 139:7-10). He always strengthens, helps, protects, guides, and teaches us the truth.

But the Counselor, the Holy Spirit, whom the Father will send in my name, will teach you all things and will remind you of everything I have said to you. —John 14:26 NIV

The Counselor instructs us concerning the nature of our Beloved. Through His divine wisdom, God's power equips us with everything we need concerning life and godliness (2 PET 1:3). The Spirit is truly a Friend of our Bridegroom. He stands and listens, that He may lead us according to the Lord's will.

> *He who has the bride is the bridegroom; but the friend of the bridegroom, who stands and hears him, rejoices greatly because of the bridegroom's voice. Therefore this joy of mine is fulfilled.* —John 3:29

Greatly does the Holy Spirit rejoice upon hearing the Bridegroom's voice. His joy will be fulfilled on the day He presents us to Christ as a radiant Bride. Our Bridegroom is returning soon. We will join our Beloved at the Marriage Supper of the Lamb. Let us lean upon Jesus' Friend, the Holy Spirit. He will help make us ready so we might say, "My Beloved, Your love is more exhilarating than all the pleasures of the world. I enjoy Your affections more than life itself. I am Yours. You are mine. Come into Your inheritance and take delight in me!" Let us live with such wholehearted abandonment that Jesus may respond, "My Beloved, truly you ravish my heart. Your life is a beautiful song of love. Your eyes of loving devotion overwhelm Me. I am undone."

Let us continually remember God's Love. What is our Beloved more than another? Have we met another like this before? He is dazzling. Jesus is God's Beloved Son in whom the Father is well pleased. In Him the fullness of God dwells. Who is like Him? This One is fully God and fully Man. He is Chief among ten thousand, fairer than all the sons of men, and more excellent than any other. Oh, to gaze upon His beauty! Our Beloved is more glorious than diamonds. He is more costly than the finest gold. He is clothed in unapproachable light. Truly His splendor is incomparable. This is the glorious exaltation that provokes others to ask, "Where has your Beloved turned aside, that we may seek Him with you?" (SONG 6:1). When we make intimacy with Jesus our life ambition, others cannot help but notice. Our passion splashes on everyone who comes near. People feel the refreshing waters that spring forth. Our lives impact others unto transformation.

We first make ourselves ready by seeking God's Kingdom. His glory radiates from our inmost beings preparing others for Jesus' return. This is the forerunner calling. John the Baptist was a forerunner sent ahead of Christ to make the people ready (JOHN 3:28; LUKE 1:17). He announced our Messiah's coming, "Behold! The Lamb of

The forerunner has entered for us, even Jesus, having become High Priest forever ...

HEBREWS 6:20

God who takes away the sin of the world!" (JOHN 1:29). When Jesus rose from the grave, He became the ultimate Forerunner (HEB 6:20). Our Beloved went before us to make a way that we might enter our eternal inheritance. During this present age He calls us forerunners. We are in partnership with the Holy Spirit in preparing the corporate Bride of Christ. Our role is to make straight a path for our King's triumphant return.

Christ also loved the church and gave Himself for her, that He might sanctify and cleanse her with the washing of water by the word, that He might present her to Himself a glorious church, not having spot or wrinkle or any such thing, but that she should be holy and without blemish. –Ephesians 5:25-27

We too are friends of the Bridegroom who hear His voice. And so we proclaim His Word to believers and unbelievers alike. As His friends, we labor with the Holy Spirit to present His Church as a holy Bride. Together with His Spirit, we call out to our Beloved Friend, saying, "Come, Lord Jesus! Your Bride has made herself ready. We long for Your return. We open wide our hearts. King of Glory enter into Your inheritance. Even so, come quickly!"

> *And the Spirit and the bride say, "Come!" And let him who hears say, "Come!" ... He who testifies to these things says, "Surely I am coming quickly." Amen. Even so, come, Lord Jesus!* —Revelation 22:17, 20

When the revelation of my friendship with God significantly impacted my identity, I created *personal* cards with the title, "Artist, adventurer, dreamer, friend of God." Not long afterward, He awakened me to the reality that I am His Bride. This journey into Jesus' affections is greater than any adventure I could have ever dreamt. Once again I find myself falling in Love with this Beautiful Man.

There is no one like our Beloved God. His Love endures forever. We are our Beloved's and His desire is for us. He relentlessly pursues our hearts. No one else loves the way He does. Nothing is more enjoyable than intimacy with Him, which explains our lovesickness. Rightly do we love this Perfect Man (SONG 1:4). Rightly do we cherish Jesus. He is our reward and we are His. This is our Beloved! This is our Friend! Let us prepare to meet our Bridegroom. He is *Altogether Lovely!*

Keep these words ...

in your *heart*.

⅋

Deuteronomy 6:6 NRSV

Listen to me,
O royal *daughter*;
take to heart what I say.

Forget your people and your family far away.

For your royal *husband*
delights in your beauty;
honor him, for he is your *lord*.

∽

Psalm 45:10-11 NLT

Invitation

Encounter Your Bridegroom

WRAP YOUR FACE IN HIS NAME

This book was birthed from the place of encounter with Jesus. I had been studying the Song of Solomon with a small group for more than a year. Upon discussing Song 5:9-16, we discovered what little revelation we had on this dynamic passage. This caused us to extend our study an extra week. I decided that if this is the most extravagant expression of love describing my Beloved, I would need to spend time searching it out further. In December of 2007, the Lord invited me to seek His face by writing *Altogether Lovely—The Perfect Man* using this passage.

I had desired to write a book for more than ten years. If I would have done so earlier, it would have been all about *me*. The concept for this text redirected my focus to *God*. I did not consider myself qualified to present any sort of explanation on His attributes. This would require complete dependency. The Lord would have to reveal His nature. His Holy Spirit would have to give me utterance. I accepted the challenge knowing it would force me to lean upon my Beloved.

For three months, my heart was steadily focused on this assignment. Then numerous activities began to compete for my attention. During the next four months it took great effort to squeeze in a few sporadic hours. I went about my weekly routine occasionally expressing the longing in my heart for time to write. In June, the Lord answered my cry and began preparing me for a season change.

*My beloved spoke, and said to me: "Rise up, my love, my fair
one, and come away. For lo, the winter is past, the rain is
over and gone. The flowers appear on the earth; the time
of singing has come ..."*   *–Song of Solomon 2:10-12*

I was enjoying a weekly Sabbath rest at my favorite park where the roses
were in full bloom. As I sang from Song 2:10-12, the Lord encouraged
me that winter was past and spring was almost here. I remembered the
roses that blossomed the previous year and died because of a late freeze.
I continued singing as the Lord revealed that there was still one more
snowfall and another *freeze* to come in my personal journey.

Within a week, the worship team that I had been singing on for five
months disbanded. I knew this was the beginning of the *snowfall*.
Three days later, Lou Engle called the IHOP–KC community to a
corporate forty-day fast from June 30 to August 8, 2008. This would
be the *freeze*. I immediately saw this as my window of opportunity to
lay aside every distracting activity. Our corporate focus confirmed my
personal direction of searching out the nature of Jesus. Mike Bickle
called our attention to the story of Elijah.

*And the angel of the LORD ... said, "Arise and eat, because
the journey is too great for you." So he arose, and ate and
drank; and he went in the strength of that food forty days
and forty nights as far as Horeb, the mountain of God. And
there he went into a cave, and spent the night in that place;
and behold, the word of the LORD came to him, and He said
to him, "What are you doing here, Elijah?" So he said, "I have
been very zealous for the LORD God of hosts; for the children
of Israel have forsaken Your covenant, torn down Your altars,*

and killed Your prophets with the sword. I alone am left; and
they seek to take my life." Then He said, "Go out, and stand on
the mountain before the LORD." And behold, the LORD passed
by, and a great and strong wind tore into the mountains and
broke the rocks in pieces before the LORD, but the LORD was
not in the wind; and after the wind an earthquake, but the
LORD was not in the earthquake; and after the earthquake
a fire, but the LORD was not in the fire; and after the fire a still
small voice. So it was, when Elijah heard it, that he wrapped
his face in his mantle and went out and stood in the entrance
of the cave. Suddenly a voice came to him, and said, "What
are you doing here, Elijah?" —1 Kings 19:7-13

The Lord instructed Elijah to stand on the mountain of the Lord. He then revealed Himself in a still small voice. When Elijah heard it, he wrapped his face in his cloak and went to the entrance of the cave. Mike spoke of the Lord's invitation for us to come up the mountain of the Lord and contend for His name. As we wrap our face in the mantle of His name, the Lord will reveal His nature. He will also ask the same question He posed to Elijah, "What are you doing here?" Are we doing what He has called us to? Or are we distracted by other things?

Mike's message verified that I was to meditate on the name of Jesus: *Altogether Lovely!* What an incredible invitation to encounter my Bridegroom. This gave me *permission* to stop being occupied with so many things. The Lord showed me what activities were unnecessary during this time. I could actually spend forty days sitting at His feet in undistracted devotion and wrap my face in His name.

I responded to my Beloved's invitation by asking Him to consume all my senses in His glory. I prayed for every distraction to be removed so

I could fix my gaze upon Him. I desired to see and hear Jesus, to think about my Beloved, to be entirely captivated by His presence, and to focus on Him alone.

Of course I could not do this in my own strength. He would have to give me supernatural grace to fast and wrap my face completely in His name so that nothing could divert me from seeking Him. Before the fast began, the Lord spoke to my heart, promising that I would come up from the wilderness leaning on my Beloved. This time of consecration is His gift. He said that He would surround me in the mantle of His name as I seek His face. And so I embarked on my forty-day journey into the wilderness with a simple commitment:

I will consider and incline my ear. The King greatly desires my beauty. Therefore, I will forget my people and my father's house (Ps 45:10-11). I will forget all the tasks I have been going about doing. I will forget all my other activities and emotions. I will forget all that is comfortable. I will leave it all behind. I will incline my ear. I will let all other lovers and distractions fade away. My soul will wait silently on the Lord (Ps 62:5). I will open up my ear and hear His still small voice. I will be attentive to wisdom. I have an ear to hear and I will not miss a word that He's saying. I will listen as He speaks to my heart. I will take these forty days to stand in the counsel of the Lord. He is Altogether Lovely! I want to know Him. I will incline my ear and wrap my face in His name!

Now He offers this invitation to you. Your Beloved beckons, "Listen, My love. Forget what seems so important and seek My Kingdom first. Lose sight of earthly pursuits. Live for another age. Make Me your first priority. I desire fellowship with you. Let Me hear your voice. Let Me see your face, for you are lovely. Love me with all your heart, soul, mind, and strength. Honor Me with all your time, emotions, energy, abilities, and thoughts. Yes, Beloved, pour out your entire life as an extravagant offering of worship at My feet."

> *Listen, O daughter, consider and incline your ear; forget your own people also, and your father's house; so the King will greatly desire your beauty; because He is your Lord, worship Him.* —Psalm 45:10-11

Will you consider Your Beloved's invitation? Whether you choose an extended time of consecration or a focused time in your daily routine, please accept this invitation to encounter your Bridegroom. Will you leave it all behind to seek Him and wrap your face in His name?

SALVATION INVITATION

If you have not yet asked Jesus Christ to be Lord and Savior of your life, why wait any longer? You can ask Him today! Too often we tell ourselves, "Maybe tomorrow I will turn my life over to God." For many *tomorrow* never comes. "As God's fellow workers we urge you not to receive God's grace in vain ... I tell you, now is the time of God's favor, now is the day of salvation" (2 COR 6:1-2).

The Bible tells us that we live and die once (HEB 9:27). Scripture says, "For the wages of sin is death, but the gift of God is eternal life in Christ Jesus our Lord" (ROM 6:23). God's Word also states, "If you confess with your mouth, 'Jesus is Lord,' and believe in your heart that God raised him from the dead, you will be saved" (ROM 10:9 NIV). God has given each of us a free will. He sets before us a choice between life and death (DEUT 30:19). We can choose eternal life by believing in Jesus, making Him Lord of our lives, and obeying His commands in Scripture; or we can choose to spend eternity in hell by denying Jesus and living life our own way apart from God and His commands. Please do not put off making the most important decision of your life, which will determine your eternal destiny.

Jesus tells us, "I am the way, the truth, and the life. No one comes to the Father except through Me" (JOHN 14:6). There is no other way to God except through His Son, Jesus Christ. God loves you deeply and wants you to live with Him for eternity. There is *nothing* you have done that God will not forgive. If you confess your sins, He is faithful to forgive you and cleanse you from unrighteousness (1 JOHN 1:9). "While we were still sinners, Christ died for us" on the cross, and then God raised Jesus from the dead (ROM 5:8; GAL 1:1). "Salvation is found in no one else, for there is no other name under heaven given to men by which we must be saved" (ACTS 4:12 NIV).

Please do not wait another moment to surrender your life to God. He is knocking on the door of your heart. Will you open to Him? Allow Jesus to bring joy, peace, and freedom to your heart like you have never experienced. Use this simple prayer to commit your life to Christ.

Dear God, I admit that I am a sinner and need You to be my Savior. I am sorry for all the wrong things that I have done in my life. Please forgive me for all my sins (name specific sins that come to mind): _____ .
I repent for not keeping your commandments. I turn away from doing wrong and commit my heart to obey You. Father God, I confess with my mouth and believe in my heart that Your Son, Jesus Christ, died on the cross, was raised from the

dead, and shed His precious blood for my salvation, healing,
and total freedom. I receive Your free gift of eternal life. Jesus,
come live in my heart. Be Lord and Savior of my life. Please
help me to live my life according to Your commandments
in the Bible. I commit to abide daily in Your Word. I love You.
In Your name, Jesus, Amen!

Remember this is only the beginning of your journey into encounter with your Beloved. As you cultivate your relationship with Jesus on a daily basis, He will reveal Himself to you more and more.

Fruitful Encounter

Turning the Song of Solomon into ongoing prayerful dialogue with Jesus Christ has profoundly impacted my heart. I encourage you to paraphrase these Scriptures using your own words. Express both your prayers to Jesus along with His responses to you. I journal from the same passage repeatedly, sometimes even years apart. Often my focus differs depending on what the Lord is highlighting in my life at the time. The more you meditate on specific verses the more they will be infused into your heart (Ps 119:11). I have enjoyed writing down thoughts and prayers, singing through certain passages, and interpreting His Word through dance, art, drama, and various forms of creativity. Let this love song become your own song of love to Jesus. The Lord will amaze you as He imparts greater revelation of His Word!

I was having a difficult time understanding Song 5:10-16 and decided to paint while meditating on this glorious declaration. As I turned it into a prayer dialogue with the Majestic God, I chose to interpret its symbolic description mostly with colors, shapes, and movement. I sang through each phrase progressing slowly through the passage. In doing so, I noticed something new! I was thanking the Lord for His perfect leadership depicted by His head of finest gold. Discouraged that I could not quite mix the right colors to portray a regal gold, I looked through my supplies. Just then I discovered some sheets of gold leaf for which I had not yet found a good use. I began tearing and gluing them along the top of my canvas to represent His perfect headship. Artistically, however, I did not like the fact that the gold would be confined to the top edge. I continued through the Scripture eventually coming to the description of His arms as rods of gold. Immediately, I began covering the right and left edges of the canvas with gold leaf—still disappointed that the bottom would remain dull. It did not take long to discover His legs were set on a foundation of fine gold. With excitement, I quickly added gold to the lower edge of the canvas before connecting the base and upper edge with two pillars. I had somehow failed to notice the multiple references to gold in this description before. This time I was struck with the sudden realization that His leadership is not the only attribute depicted as perfection. All of Jesus' attributes are surrounded in gold. He is entirely perfect, not only His headship and authority but also His strength. He acts on my behalf with precision. His strong foundation is flawless. There is no spot in Him. My Beloved is Christ, the solid Rock on which I stand. He is truly the only One worthy. What an amazing revelation to behold simply by painting and singing my songs of love to Jesus! He is worthy to receive blessing and honor!

Then I looked, and I heard the voice of many angels around the throne, the living creatures, and the elders; and the number of them was ten thousand times ten thousand, and thousands of thousands, saying with a loud voice:

"Worthy is the Lamb who was slain to receive power and riches and wisdom, and strength and honor and glory and blessing!" And every creature which is in heaven and on the earth and under the earth and such as are in the sea, and all that are in them, I heard saying: "Blessing and honor and glory and power be to Him who sits on the throne, and to the Lamb, forever and ever!" Then the four living creatures said, "Amen!" And the twenty-four elders fell down and worshiped Him who lives forever and ever. —Revelation 5:11-14

May we join in with the choir of heaven singing of His glory forever and ever! We have been made in the image of our Creator. The Lord wants to release creativity among artists, writers, singers, musicians, dancers, actors, preachers, and so many others to declare His beauty.

What has the Lord put in your heart to do? If you have ever considered writing you can start by setting aside time today. Begin compiling your thoughts and typing them into a document. In whatever media you express creatively, ask the Lord for direction. As you spend time in communion with the Living God, He will release His Spirit of Prophecy, which is the testimony of Jesus (REV 19:10). Seek Him! He

Awake, O north wind, and come, O south! Blow upon my garden, that its spices may flow out ...
SONG 4:16

will send His north winds of adversity and south winds of blessing to blow upon your garden until you become the aroma of Christ. He will draw you after Himself in intimacy. You will run with Him in ministry. In His perfect timing your Beloved will cause a fragrance to arise from your life of abiding in Him (SONG 4:16).

Now thanks be to God who always leads us in triumph in Christ, and through us diffuses the fragrance of His knowledge in every place. For we are to God the fragrance of Christ among those who are being saved and among those who are perishing. —2 Corinthians 2:14-15

PRAYERFUL CONVERSATION

May our Bridegroom King continue revealing His divine attributes to our hearts. Let us commit our hearts to stay connected to the Vine and seek first His Kingdom. Without Him we can do nothing. I am reminded of a phrase continually repeated by Heidi Baker, "All fruitfulness flows from intimacy." We must daily drink from the Eternal Fountain of Living Water. As we drink of this Living Water that flows from the sanctuary, it will pour out of our hearts. We will bear fruit every season of the year. Let us drink deeply by turning the Scriptures into dialogue with Jesus every day!

Open my eyes, that I may see wondrous things from Your law.
PSALM 119:18

Following are pages for you to begin journaling to and from your Beloved. May the Lord open the eyes of your understanding as you turn His Word into prayerful conversation with the Living God. He will reveal wondrous truth to your heart and soul (Ps 119:18).

Closing Word

By Audra D. Close

After reading *Altogether Lovely—The Perfect Man,* I realized that this amazing book cannot be quickly inhaled in one sitting but must be read and reread, prayed through, pondered and digested slowly for the reader's maximum benefit. *Altogether Lovely* is truly a spiritual feast, which we will want to take the time to taste, savor and enjoy. In our day of convenience, we would like to go through the drive through and eat our *fast-food spiritual meals* without a lot of fuss. However, just like its physical counterpart, a fast-food spiritual meal gives you lots of *fluff,* empty calories taking up space, and hardly any nutritional value. Just as physical fast-food diets lead to poor physical health, spiritual fast-food diets lead to poor spiritual health.

Think back to the feasts and celebrations that people thousands of years ago participated in. Even in the days of Esther, King Ahasuerus (Xerxes I) gave a banquet lasting seven days. Can you imagine what it must have been like sitting around all day, eating, drinking, relaxing, talking, and laughing for a whole week? I think that most of us would not be used to taking that much time for resting and relishing each moment. Many of us are more accustomed to fourteen hour days working, cleaning, caring for children, literally *running* from thing to thing, and making sure *everything gets done.* We need our conversations to be quick and to the point; our meals are usually fast and as convenient as possible. We live as if we are going for the gold in errands, efficiency and productivity, and then we fall wearily into bed only to get up and do it all over again the next day. So between filling our spirits with the wrong *foods* and racing through life at breakneck speed we wake up feeling physically and spiritually exhausted.

Sometimes we are just so tired that we try and get a nutritious spiritual meal on Sunday or by snacking on a few verses in the Bible here and there. However, just as we cannot live off of physical food that we ate a week ago, let alone twenty years ago, we cannot live off of spiritual food from last month or ten years ago. We need fresh *spiritual Bread* every day. Much of the time we find ourselves trying to supplement with the world's *spiritual junk food*, which includes television, news, movies, fantasy, magazines, entertainment, shopping, sports, work, time-consuming hobbies, food, caffeine, drugs, alcohol, sex outside of marriage, pornography, and the like. We are all trying desperately to fill our empty, spiritual stomachs with something, *anything*. However, there is only one thing that will truly satisfy us. There is only One in whom we will find our rest. His name is Jesus Christ. Jesus gave us the key to satisfaction when He emphasized putting the first commandment first. Jesus said, "Love the Lord your God with all your heart, with all your soul, and with all your mind." (MATT 22:37). In other words, fill your heart, soul and mind with God. Be consumed entirely with love for God in the way He loves you. God loves us so much He gave His very life for us. As fully God and fully Man, Jesus Christ came as our servant, suffering for us and even purchasing us from eternal death with His precious blood.

> *Love the LORD your God with all your heart ...*
> MATTHEW 22:37

Altogether Lovely is not only like a highly nutritious meal full of spiritual vitamins ready to impart health to its participants, but it is a banqueting table laid out for the reader by the Lord who says, "You are cordially invited to My *feast*. Come and feast on Me." Someday we will eat the Marriage Supper of the Lamb with Jesus. In this age, the Bread of Life gives us a feast *before our enemies* by providing the Bread

> *They feast on the abundance of your house.*
> PSALM 36:8 NIV

of His Word. He says, "Come and enjoy, take your time, stay for a while and relax. Close your eyes, breathe, and make the time to gaze on My beauty. Don't rush. Go slow. Enjoy the journey. Ponder My Love for you. Let Me whisper in your ear Who 'I AM.' Let me tell you what I am really like."

God is longing for a people who love Him as much as He loves them. How do we do meet all these seemingly lofty, spiritual goals of gazing upon God and loving Him totally? Reading, meditating, singing, pondering, memorizing and studying His Word is how we do it! It is so simple and easy but it actually takes time to *sit down to dinner* and see that we are at a wonderful feast lasting for days and days to come. There is no lack in spiritual food, delight, enjoyment and wonder when we just sit at Jesus' feet gathering the sacred oil of intimacy through worshiping Him, praying to Him through His Word, studying His Word and loving Him with our whole heart, soul and mind. It is difficult to participate in a feast if we are already full on *junk food*. How do we find time to spend with Him? This could mean that we do not watch as much television, see as many movies, seek out as much entertainment, or spend as much time watching sports or shopping. We may have to get a little radical and adjust our work schedule or even do some fasting from sweets, caffeine and/or food. It could mean that we actually say "No" to some requests and redefine our priorities so that our boundary lines can fall in pleasant places (Ps 16:6).

Closing Word: By Audra D. Close

Altogether Lovely is a wonderful companion for the one who is *on a pilgrimage*, pointing the way to greater depths of knowing and loving Jesus without wavering or distracting. As you read through this book and read it again, I encourage you to take time to go slowly, praying and asking God to give you the *spirit of wisdom and revelation* to more fully understand all that is shared in each lovingly penned sentence and verse. Practice journaling your thoughts and revelations about Jesus that you receive from God as you read *Altogether Lovely*. Turn the thoughts, concepts and verses into your own prayers, songs and love letters to Jesus. Enjoy the feast!

Bon Appetit!

Audra D. Close

Intercessory Missionary
International House of Prayer
Kansas City, Missouri

May Your Fragrance Arise

READ

Choose one Bible version to read from consistently. Read from other translations for comparison. When studying a particular passage, start by reading the entire chapter or book three times. After learning the context, begin to focus on only a few verses at a time.

WRITE

Keep a blank journal or notebook to record Scriptures, observations, questions, thoughts, and prayers. Copy a few verses directly from your Bible to your journal. Write the verses again in your own words adding insights and other Scriptural references to look up later.

SPEAK

Speak the Scriptures aloud and then turn them into melodies as you spontaneously sing through a passage. Join others in small groups to discuss what God is teaching you.

PRAY

Pray each Scripture by thanking the Lord for particular truths and committing to obey His instruction. Then turn each passage into a response from Jesus. Highlight realities in His Word that He would say to encourage your heart. You may enjoy expressing your prayers creatively through music, dance, and various forms of visual art.

Song 5:8

I charge you, O daughters of Jerusalem,
if you find my beloved,
that you tell him I am lovesick!

Song 5:9

What is your beloved more than another beloved,
O fairest among women? What is your beloved
more than another beloved, that you so charge us?

Song 5:10

My beloved is white and ruddy,
chief among ten thousand.

Song 5:11

His head is like the finest gold;
his locks are wavy, and black as a raven.

Song 5:12

His eyes are like doves by the rivers of waters,
washed with milk, and fitly set.

Song 5:13

His cheeks are like a bed of spices,
banks of scented herbs. His lips are lilies,
dripping liquid myrrh.

Song 5:14

His hands are rods of gold set with beryl.
His body is carved ivory inlaid with sapphires.

Altogether Lovely—The Perfect Man

Song 5:15

His legs are pillars of marble set on bases of fine gold.
His countenance is like Lebanon,
excellent as the cedars.

_____

_____

_____

_____

_____

_____

_____

_____

_____

_____

_____

_____

_____

_____

_____

_____

_____

_____

_____

_____

_____

Song 5:16

His mouth is most sweet, yes, he is altogether lovely.
This is my beloved, and this is my friend,
O daughters of Jerusalem!

End Notes

1. Edwards, Misty. "Dove's Eyes." *Relentless/Unplugged.* Forerunner Music, 2007. CD. Used by permission.

2. Ford, William. "Don't You Remember?" New Life in Christ International Ministries, Grandview, Missouri. December 16, 2007.

3. Lockridge, Dr. Shadrach Meshach (S.M.). "That's My King!" Sermon delivered in Detroit, 1976. URL: http://en.wikipedia.org/wiki/S._M._Lockridge

4. Geisel, Theodor Seuss (Dr. Suess). *Oh, the Places You'll Go!* New York City, USA: Random House, Inc., 1990.

5. "Jamie's Recovery." URL: http://www.youtube.com/user/shartman007. Used by permission.

To purchase Chérie's books, devotionals, and artwork;
or to make a donation, please visit:

www.uniquedove.com

About Chérie

Uniquedove Creations

Chérie Lynn Blair

Uniquedove Creations

www.uniquedove.com

Chérie has been involved in ministry at the International House of Prayer (IHOP–KC) Missions Base in Kansas City, Missouri, since 2003. She first encountered Jesus as her Eternal Bridegroom after reading the Song of Solomon as a love letter from Him. This revelation has profoundly transformed her life. During times of worship she expresses the testimony of Jesus in music, dance, and art. Through her own journey Chérie has been equipped with tools to help others deepen their walk with the Lord. Her prayer is that you may experience the love of Jesus Christ and be filled with the Spirit of God (EPH 3:19).

Journey through the Song of Solomon: a devotional by Chérie Blair

ISBN 978-0-615-17374-0

This devotional journal is intended to help you mature in intimacy and partnership with Jesus Christ through His Word. The Song of Solomon illustrates the Romance of the Gospel. Jesus Christ, King of all kings, passionately pursues each of us, His Bride. The goal in studying this divine love song is to cultivate lifestyles of communion with our Beloved. Men, women, married couples, and singles will all grow in greater passion for Jesus as they turn this Song into devotional prayer!

Road Maps

Tools for Your Journey

1. Turn the Song of Solomon into devotional prayer (see page 301).

   Journey through the Song of Solomon by Chérie Blair

2. The Song of Songs is Mike Bickle's most popular teaching series.

   Song of Songs (Study Guide / MP3 / CD) by Mike Bickle

3. What is the nature of God? This modern classic shows how we can recapture a real sense of God's majesty and truly live in the Spirit.

   The Knowledge of the Holy by A.W. Tozer

4. God has placed longings in our hearts that only He can fulfill.

   The Seven Longings of the Human Heart by Mike Bickle

5. Fasting is a gift that can increase our receptivity to God's Word.

   The Rewards of Fasting by Mike Bickle and Dana Candler

6. What is God's purpose for Israel? If we make the covenant with Israel that Ruth made with Naomi, the Church will never be the same.

   Your People Shall Be My People by Don Finto

7. This introduction is a perfect entry point to end-times subjects.

   Omega Personal kit by Mike Bickle

8. This gripping story is a dramatic autobiography of one of China's dedicated, courageous, and intensely persecuted house church leaders.

   The Heavenly Man by Paul Hattaway

Printed in the United States
128087LV00005BA/4/P